Cooperative Learning in Higher Education

New Pedagogies and Practices for Teaching in Higher Education series

In the same series:

Blended Learning
Across the Disciplines, Across the Academy
Edited by Francine S. Glazer

Just-in-Time Teaching
Across the Disciplines, Across the Academy
Edited by Scott Simkins and Mark H. Maier

Published in Association with The National Teaching and Learning Forum

Cooperative Learning in Higher Education

Across the Disciplines, Across the Academy

Edited by Barbara J. Millis

Foreword By James Rhem

Published in Association with The National Teaching and Learning Forum

Sty/us

STERLING, VIRGINIA

Sty/us

COPYRIGHT © 2010 BY
STYLUS PUBLISHING, LLC.

Published by Stylus Publishing, LLC
22883 Quicksilver Drive
Sterling, Virginia 20166–2102

Library of Congress Cataloging-in-Publication-Data

Cooperative learning in higher education : across the
disciplines, across the academy / edited by Barbara J.
Millis ; foreword by James Rhem.
    p. cm. — (New pedagogies and practices for
teaching in higher education series)
  Includes bibliographical references and index.
    ISBN 978–1-57922–328–1 (cloth : alk. paper)—
ISBN 978–1-57922–329–8 (pbk. : alk. paper)
  1. Group work in education—United States.
  2. Education, Higher—United States.   I. Millis,
Barbara J.
  LB1032.C596 2010
    378.1'76—dc22   2009041906

13-digit ISBN: 978–1-57922–328–1 (cloth)
13-digit ISBN: 978–1-57922–329–8 (paper)

Printed in the United States of America

All first editions printed on acid free paper
that meets the American National Standards Institute
Z39–48 Standard.

> Bulk Purchases
>
> Quantity discounts are available for use in
> workshops and for staff development.
> Call 1–800–232–0223

First Edition, 2010

10 9 8 7 6 5 4 3 2 1

Dedication

This book is lovingly dedicated to Neil Davidson, a man described as "good with groups," who started me on my lifelong love of cooperative learning, and to the fifteen creative, cooperative chapter authors who continue to inspire and lead.

Contents

Foreword

James Rhem

Not that long ago, the word "pedagogy" didn't occur very often in faculty conversations about teaching. Today, one hears it frequently. Without putting too much weight on the prominence of a single word, subtle shifts in discourse, in vocabulary, often do mark significant shifts in thinking, and faculty thinking about teaching has changed over the last several decades. Faculty have always wanted to teach well, wanted their students to learn and succeed, but for a very long time faculty have taught as they were taught; for the students who were like them in temperament and intelligence, the approach worked well enough. When only a highly filtered population of students sought higher education, the need to look beyond those approaches to teaching lay dormant. When a much larger and more diverse population began enrolling, the limits of traditional teaching emerged more sharply.

At the same time, intelligence itself became a more deeply understood phenomenon. Recognition of multiple kinds of intelligence—visual, auditory, kinesthetic, etc.—found wide acceptance, as did different styles of learning even within those different kinds of intelligence (as measured, for example, by the Myers-Briggs Type Indicator (MBTI) developed by Katharine Cooks Briggs and Isabel Myers Briggs). Efforts to build ever more effective "thinking machines," that is to say, computers, through artificial intelligence sharpened understanding of how information needed to be processed in order for it to be assembled and utilized effectively. The seminal article, "Cognitive Apprenticeship: Teaching the Craft of Reading, Writing and Mathematics" was one by-product of this research, and one instructive aspect of this work lay in how it looked back to accumulated wisdom to lay its foundations for moving forward. Public schools had long dealt with large, diverse populations rather than highly filtered ones. Teachers there understood "scaffolding," "wait time," and "chunking" in conscious ways that were new to teachers at more advanced levels in education. Now, many of these terms, and more importantly these conscious and deliberate ways of thinking about teaching, have become commonplace in higher education.

Even more recently all this work has found support and expansion in the findings of neurobiological research into the human brain and how it operates, and in the study of groups and how they operate.

If renewed attention to teaching in higher education began as something of a "fix-it" shop approach aimed at helping individual faculty having problems with their teaching, it didn't stay that way very long. As Gaff and Simpson detail in their history of faculty development in the United States, pressure from the burgeoning "baby boom" population brought the whole business of university teaching up for reconsideration. What was relevance? What were appropriate educational goals, and what were the most effective means of meeting them? Traditionally, the primary expectation of faculty was that they remain current in their fields of expertise. Now, a whole new set of still forming expectations began to spring up on campuses all over the country.

Change often fails to come easily and smoothly. Generational and social conflicts, together with passionate political conflicts centering on the unpopular war in Vietnam, may have fueled the pressure for changes in teaching while making them more conflict-ridden than they needed to be. It is important to repeat: faculty have always wanted to teach well and have their students succeed. As the clouds of conflict from those decades have passed, the intellectual fruits have remained and grown. Some ascribe credit for change in faculty attitudes toward teaching to the social pressures of those decades. Whatever truth lies in that ascription, it seems equally clear that faculty's innate intellectual curiosity and eagerness to succeed in their life's work deserve as much credit, certainly for today's faculty interest in improved teaching.

Faculty face a challenge in embracing new understandings of effective teaching not unlike the challenge of any population of diverse intelligences in learning and applying new information. Some understanding emerging in the 1980s (in which much of the new thinking on teaching and learning began to appear) has cross-disciplinary, universal applicability, for example, the "Seven Principles of Good Practice in Higher Education" by Chickering and Gamson. But just as diverse people learn in diverse ways, diverse faculty will apply even universal principles in different ways, because both personalities and disciplinary cultures vary. Perhaps that is why many pedagogical insights into effective teaching have not aggregated into one universal, best way to teach. Instead, the forward moving inquiry into effective teaching has spawned a variety of pedagogical approaches, each with strengths appropriate to particular teaching styles and situations.

While faculty today have greater curiosity about new understandings of effective ways to teach, they remain as cautious as anyone else about change.

If they teach biology, they wonder how a particular approach might play out in teaching biology rather than how it works in teaching English literature. If they teach English literature, they may wonder if problem-based teaching (an approach highly effective in the sciences) has anything to offer their teaching and if anyone in their discipline has tried it. Every new idea requires translation and receives it in the hands of the next person to take it up and apply it in his or her work. And this is as it should be. Thus, this series of books strives to give faculty examples of new approaches to teaching as they are being applied in a representative sample of academic disciplines. In that, it extends the basic idea of The National Teaching and Learning FORUM. For roughly 20 years, the central goal of FORUM has been to offer faculty ideas in contexts: that is to say, to present them enough theory so that whatever idea about teaching and learning being discussed makes sense intellectually, but then to present that idea in an applied context. From this combination, faculty can see how an approach might fit in their own practice. Faculty do not need formulae; they need only to see ideas in contexts. They'll take it from there. And so our series of books offers faculty a multipaned window into a variety of nontraditional pedagogical approaches now being applied with success in different disciplines in higher education. Faculty will look in and find something of value for their own teaching. As I've said and believe with all my heart, faculty have always wanted to teach well and see their students succeed.

—James Rhem,
Executive Editor,
The National Teaching and Learning FORUM

Editor's Preface

This book was a labor of love, put together by carefully selected experts who, in workplace parlance, "exceeded expectations." I encourage readers to read widely, rather than only dipping into the chapters relevant to their disciplines. This volume was written by master teachers, and virtually every chapter can be mined for pedagogical gold and teaching practices easily adapted to a wide range of topics. I was struck by the level of reflection and assessment data-gathering that the authors put into their classroom practices. The authors have many things in common, such as a commitment to structured group work, learning-centered teaching, and student accountability, but this volume does not offer a cookie-cutter, one-size-fits-all approach to cooperative learning. For example, the authors differ on the size of the groups and on the group selection process. By and large, however, the authors agree on key underlying principles and practices that are emphasized by the cooperative cross references in each chapter, an approach that is not often seen in edited books.

The authors teach in a range of settings, including research institutions and community colleges. However, most of their classes are face-to-face and relatively small, which might lead some readers to mistakenly believe that cooperative learning is effective or viable only under those conditions. Accordingly, the introductory chapter emphasizes that cooperative learning is equally effective in large classes, particularly when using team folders and approaches such as the "Quick-Thinks" described by Robinson and Cooper. Personal response systems ("clickers") are effective in large classes, as Eric Mazur and others have shown, because they engage students, but, more important to learning, because they also encourage peer collaboration and debate about possible solutions in cooperative pairs or small groups. The introductory chapter also emphasizes that online or hybrid courses can use cooperative learning approaches by applying the same key principles, but by changing the delivery modality—through threaded discussions, cooperative wikis, and other online modalities.

Philip G. Cottell, in the first edited chapter, lays the groundwork for cooperative learning with major principles such as individual accountability, positive interdependence, heterogeneous teams (not a given in the literature), group processing, and social or leadership skills. He links these cooperative principles to unfolding problems in problem-based learning (PBL). Focusing on a financial accounting research class, Phil shares practices such as the use of team folders and playing cards, team roles, group monitoring, team reformation, and a review for the final. The structures that he uses—Value line; Think-Pair-Share; Within-Team Jigsaw; Cooperative Examination Critique; Visible Quiz, Quizo, a variation of Bingo; Three-Stay, One Stray; and Quality Control Circles—can be adapted to virtually any discipline.

Susan Shadle focuses on general chemistry and introduces sound pedagogical practices, such as effective student interaction, scaffolding, teacher-selected teams, group roles, and inquiry-based activities. Like Phil, she uses assigned identities within teams and team folders. She also links cooperative learning to other pedagogies, seeing it as central to a group-based model called "Process-Oriented Guided Inquiry Learning" (POGIL). Susan emphasizes the value of having two different recorders in each team: the "activity recorder," who focuses on the answers to routine questions, and the "big idea recorder," who focuses on breakthrough ideas. She also adds a "reflector" role to monitor and share with the team members or the instructor how well the group is working together. In addition to a discussion of the structured inquiry process that leads students through learning cycles, Susan's chapter emphasizes accountability by coaching students to learn group skills, by making certain that group members all "get it," by having students come to class prepared, and by student anxieties and resistance. Her practices—such as combining individual work through quizzes, homework, and exams, with group work that is focused by clear instructions and a group performance rubric—could be adapted to many disciplines.

Theodore "Ted" Panitz, who teaches developmental mathematics at a community college, focuses, like Susan, on overcoming student anxieties and ensuring accountability. He encourages students to come to class prepared by assigning extra-credit worksheets "that ask students to write out the chapter section's outcomes, record crucial vocabulary definitions," and solve six to ten math problems from the chapter. Individual and group-based quizzes also count as extra credit. Some of the specific activities that Ted employs, such as a welcoming letter, a math autobiography, Pair-Reading, and Math Olympics, could also be adapted to other disciplines.

Margaret "Peggy" Cohen uses cooperative learning in an educational psychology course for graduate and undergraduate students who plan to earn a state teaching certificate. This particular audience presents three unique challenges for Peggy: (1) she feels compelled to model exemplary teaching; (2) she needs to help students understand how the literature informs this learning-centered teaching so that they can apply the principles and practices to their own classrooms; and (3) she strives to create a learning environment that encourages students to adopt these exemplary practices. To add structure to the course, Peggy relies on "cooperative group agreements, guidelines, descriptions of roles and responsibilities, and monitoring sheets" that are made accessible through the course management system. Student buy-in is important to enhance motivation in this course. Peggy relies on her students, for example, to select a "quiet signal," and, in small groups, team members define three course requirements on which they will be evaluated: attendance, participation, and professionalism. She uses peer review for Critical Response Journals that are intended to encourage students to be self-reflective about their professional progress as teachers. Her course culminates with a complex group project requiring students to develop hands-on, interactive assessments that they apply to one student.

Karl Smith, Holly Matusovich, Kerry Meyers, and Llewellyn Mann also teach graduate students, but in a doctoral course, the History and Philosophy of Engineering Education, in the first engineering education program in the United States. Their teaching is focused on this key question: "Through the use of cooperative learning strategies such as Constructive Controversy, can we increase the rate of development of the theory and practice needed to prepare engineering graduates for 21st-century opportunities and challenges?" Accordingly, their chapter focuses on their use of the Constructive Controversy cooperative learning strategy and its impact on future engineering educators.

Pamela Robinson and James "Jim" L. Cooper offer a wide range of useful cooperative activities for virtually any course. To make lectures interactive, they use Quick-Thinks and cognitive scaffolding. Pamela and Jim define Quick-Thinks as "classroom assessment procedures in which the instructor stops the presentation every 10–20 minutes and poses a question or issue to students that requires them to process information individually or collaboratively." They offer nine of these brief interactive techniques—with examples from their research methods and statistics classes—such as Select the Best Response, Correct the Error, Complete a Sentence Starter, and Reorder the Steps. They describe scaffolds as "forms of support temporarily provided by instructors when introducing new content and making assignments." Pamela and Jim discuss five techniques in particular—Procedural Guidelines, Partial Solutions, Think-Alouds, Anticipate Student Errors, and Comprehension Check—making this chapter chock-full of practical strategies that are useful for both small and large classes. They also share other cooperative-learning–based procedures such as Scaffolding and Rubrics for Student Papers, Workbooks, Team Folders, Checklists, and Peer Editing. Their final advice focuses on the importance of clarity in grading and assignments, the value of in-class group work, and the need for structure and student interactions.

Craig Nelson's reflective but practical chapter is a personal odyssey of his pedagogical journeys, beginning with his discovery of William Perry's "Stages of Intellectual Development" and the implications for teaching biology courses. Drawing on extended research, including Hake's, Craig makes a strong case for the fact that "cooperative learning is essential to maximizing learning in science." He reviews the research by Mazur and others on Peer Instruction, noting that he independently came to the same approaches while both scholars, ironically, were unaware of the voluminous research on cooperative learning.

I particularly like Craig's emphasis on the success of these approaches in both large and small classes. I have already shared at a teaching conference his pre-class worksheet technique: students bring to class a step-by-step analysis of cognitively complex material requiring critical thinking. He grades—rapidly, credit/no-credit—only on their preparation but allows students to add to their thoughts using red pens he distributes as they work together in groups of five. The worksheet is highly structured with these instructions: (1) summarize the author's arguments, (2) evaluate the strength of evidence and the overall evidence, (3) discuss the burden of proof, and (4) make decisions (accept/reject) about each main point and the overall argument. He uses the same red-pen technique with quizzes.

Shifting gears, Craig discusses his use of cooperative learning in first-year seminar courses where he uses personal, developmental, and academic maps that students develop in pairs and small groups. In a graduate biology class, he uses journal-based cooperative learning. Like other experienced teachers in this volume, he emphasizes learning cycles.

My own chapter on literature applications starts, like Nelson's, with a personal teaching odyssey— beginning with my exposure to cooperative learning, which was later augmented by the international model on deep learning. This synergy led to an awareness of the importance of using cooperative learning approaches as a means to sequence activities and assignments to build in the repetition needed for learning. The chapter then becomes quite practical, focusing on a series of complex cooperative learning structures that can nonetheless be adopted for 50-minute classes: the Double Entry Journal, Jigsaw, Send-a-Problem (including some report-out methods), Cooperative Debates, Guided Reciprocal Peer Questioning, and BINGO.

Mark H. Maier, KimMarie McGoldrick, and Scott Simkins discuss their use of cooperative learning in introductory economics courses, touching on some of the issues such as "free riders," that discourage more economics teachers from adapting cooperative learning. They discuss four specific approaches: Think-Pair-Share (often in the guise of Quick-Thinks), Send-a-Problem, Jigsaw, and Cooperative Controversy. I find their discipline-specific applications of Send-a-Problem particularly interesting because their variations can be used in many disciplines. The authors also give two variations of the Jigsaw approach. Their discussion of Cooperative Controversy can be compared with the approach used in Smith et al.'s engineering application.

Mark, KimMarie, and Scott, like other authors, emphasize the versatility of cooperative learning, noting that it complements classroom experiments, simple games, simulations, surveys, Just-in-Time Teaching (JiTT), service learning, and undergraduate research, providing discussions and examples of each.

In the final chapter, Edward "Ed" Nuhfer presents cooperative learning applied within a sophisticated, holistic teaching philosophy that arises in part from the character of his discipline's ways of knowing. Ed examines the research on cooperative learning by applying the scientific method of multiple working hypotheses, the "historical method" of science through which field scientists gain an understanding of the physical world. After using that reasoning to conclude that cooperative learning was worth adopting, he began to integrate it into diverse lesson designs. These cooperative lessons range from simple rock and mineral identification to the design of deep learning exercises that move students toward conceptual thinking about change through time and reflection on how major theories develop in science.

This volume, then, provides theoretical overviews of teaching and learning, but it is also opens a treasure trove of discipline-specific activities that can be applied to virtually all disciplines within the framework of cooperative learning. Readers of this book can appreciate both the power and the versatility of structured group work, as well as a sincere appreciation for the commitment and experience of these fifteen authors.

—Barbara J. Millis
The University of Texas, San Antonio
March 8, 2010

Why Faculty Should Adopt Cooperative Learning Approaches

Barbara J. Millis

It is a cliché now that "Change is the only constant." Even in academia, where change is notoriously slow, most faculty members are aware of the challenges that incoming students represent with their increasing numbers and diversity, their varying levels of preparation, and their expectations or naïveté about academic rigor. Faculty also face a complex range of technology options and burgeoning class sizes. Many faculty recognize that "business as usual" will not result in significant learning gains.

Barr and Tagg's (1995) influential *Change* magazine article, "From Teaching to Learning: A New Paradigm for Undergraduate Education," started a healthy movement toward rethinking the nature of teaching and learning. Subsequent books, such as Weimer's (2002) *Learner-Centered Teaching* and Fink's (2003) *Creating Significant Learning Experiences*, as well as numerous articles, provide useful models and convincing research. Bransford, Brown, & Cocking's (2000) *How People Learn* makes it difficult for even the most lecture-committed faculty member to ignore research with clear implications for a more learning-centered basis of teaching. In fact, Finkel (2000) concludes, "Educational research over the past twenty-five years has established beyond a doubt a simple fact: What is transmitted to students through lecturing is simply not retained for any significant length of time" (p. 3).

Application and execution, however, remain key issues for faculty. Even faculty who are philosophically committed to the new paradigms often lack the know-how to successfully adapt the teaching techniques and classroom management practices that can lead to more learning-oriented approaches, particularly in content-driven courses. As Nilson (2003) points out, change is not easy, because "old teaching paradigms and habits die hard. If *we* had no trouble learning with them when we were in college, we can't understand why our students do" (p. 128). Fortunately, if faculty are open to change—a topic addressed throughout this book—these goals can be realized through a time-tested, increasingly well-known pedagogy called *cooperative learning*.

THE NEED FOR COOPERATIVE AND ACTIVE LEARNING APPROACHES

Countless studies, including the National Survey of Student Engagement (NSSE), emphasize the need for student engagement. In fact, recent research from the NSSE "found that student engagement had a 'compensatory effect' on grades and students' likelihood of returning for a second year of college, particularly among underserved minority populations and students entering college with lower levels of achievement" (Wasley, 2006, p. A39). Furthermore, a newer study, "The Role of Active Learning in College Student Persistence," finds that "Faculty use of active learning practices plays a significant role in the retention of first-year college students." According to the study,

> The pattern of findings of this study tends to indicate that active learning practices that faculty use shape in students the perception that their college or university is committed to their welfare in general and their growth and development in particular, a perception that leads to their sense of social integration. The greater a student's degree of social integration, the greater is his or her level of subsequent commitment to the college or university. The greater the student's level of subsequent commitment to the college or university, the greater is his or her likelihood of persistence in the college of initial choice. (Braxton, Jones, Hirschy, & Hartley, 2008, p. 81)

The Association of American Colleges and University's recent report *College Learning for the New Global Century* concludes that "the commitment to expanded college access needs to be anchored in an equally strong commitment to educational excellence" (2007, p. 10).

The classroom-based cooperative approaches that lead to increased learning are well-documented (Cooper & Mueck, 1989; Cooper, Robinson, & Ball, 2003; Johnson, Johnson, & Smith, 1991; Millis, B. J., 2002, 2005, 2006; Millis & Cottell, 1998). Cooperative learning is founded on a deep historical research base, with new research on how people learn and on deep learning providing added insights into its efficacy. Faculty members, however, not only must recognize the value of cooperative approaches but also must have access to the tools, pedagogical support, and inspiration—particularly in their own disciplines—that will enable them to implement cooperative approaches. This book addresses those needs.

In addition to the fact that more and more students are now seeking access to higher education—and justifiably expecting opportunities for success—the current challenges are compounded by two specific factors: (1) increasing faculty reliance on technology and the need to use it "wisely and well," and (2) the increasing size of classes at virtually all public universities, the institutions with the greatest need to support underserved student populations.

These two challenges are intimately intertwined. Currently, many large classes are taught with a minimum of student engagement ("death by Power-Point" or "PowerPoint karaoke"), often because faculty members and graduate teaching assistants assume that only passive approaches are feasible when numbers grow beyond eighty. At best, faculty use a whole-class discussion model for trying to involve students and then lament the fact that only a few students—usually in the front rows—respond.

Even when faculty members introduce new technology such as course management systems or personal response systems ("clickers"), they often do not use these tools to maximize the peer interactions that, according to Crouch and Mazur (2001) and others, lead to increased student learning. The growing body of literature on how people learn emphasizes that "Learning is defined as stabilizing, through repeated use, certain appropriate and desirable synapses in the brain" (Leamnson, 2000, p. 5). This means that active student engagements and cooperative interactions are essential.

Thus, in all classes, including large ones with enrollments exceeding one hundred and sometimes ballooning to four hundred or more, the students themselves—not the faculty members who are lecturing—must grapple with complex material. Cooperative learning can work in large classes. Jeanne Hilton (Hilton, Millis, & Kopera-Frye, 2007), for example, began using team folders and playing cards and introduced color-coded Visible Quiz cards—(A, B, C, D, and TF)—to test for understanding (Cottell, chapter 2) in her Marriage and the Family class of more than 150 students at the University of Nevada, Reno. This approach transformed her large lecture class by making every team accountable for the group in-class assignments, which were collected in the folders, and by making every student in class potentially accountable for giving a team report. She asked students to discuss questions with multiple choice or true/false answers in their teams and then hold up the colored Visible Quiz cards (sometimes called the "cheap" answer to clickers [personal response systems]), giving her and the students immediate feedback as she discussed—or had the students discuss—correct answers.

Through the use of clickers, classroom management systems, and even more radical technological options such as *Second Life*, faculty members have increasing opportunities to use technology creatively to build community and foster engagement. The same tenets identified for cooperative face-to-face classrooms also apply to online applications: structure, relevance, positive interdependence, individual accountability, attention to group skills and social dynamics. A huge number of technology-based approaches in large classes lend themselves to cooperative learning approaches: threaded discussions, clickers, technology-enabled academic games, wikis, blogs, Twitter, distance learning, etc. Not only do faculty need to adopt more creative ways to engage students through technology, but students themselves need to learn these new ways of doing business if they are to be functional in the 21st century.

Furthermore, using both class time and online time for active learning and interaction through group work (cooperative learning) accomplishes many other objectives that are important to those teaching a broad range of students in a variety of settings:

1. Teachers who deliberately form teams or pairs based on student hetero-geneity set the stage for critical thinking. Brookfield (1987) and others have emphasized that critical thinking depends on identifying and chal-lenging assumptions and subsequently exploring and conceptualizing alternatives. These challenges will not occur when students all think alike.

2. Group heterogeneity also helps students build needed workforce and community skills by learning to value the contributions of others. Teachers who help students see the value of cooperative behaviors can significantly affect their later success in a world where the Lone Ranger is no longer a viable model.

3. It is also important to build in processing activities so that students acquire not only teamwork skills, but also the metacognitive skills advocated by Bransford et al. (2000). Cuseo (1992) notes: "Such meta-cognitive processing involves student reflection on (a) individual steps involved in their thinking or problem-solving, (b) specific strategies or approaches they used in the process of reaching problem solutions, and, (c) underlying rationales for their ideas" (p. 73).

4. Structured group work (active learning and interactions) can also pro-mote problem-solving at a higher level than possible with individual effort alone. Springer, Stanne, and Donovan (1999) provide strong evi-dence that the use of small groups can result in greater academic achievement, more favorable attitudes, and increased persistence. Webb (1989) has found that giving detailed, elaborate explanations—activities that occur with cooperative learning small group discus-sions—increases student achievement.

Bransford et al. (2000) conclude: "The emerging science of learning underscores the importance of rethinking what is taught, how it is taught, and how learning is assessed" (p. 13). Teachers who understand this emerging science of learning—including the premises behind deep learning and cooperative learning—are prepared to bring theory into practice. Cooperative learning offers a concrete, coherent way to strengthen classroom and online practices that "operationalize the principles of learning."

AN OVERVIEW OF COOPERATIVE LEARNING

Most experts agree that several components distinguish cooperative learning from other small group or paired procedures, including collaborative learning. In a nutshell, cooperative learning is a highly structured form of group work that focuses on the problem solving that—when directed by an effective teacher—can lead to deep learning, critical thinking, and genuine paradigm shifts in students' thinking. Two givens in the cooperative learning literature are positive interdependence and individual accountability.

Positive interdependence means that teachers give students a vested reason to work together on a task, usually through the nature and structure of a task that has been designed to encourage cooperation and provide challenges a single student could not meet. Individual accountability probably the most abused principle in other less-structured forms of group work—means that students receive the grades they earn. They are not allowed to "coast" on the work of others. Teachers do not "rubber stamp" grades for projects in which the product is assigned a group grade without taking into account the contributions of the individual students.

In cooperative learning classrooms, students can be graded on their own homework submissions, papers, and exams. When group projects are submitted, individual accountability is especially important to prevent "freeloading" or "social loafing." To counter this, every group member can submit for consideration a peer critique of the other group members' contributions, a self-critique, and an overall critique of the group's overall functioning.

Cooperative learning also requires "group processing": the teacher and the students pay attention to what is going on in the groups and actively work to make the groups more productive. There is also an emphasis on the development of social and leadership skills: students learn to conduct an effective work session by drawing contributions from all group members, making certain that everyone's ideas are heard and treated respectfully, and drawing out reluctant contributors.

Although it is not a given in the cooperative learning literature, many cooperative learning practitioners are passionately committed to heterogeneous teams. Teachers thus consider factors that are relevant to the course, such as majors and grade-point averages, but they can also mix students by gender, ethnicity, age, and any other obvious demographic features. This means that instructors need to assign students to groups.

Four people, a common team number, can remain together for a semester in a large class or be remixed at the midterm point in smaller classes. Instructor-selected, diverse groups increase the likelihood that students will face challenges to their assumptions and experience the diverse approaches to problem solving needed for critical thinking. Students also learn to work with people unlike themselves, an important workplace skill.

Classroom management tools are also important as the "grease" that makes everything flow smoothly in a cooperative classroom. The quiet signal, a raised hand to bring the class back to attention, can help everyone transition from group work to whole-class discussion or mini-lecture. "Sponge" or "extension" activities help fast-working groups move on to other challenging problems, case studies, or assignments rather than waste time waiting for other groups to finish. (See chapter 2 for an extensive discussion of cooperative learning elements.)

Adopting a structured, cooperative approach with these components offers faculty members both the philosophical approach and the specific tools to transform their teaching. The philosophy is a constructivist theory of learning that places the responsibility for students' learning on the students themselves, situating cooperative learning clearly in the learning-centered camp.

Students are not left to flounder: they receive support from their teachers and from their peers. The tools are carefully delineated structures—the empty shells that faculty can fill with their discipline-specific course content. This book gives many examples of cooperative learning from a variety of disciplines.

CONCLUSION

Cooperative learning offers a systematic, learning-centered approach to instruction without putting anyone into a pedagogical strait jacket. Lecturing and other approaches thus complement the coopcrative tenels. One of the strengths of cooperative learning lies in its versatility. Following highly structured practices for responsible group work can augment a host of other pedagogical approaches and can result in both deep learning and critical thinking.

Classroom debates, classroom assessment techniques, problem-based learning (Cottell, chapter 2), Just-in-Time Teaching (Maier, McGoldrick, and Simkins, chapter 10), POGIL (Shadle, chapter 3), team-based learning, and academic games can all be enhanced through a cooperative approach. As emphasized earlier, technology and cooperative learning are natural partners.

Cooperative learning satisfies the deepest longings of teachers. It allows faculty members to be learning-centered with an emphasis on building community in classes without abrogating the responsibility for shaping a class based on their experience and expertise. Cooperative learning provides teachers with very specific tools—the structures and the classroom management approaches—that allow them to sequence activities to maximize learning. It helps teachers foster not only learning but also a host of other positive outcomes, such as increased self-esteem, respect for others, and civility. Cooperative learning can transform large, diverse lecture classes into a community of supportive teams.

Cooperative learning satisfies for students the human desire for connection and social support. In addition to keeping students energized and awake, it provides them with the academic resources—their peers—to tackle complex tasks impossible to complete alone. It also gives them essential social and communication skills needed for success in the workplace.

Faculty members find comfort in knowing that they are putting into practice compelling research about how people learn. They can exercise creativity in designing and implementing structured activities. Finally, for both teachers and students, cooperative learning makes deep learning both feasible and fun.

References

Association of American Colleges and Universities. (2007). *College learning for the new global century: A report from the National Leadership Council for Liberal Education & America's Promise*. Washington, DC: Association of American Colleges and Universities.

Barr, R. B., & Tagg, J. (1995, November/December). From teaching to learning: A new paradigm for undergraduate education. *Change: The Magazine of Higher Learning, 27*(6), 13–25.

Bransford, J. D., Brown, A. L., & Cocking, R. R. (Eds.) (2000). *How people learn: Brain, mind, experience, and school*. Commission on Behavioral and Social Sciences and Education National Research Council. Washington, DC: National Academy Press.

Braxton, J. M., Jones, W. A., Hirschy, A. S., & Hartley, H. V., III. (2008). The role of active learning in college persistence. In J. M. Braxton (Ed.), *The role of the classroom in college student persistence: New directions for teaching and learning, no. 115* (pp. 71–83). San Francisco: Jossey-Bass.

Brookfield, S. D. (1987). *Developing critical thinkers: Challenging adults to explore alternative ways of thinking and acting.* San Francisco: Jossey-Bass.

Cooper, J. L., & Mueck, R. (1989). Cooperative/collaborative learning: Research and practice (primarily) at the collegiate level. *The Journal of Staff, Program, and Organization Development, 7*(3), 149–151.

Cooper, J. L., Robinson, P., & Ball, D. (Eds.) (2003). *Small group instruction in higher education: Lessons from the past, visions of the future.* Stillwater, OK: New Forums.

Crouch, C. H., & Mazur, E. (2001). Peer instruction: Ten years of experience and results. *American Journal of Physics, 69,* 970–977.

Cuseo, J. (1992, Winter). Collaborative & cooperative learning in higher education: A proposed taxonomy. *Cooperative Learning and College Teaching, 2*(2), 2–4. Reprinted in J. L. Cooper, P. Robinson, & D. Ball (Eds.), *Small group instruction in higher education: Lessons from the past, visions of the future* (pp. 18–26). Stillwater, OK: New Forums.

Fink, L. D. (2003). *Creating significant learning experiences: An integrated approach to designing college courses.* San Francisco: Jossey-Bass.

Finkel, D. (2000). *Teaching with your mouth shut.* Portsmouth, NH: Heinemann.

Hilton, J. M., Kopera-Frye, K., & Millis, B. (2007). Techniques for student engagement and classroom management in large (and small) classes. *Journal of Teaching in Marriage and Family, 6,* 490–505.

Johnson, D. W., Johnson, R. T., & Smith, K. A. (1991). *Cooperative learning: Increasing college faculty instructional productivity.* ASHE-ERIC Higher Education Report No. 4. Washington, DC: The George Washington University School of Education and Human Development.

Leamnson, R. (2000). *Thinking about teaching and learning: Developing habits of learning with first year college and university students.* Sterling, VA: Stylus.

Millis, B. J. (2002, October) Enhancing learning—and more!—through cooperative learning. IDEA Paper #38. Kansas State University: IDEA Center. Retrieved February 13, 2010, from http://www.theideacenter.org/sites/default/files/IDEA_Paper_38.pdf.

Millis, B. J. (2005). Helping faculty learn to teach better and "smarter" through sequenced activities. In S. Chadwick-Blossy & D. R. Robertson (Eds.), *To improve the academy: Resources for faculty, instructional, and organizational development, 24* (pp. 216–230). Bolton, MA: POD Network and Anker.

Millis, B. J. (2006). Structuring complex cooperative learning activities in 50-minute classes. In S. Chadwick-Blossy & D. R. Robertson (Eds.), *To improve the academy: Resources for faculty, instructional, and organization development* (pp. 153–171). Bolton, MA: POD Network and Anker.

Millis, B. J., & Cottell, P. G. (1998). *Cooperative learning for higher education faculty.* Phoenix, AZ: American Council on Education/Oryx.

Nilson, L. B. (2003). *Teaching at its best: A research-based resource for college instructors* (2nd ed.). Bolton, MA: Anker.

Springer, L., Stanne, M., & Donovan, S. (1999, Spring). Effects of small-group learning on undergraduates in science, mathematics, engineering, and technology: A meta-analysis. *Review of Educational Research, 69*(1), 21–51.

Wasley, P. (2006, November 17). Underprepared students benefit most from "engagement." *Chronicle of Higher Education*, pp. A39–A40.

Webb, N. M. (1989). Peer interaction and learning in small groups. *International Journal of Educational Research, 13,* 21–39.

Weimer, M. (2002). *Learner-centered teaching: Five key changes to practice.* San Francisco: Jossey-Bass.

2

Cooperative Learning in Accounting

Philip G. Cottell, Jr.

In October 1987, I attended a conference of the Professional and Organizational Development Network in Higher Education (POD), an organization dedicated to the improvement of college teaching. The conference included a workshop on cooperative learning conducted by Dr. Barbara Millis. I have attended many well-presented, interesting conference sessions, but this one changed the direction of my career. The week after Barbara's workshop, I returned to my campus and tried one cooperative learning structure, following her advice to "start small." I have never looked back. Since that time, my teaching has evolved to the point where I use cooperative learning over 90% of the time in my classes. This chapter describes my use of cooperative learning in my financial accounting research class at Miami University (Ohio).

COURSE DESCRIPTION

The subject matter in financial accounting research mirrors the material that is typically found in a second intermediate financial accounting course at most colleges and universities. Earlier, the Miami accounting faculty had introduced case based learning in this course. When I took the course over, I discovered that this approach did not help me teach either financial accounting or financial accounting research. At the same time, shifts in department personnel had caused a dramatic increase in class size, making the writing-intensive component impractical. To address these problems, I introduced cooperative learning, a pedagogy that I had used successfully in my other courses. Recognizing the close kinship between cooperative learning and problem-based learning (PBL)—both rely on highly structured group work—I introduced into the course unfolding PBL problems for financial accounting topics.

DESCRIPTION OF PEDAGOGIES

Cooperative learning and PBL are ideally suited for each other. I think of cooperative learning as a frame into which an instructor can fit other pedagogies. For me, PBL fits into the cooperative learning framework like a hand in a glove. Used together, they create a classroom environment where dynamic, student-driven learning occurs.

Cooperative Learning

As indicated in the opening chapter, cooperative learning employs a structured form of small group problem solving that incorporates the use of heterogeneous teams, maintains individual accountability, promotes positive interdependence, instills group processing, and sharpens social and leadership skills. The emphasis on structure provides a firm foundation. A longtime cooperative learning practitioner, Cooper (chapter 7), asserts that the three most important aspects of cooperative learning are "structure, structure, and structure" (Cooper, 1990).

Through careful planning and execution, the classroom instructor can create a comfortable yet controlled environment where student teaching and learning flourish. This environment emerges through cooperative learning structures, which are described in detail in *Cooperative Learning for Higher Education Faculty* by Millis and Cottell (1998). I have used several of these structures in my financial accounting research course with great success.

In addition to structure, appropriately formed teams constitute a second pillar of successful cooperative learning. Cooperative learning researchers and practitioners agree nearly unanimously that diverse teams result in learning environments that are superior to those created with homogeneous teams. We do, in fact, learn more from people with experiences and backgrounds that are different than our own. Because students left to their own devices tend to cluster into homogeneous teams, the classroom instructor must take an active role in team formation.

As emphasized throughout this volume, individual accountability remains a critical aspect of cooperative learning. Students working in groups often expect to receive the same grade as their teammates, regardless of their individual contributions. The practice of handing out undifferentiated group grades, however, undermines cooperative learning. Many cooperative learning proponents consider the assignment of group grades to be not only poor pedagogical practice, but also poor ethical practice. The rule to remember and to communicate to students is this: learning occurs in groups, but the gauge of each student's learning is determined on an individual basis. The individual accountability component of cooperative learning motivates students to work hard in the cooperative effort.

Positive interdependence, an important element of cooperative learning, poses a challenge for instructors. Johnson, Johnson, & Smith (n.d.) describe this as an environment where "We sink or swim together." The dilemma occurs because the most obvious way to achieve positive interdependence is the assignment of undifferentiated group grades. Yet, as already stated, that option is not viable because of the individual accountability component. Instructors must take the more difficult and, at the same time, more rewarding path of demonstrating to students that their own learning is enhanced by working cooperatively with their peers. This process occurs through carefully designed cooperative learning structures.

Group processing supports positive interdependence. This component of cooperative learning helps students assess their own learning, an ability that Bransford, Brown, & Cocking (2000) describe as "metacognition" and regard as one of three key learning principles. Group processing skills are lifetime learning enhancers that may be more valuable to students than mastering specific ephemeral course material.

Social or leadership skills comprise the final critical ingredient of the cooperative learning classroom. Cooperative learning practitioners embed writing, speaking, appreciation of differences, and other intellectual skills in their cooperative learning structures and thus teach them alongside the course material. Many employers hiring students value the social skills they master in college more than specific course content.

Problem-Based Learning (PBL)

A pedagogy known as PBL gives college teachers another tool that produces a learning-centered environment. Because PBL contains a strong small group component, I decided to use PBL hand-in-hand with cooperative learning. It has turned out to be a marriage made in educational heaven.

In PBL, the students confront a problem before they are given any information about how to solve it. This turns on its head the typical pedagogy where students receive given methods—usually through lectures or demonstrations—and then they solve problems. This often results in a "plug and chug" approach in which students don't apply critical thinking but merely grope for the appropriate formula. Students who receive a given problem-solving method initially remain unclear about its usefulness until they also receive an appropriate problem.

With PBL, before they receive any problem-solving methods, students confront a problem that closely resembles a workday situation. They then seek ways to resolve it, often by determining the missing information they need and a logical problem-solving approach. At the end of their quest, students value the knowledge they glean because it is applied and because they discovered it constructively and cooperatively.

In a PBL environment, students typically learn how to learn. Johnstone and Biggs (1998) propose PBL as a curricular structure that integrates technical accounting information, practical experience, and lifelong learning skills to promote accounting expertise. Instructors may consult Duch, Groh, and Allen (2001) for in-depth perspectives about PBL.

Duch (2001) describes the characteristics of good PBL problems. She notes that many PBL problems are designed with multiple stages. In explaining these multistage problems, Bellas, Marshall, Reed, Venable, and Whelan-Berry (2000) call them "unfolding problems." Essentially, an unfolding problem differs from the traditional classroom problem or case in that the problem itself does not contain sufficient information for the student to solve it. In the initial stage, the problem is vague and ill-defined. As students wrestle with the accounting issue, they first determine what additional information they need. The problem "unfolds" as students receive or discover information that allows them to approach the problem at an increasingly concrete level. As the students work together on the various stages of the problem, they simultaneously learn both course-related concepts and problem-solving skills.

As in cooperative learning, PBL students work in small groups to solve the problems. For this purpose, cooperative learning structures, as explained by Cottell and Millis (1993), are helpful. Instructors wishing an overview of cooperative learning may consult Johnson, Johnson, and Smith (1991) or Millis and Cottell (1998).

I have discovered that many students can properly recite the way to account for a transaction, but they can't accomplish the underlying arithmetic to compute cash flows or to make a journal entry unless they see the instructor complete an example. Duch (2001) aptly labels this kind of student learning as "pattern match, plug and chug." Often, this kind of learning results in short-term memorization rather than long-term understanding. PBL alleviates this approach because students must make their own calculations before seeing a template example.

HETEROGENEOUS TEAMS

As noted previously, successful cooperative learning depends on heterogeneous teams. Because Miami University has been largely unsuccessful in attracting minorities, particularly to the business school, I focus on gender, ability, and scholastic interest to achieve heterogeneity. The student population is equally divided between male and female, so I try to have my groups reflect that ratio.

As to ability, I use the student's undergraduate grade-point average (GPA) as a surrogate measure. This crude statistic may measure motivation as well as ability. I determine scholastic interest by the student's declared major. Because this is a senior-level accounting course, few nonaccounting majors are represented, but I want those students spread among the groups where they will receive coaching from accounting peers.

My groups are organized with a deck of playing cards. I use a seating chart that assigns a playing card to each seat in the class (Figure 2.1). Before the first class period, I place playing cards on these seats so that the students will find them when they enter. Often, students quip, "Are we going to play Texas Holdem?" when they find these cards. To build rapport, I respond to their jokes. A second deck of playing cards in my pocket assists me with group formation.

The Value Line

A Value Line is a cooperative learning structure in which students are first organized homogeneously and then split into heterogeneous teams. Although it has multiple uses, I employ it primarily for group formation. The term "Value Line" originated from a lineup based on students' opinion about a controversial issue. However, the lineup can occur using any designated criteria

I use gender and ability or motivation to form teams. Following a brief explanation of the course, PBL, and cooperative learning, I have students derive an individual score by adding numbers. First I tell the students, "If you are a woman, write the number one thousand on a piece of paper; if you are a man, write the number five hundred." Next, I ask the students to multiply their undergraduate GPA by one hundred and add that to the number they have on their paper. To the resulting sum, I tell them, "Add one hundred if you are a double major in accounting and finance. Add seventy-five if you are either an accounting major with some other major as a double or if you are a singular accounting major. Add fifty if you have a business school major other than accounting. Add twenty-five if you have a major outside the business school." Finally, I tell them to sum the digits of their social security number and add the result. This final step creates randomness to break any ties.

I then tell the students to line up in the hall based on their derived number, lowest to highest. I tell them to take all their belongings with them but leave the playing cards in place. At this point, the students realize that this is not a business-as-usual accounting course and begin to relax. Occasionally, a male finds himself in the middle of the women and realizes that he must not have been paying attention. I just smile.

Seating Chart
Room 301 & 303 Laws Hall

Course: _____   **Section:** _____

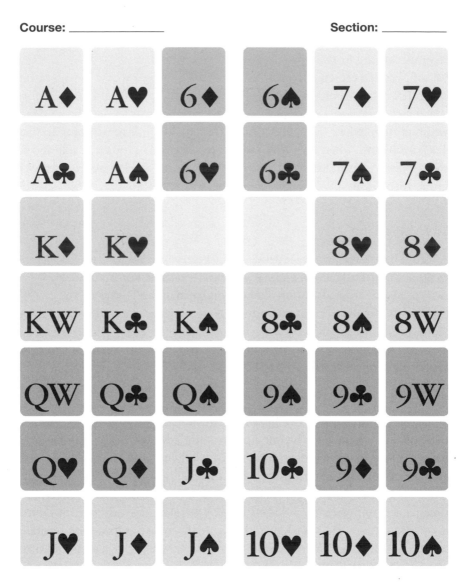

Front

Figure 2.1

I tell the students to forget the number they just added because they are going to get a new number. "I was never good at arithmetic," I tell them. "You must help me discover how many students are in the class by counting off, left to right—one, two, and so forth—until the last student informs me how many are present. I learned this count-off trick in the Army." After I remind them to remember their new number, we proceed with the count-off.

After the last student announces his or her number, I write it on a tablet and quickly divide by two. Then I create four columns of numbers. The first starts with one, the second with the median, the third with one plus the median, and the final column starts with the number of students in the class.

"I will call out numbers," I tell them. "When I call your number, approach me to receive a playing card. When you have your card, return to the classroom and sit in the seat with the matching card. That is your permanent assigned seat."

I then proceed to announce numbers, four at a time. The first set of numbers are the numbers at the head of the four columns on my tablet. I then scratch off each of these numbers, add one to columns one and three, and subtract one from columns two and four. This process continues until each student has a playing card and therefore a seat, and, as I explain in the following, a group assignment. Figure 2.2 depicts the procedure of distributing playing cards.

A special caution is in order here. Never assign a spade to an African American student. A participant in one of my workshops reminded me years ago that a spade can be a highly offensive symbol in that culture. So take care when handing out the cards.

Valve Line Formation			
Class of Thirty-Five			
Ace	1	18	19	35
King	2	17	20	34
Queen	3	16	21	33
Jack	4	15	22	32
Ten	5	14	23	31
Nine	6	13	24	30
Eight	7	12	25	29
Seven	8	11	26	28
Wild card*	9	10		27

*The students left after the last group of four receive a wild card. They are assigned to random groups as fifth members.

Figure 2.2

GROUP ORGANIZATION

I deliberately assign students to groups of four, even though cooperative learning practitioners and theorists differ about whether the appropriate group size should be three, four, five, or six. I strongly prefer groups of four. With three students, if a student is absent, the group is reduced to a nearly dysfunctional level of two. Six becomes unwieldy in my experience, allowing some students to freeload. I therefore use four and five. I prefer four because I often pair students; however, I rarely have classes that divide evenly by four, so I use the spillover to form groups of five.

The playing cards are not a cute attention-getter: the rank of the playing card represents the group to which the student has been assigned. The color of the suit represents the unique partner with whom the student will work in cases where I use paired structures. The suit itself represents roles that I assign to students from time to time on a rotating basis.

For groups of five, I introduce "wild cards." These wild cards constitute a fifth suit in the group of five. For this purpose, I use jokers with card ranks written on them. In Figure 2.1, the "W" designates the seats assigned to students holding wild cards. In Figure 2.2, the students left after the last group of four receive a wild card. They are assigned to random groups as fifth members.

I use rotating roles, which are typically the discussion leader or facilitator, the recorder or scribe, and the reporter or spokesperson. I sometimes put an accounting spin on these by calling the discussion leader or facilitator, for example, the chief executive officer (CEO).

In my early days using cooperative learning, I used these student roles much more prominently than I do today. Rotating roles reinforce the social skills component of cooperative learning; however, these group roles tended to hurt the positive interdependence aspect of cooperative learning. Because I have found other ways to promote social skills, I have gradually backed away from assigned roles in order to foster more positive interdependence. But I still use roles from time to time. In fact, I have discovered that doing the unexpected (such as assigning roles for the day) makes class more enjoyable for the students and for me.

New Group Formation

Because I have relatively small classes (typically, 30–50 students), I form new groups at least once during the semester. I can defuse the one or two dysfunctional groups that usually emerge early in the semester by forming new groups at approximately the midterm point. Students in well-functioning groups often hate to leave cooperative friends, but I explain that working in new groups gives them the opportunity to work with new people and learn good workplace skills. Most accept this explanation.

The first test provides data for the group switch. In this case, I develop a virtual line-up based on student test scores. I arrange the students by their test scores, highest to lowest. Then I form groups as described earlier, but now in the privacy of my office. I pay attention to gender, trying not to have an isolated male or female in a group where all the rest are the opposite sex. The groups of five make this mix easier.

COOPERATIVE LEARNING STRUCTURES

My combined PBL and cooperative learning classroom is a fluid, dynamic environment. Any one class likely has group work, followed by whole-class discussion. On occasion, I throw in an old-fashioned lecture. As a constant, I always use cooperative learning structures because of their power to drive learning.

I use team folders, described by Millis and Cottell (1998), as a classroom management tool. On a typical day, the students pick up their team folders and discover a new PBL problem or a new phase to an unfolding problem. To begin the class, I ask the students to discuss this problem with two questions in mind: "What do we know?" and "What do we need to know?"

I have designed a PBL worksheet (Figure 2.3) to help the students organize their thoughts, including how to use the necessary information. A single copy of this worksheet is in the folder to promote positive interdependence: the students have to work together to complete the one worksheet.

The second page of the worksheet contains a block with the question "What have we learned?" To assess their own learning at the end of the class session, students respond to this question. Each team then turns in its folder with the completed PBL worksheets. Later I read them and comment, particularly on the portion that addresses the question, "What have we learned?" I clip the completed worksheets with my comments into the team folders as a permanent learning record.

While the students are in groups, I sit in as an observer, randomly determining the selected group by drawing a card. From the beginning of the semester, I discourage students from viewing me as the authority with "the right answer." When they question me, like Shadle (chapter 3), I gently return the question back to the group. I limit myself to five minutes with each cooperative team before drawing another card and moving to a new team.

Once the students have worked on the problem for a sufficient period, I gain their attention by using an agreed-upon quiet signal. Whole-class discussion follows. I use the same questions—"What do we know?" and "What do we

Pertinent, Known Information

Group: _____   Date: _____

What do we know?	How will what we know help us solve this problem?

Additional Information Required

Group: _____   Date: _____

What do we need to know?	How will what we need to know help us solve this problem?
What have we learned?	

Figure 2.3 PBL Worksheet

need to know?"—for the whole-class discussion. I do not concern myself if a critical piece of information is missed because it will emerge in subsequent phases or explorations of the problem.

Once the class has had adequate whole-class discussion, I pass out the next phase of the PBL unfolding problem, and the cycle is repeated. This process continues for several days with a single PBL unfolding problem. Throughout the process, cooperative learning structures frame both the group work and, to some extent, the whole-class discussion.

Think-Pair-Share

This cooperative learning structure is the simplest, both in terms of planning and implementation. In fact, Think-Pair-Share is so easy that at times I use it "on the fly" when I believe the class as a whole is either stuck or unwilling to respond. At other times, I have planned Think-Pair-Shares for a particular day.

I use the Think-Pair-Shares at two points in the class. One is during the mini-lectures that I deliver from time to time in areas where experience tells me students need a boost to get going on the PBL. These Think-Pair-Shares are planned. The other more common use occurs in the "on the fly" variety in order to recharge the whole-class discussion when it stalls.

To implement a Think-Pair-Share, I pose a question and give students time to compose an answer. Sometimes I tell them to write their response in their notes. I try not to rush this quiet waiting time because it is valuable for student learning. Next, I tell the students to discuss their responses with their suit partners (red suits paired and black suits paired) and to discuss and resolve any differences. In the final "share" portion, I invite students to share their responses with the entire class. Nearly always, several students volunteer with carefully thought-out responses because they have had an opportunity for rehearsal and feedback.

Think-Pair-Share is a powerful cooperative learning structure because it employs the principle of simultaneous interaction. When I call on a single student to respond, normally the rest of the students tune out, grateful that they were not "nailed." When the same question is posed as a Think-Pair-Share, all the students become simultaneously involved as they talk to one another in pairs. A Think-Pair-Share can transform a stalled whole-class discussion into a lively student exchange.

Structured Problem Solving

For me, Structured Problem Solving, called "Numbered Heads Together" in much of the cooperative learning literature, is the workhorse of cooperative learning. Because the K–12 term is a bit "cutsey" for college-level teaching, I have adopted the term coined by Millis and Cottell (1998).

Structured Problem Solving depends on students having a preplanned identity, which is determined in my class by their playing card. In this structure, the team's spokesperson is not pre-identified, thus making any student potentially responsible for explaining the group's progress and findings.

I use Structured Problem Solving in nearly every class session. As students working in their groups wrestle with each phase of my PBL unfolding problems, I closely monitor them to determine an appropriate time to switch to whole-class discussion. When that happens, I go to the front of the class, gain the students' attention with the quiet signal, and draw a card from a deck. The student whose card is selected responds to a question, often drawing on the team's thinking.

Called-upon students may decline to respond (I refer to this as a "punt" rather than a "pass"); however, because I build in a heavy class participation component, students generally respond to earn these participation points. When a student does punt, I ask the class if anyone would like that student's points. I always have several eager takers.

I emphasize that I am not looking for a "right answer" so much as a reasoned response. The open-ended responses usually elicit additional student comments, leading to a student-student class discussion. If this does not occur, I simply draw another card to begin a new discussion cycle.

At the conclusion of a whole-class discussion, I sometimes decide that additional group work will help teams complete this phase of the PBL problem, and I return the groups to it. After other discussions, I pass out the next phase of the PBL unfolding problem. At the conclusion of the last PBL phase, class discussion focuses on reflections about the learning that occurred throughout the various phases.

Within-Team Jigsaw

An old saw states, "Variety is the spice of life." This is certainly true in a classroom environment. I try to keep students engaged by offering new pedagogical approaches.

A Within-Team Jigsaw fits the bill. This cooperative learning structure works well with complex problems that have two "pieces." The problem is solved when the pieces are put together. As an example, I use a Within-Team Jigsaw for complex earnings per share computations. Here a student must calculate the numerator effect, calculate the denominator effect, and then put the pieces together by dividing the denominator into the numerator to calculate the earnings per share.

A Within-Team Jigsaw is easy to implement once instructors have organized the structured learning teams so that students have a "suit partner" with a playing card that has the same color suit (spades with clubs, hearts with diamonds, wild cards forming a triad with the black suits). I pass out a problem to the students to work with their suit partners.

I usually use a trick that Barbara Millis taught me by starting with a Think-Pair-Share that asks, "What is a suit partner?" Once this is resolved, I tell the students holding black suits to work with their suit partner to calculate the numerator of the earnings per share ratio. Simultaneously, students holding red suits calculate the denominator of the earnings per share ratio. As students complete their timed tasks, I move about the room monitoring their activity.

Once this task has been accomplished, I tell the students to re-form their structured learning teams. Here there is a critical (and difficult) aspect of Within-Team Jigsaw. Each of the pairs (triads) must now teach their portion to the other two students. In my experience, accounting students ignore the teaching element and rush to get "the right answer." Students assume that the other pair can do the calculations for the first portion on their own.

I fight this tendency in two ways. The first is with group monitoring. As I visit a group, I don't ask for the correct answer for earnings per share; instead, I ask a student to explain the portion of the calculation that the other pair did. For example, I ask a student holding a diamond to explain the calculation of the numerator in the problem. If the student is stumped (which is frequently the case), I ask the students holding the black suits to explain to me the strategy that they used to teach this portion. Students usually get the point quickly.

My second tactic is similar. I have found that students seek closure for cooperative learning structures involving problems. Whole-class discussion and follow-up accomplishes this. However, during the whole-class follow-up, as I do when monitoring, I call on the opposite suit to explain the procedure. If the designated student is unable to respond, I open up this challenge to all students holding that suit color, exempting the groups I have already monitored. If no student can give the explanation, I return students to their groups to "re-teach" the materials that they had obviously ignored or blitzed through in their focus on the final answer. This practice reinforces the importance of the teaching portion of Within-Team Jigsaw.

COOPERATIVE EXAMINATION CRITIQUE

For many students, the most pressing question in a course is "What will be on the exam?" In many cases, the question changes after the exam papers have been returned. Now the students want to know "Will you curve the grades?"

The question itself poses an immediate problem for the cooperative learning practitioner. As Millis and Cottell (1998) point out, most experts agree that grading on the curve—a practice that creates a quota system in the class and thus sets up a competitive rather than a cooperative atmosphere—should be avoided.

Yet the frequency of the students' question suggests that the issue needs further exploration. Ironically, students who ask about a curve on a test rarely mean a quota-based bell-shaped curve. They really want points added to their test score so that the class average will reach some preconceived level of fairness.

In a perfect educational world, such a notion would be absurd. The professor has written a perfect test, allowing students to demonstrate with certain accuracy their levels of knowledge and skills. Following this logic, adding points simply because of student inadequacies adds nothing to the learning environment and fosters grade inflation.

But wait! The prior response assumes that professors are experts in creating infallible tests. This professor has never been able to come close to that standard. Because I know this, I generally attempt to err on the difficult side when writing my accounting test questions. As a result, when I mark the tests, the class average is sometimes below even the "no-longer-average" C. Although disappointed with the students' low performance, I recognize my contribution to this outcome. Therefore, until "inventing" my new approach, I simply added points to student scores to get the grades to a reasonable level.

On the day that graded examinations are returned, some professors go over the exam to review the key concepts. I have never been satisfied with this procedure because the better students, who have already demonstrated their mastery of the exam material, are bored, and some students wish to challenge me on the appropriateness of test questions and my grading policy.

Moreover, this "stand-and-deliver" approach places the students in the role of passive, not active, learners and makes me a rigid authority figure handing down the "right" answers. Therefore, in the past I had typically skipped the review and instead gave students written solutions so that they could review on their own the concepts they missed.

Nevertheless, I felt that a critique of the exam might be a useful learning tool if I could engage the students in active learning. Then, after a particularly dismal exam performance, I came up with the cooperative exam critique. I now explain the cooperative exam critique in the class syllabus and also verbally explain it before the exam itself.

I tell the students that the examination is a two-day event. On the first day, they all take the exam individually, as in other courses. On the second day, they retake a portion of the examination in their groups. Scores earned by the group during the group phase are added to the individual scores of the students in that group. I tell the students that if the individual grades are sufficiently high, I will cancel the cooperative exam critique. I tell them that past grades have usually necessitated the second-day cooperative exam critique, which is intended to help their learning and boost their overall exam grade.

The cooperative exam critique gives students a second chance to revisit the exam material after gaining insights into the areas where they need to focus. Students welcome the chance to make up for deficiencies in their studies.

After the students take the individual exams, I grade them and calculate grade distributions. I then determine how many points I must add to get the grades at a level I like. I identify the question or questions where the students experienced the most difficulty and assign sufficient points that they can earn on the group response. I make copies of this question (or questions) and place them in the student folders.

Conduct of the Critique

On the day of the cooperative exam critique, I bring these materials to class. To initiate the process, I carefully explain how the critique unfolds, including team members' roles and the time allotted. Using playing card suits, I assign two special roles in each group. One, the reporter, records the teams' solution to the exam, which is taken to another group during the second phase of the cooperative exam critique. A second student, the recorder, also records the team's exam solutions, but these remain with the group during the second phase.

Because students have already taken the same test individually and have had time to re-study any weak areas that they identified during the original exam, I give the teams about one-third of the original time for this retake. Because I teach a 75-minute class, I allot 25 minutes for the group to complete the first problem-solving portion of the exercise.

With grades on the line, the group discussions during the critique become remarkably animated. In their groups, students debate accounting principles and procedures far more intensely than during the rather tame dialogues that occur in traditional exam critiques. While problem solving as a team, the students are engaged in the active learning component of cooperative learning that makes it such a powerful pedagogical tool.

After the 25 minutes have elapsed, I use the prearranged quiet signal to gain students' attention and then begin the second phase of the cooperative exam, in which I use a cooperative learning structure called "Three-Stay/One-Stray." Armed with the agreed-upon answers from his or her home group, each group reporter joins another group in the class. This is easily accomplished by instructing all reporters to rotate clockwise to the next group (the reporter from the ace group moves to the two team, the two reporter rotates to the three team, and so on). In large classes, the king reporter jumps to the ace team of the next set of teams, which is identified by a different colored folder. I inform the class that they will have ten minutes to discuss the exam in these modified groups.

This phase of the cooperative exam critique introduces a powerful critical thinking component. Most reporters are surprised to find that the new group disagrees with the well-reasoned response of their home group on at least part of the question. Because the correct answer helps each team member's individual score, all the students typically question their earlier assumptions. Again, concentrated dialogue ensues, as students wrestle with accounting principles and techniques that enable them to attain the maximum number of exam points.

After spending ten minutes with the new group, the reporters return to their home groups to give an account of what they learned. This phase of the exercise also lasts ten minutes. During this time, the group considers the findings of their own reporter who "strayed" and also discuss what they learned from the reporter who visited them. Thus, each student has been at least indirectly exposed to the perspectives of three different groups. Now teams must decide on the final response to submit. Once more, students employ critical thinking skills to maximize the points that they can earn.

After ten minutes, groups submit their solutions to the exam. In the final phase of the critique, we engage in a brief whole-class discussion of each question, a process requiring little time because, by now, most groups agree on the correct solution.

Nevertheless, one or two questions may remain in dispute. A rich whole-class discussion ensues, as the students promote their point of view—without adding the contentious elements that occur during a traditional exam review, when students sometimes fight for every point. By the end of this phase, all students understand the correct solutions to these difficult test questions. Figure 2.4 graphically illustrates the movements of the students among groups in this structure.

Benefits of the Critique

The cooperative exam critique promotes many positive results. First, it motivates students to dig into the accounting material immediately after the individual test when they can recall most of the questions. Students eager to earn higher grades become actively engaged with the material as they study and as they work the problem(s) during the critique.

Three-Stay/One-Stray

First Phase
Students retake the test in their structured learning teams.*

A♣ A♠
A♥ A♦
Q♣ Q♠
Q♥ Q♦

K♣ K♠
K♥ K♦
J♣ J♠
J♥ J♦

Second Phase
A student from each group rotates to another group to check test responses.

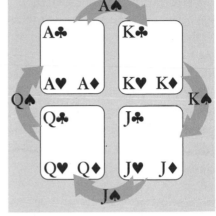

Third Phase
Students rotate to their home group to report the results of their discussions with other groups.

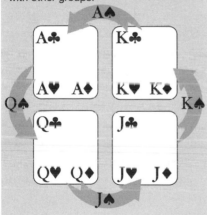

Fourth Phase
In re-formed structured learning teams, students finalize responses to turn in.

A♣ A♠
A♥ A♦
Q♣ Q♠
Q♥ Q♦

K♣ K♠
K♥ K♦
J♣ J♠
J♥ J♦

* Symbols represent playing cards (Millis & Cottell, 1998)

Figure 2.4

Second, students learn valuable critical thinking skills when they are confronted with solutions that differ from those they believed to be correct. Third, students come to appreciate the power of the group process because they realize that better test results occur in a group setting. This aspect of the structure also reinforces the positive interdependence.

Because the cooperative exam is based on the most rigorous questions in the original exam, even the most talented students in the class are challenged as they convince their teammates of their reasoning. Thus, the level of learning for all students rises. Students engage in deep, as opposed to surface, learning during the entire review process. Furthermore, they feel a sense of accomplishment because they earned the extra points, rather than receiving a gift reinforcing their failure. The cooperative exam critique transforms what could be a routine exam critique into a powerful learning tool.

REVIEW FOR THE FINAL

Early in my teaching career, I discovered that students appreciate a review of course material prior to a comprehensive final examination. Initially, I scheduled a review session where I asked students to bringing their questions about the material. I reasoned that this approach would motivate them to begin preparing early for the final.

Instead, I discovered that the vast majority of students came to the session with only one question: "What is on the exam?" I also realized over the years that, as on many other campuses, students at my institution typically cram rather than preparing early for exams. My review sessions did little to motivate them to focus on serious questions. Because I wouldn't "spoon feed" them the exam questions, both the students and I found this review time wasted.

I was determined to design a review session that would get the students actively involved in the process and stimulate their interest during the doldrums at the end of the semester. My first radical shift was to assign to myself the duty of bringing questions to the review session. I did this by drawing multiple-choice questions from past exams.

I used two cooperative learning structures to pose the questions: Visible Quiz cards (Staley, 2003) and an academic game called Quizo (Sugar, n.d.). I make the review session voluntary but entice the students by telling them, "We will play a game during the review with valuable prizes."

Preparation for the Visible Quiz

To prepare for the Visible Quiz, I make large colored cards for the students to display in teams. These cards—which allow multiple-choice responses based on a, b, c, and d—are made with a PowerPoint file with four slides. The first slide has two text boxes, each with the letter "a." The font size is 96, and the text box is rotated ninety degrees. Both text boxes are centered vertically. One text box appears about one-quarter of the way in and the other three-quarters of the way in. The remaining three slides are identical except that they contain the letters "b, c, and d."

I print these four slides and then reproduce them on colored card stock, which I cut in half to form two 8½- × 5½-inch cards. For my sets, the "a" is red, the "b" is blue, the "c" is yellow, and the "d" is green. I create new file folders, which are reserved exclusively for the final exam review. I place one set of the Visible Quiz cards (a through d) into each file folder.

Preparation for Quizo

Quizo is an academic game adapted from Bingo. Various materials are assembled for this game. The first is the marker boards, which look like the ones used in Bingo, except the letters Q-U-I-Z-O replace B-I-N-G-O across the top. Below is a 5 × 5 matrix with the numbers one through five in each column. The configuration of the numbers is scrambled so that no two cards are alike. I place one of these unique cards into each file folder with the Visible Quiz cards.

The game also requires a special deck of cards. The cards in this deck are marked Q1, Q2 . . . O4, O5, so that each square on the marker boards is represented. The deck contains five additional cards that say, "Cover any square in the Q column," "Cover any square in the U column," etc.

I use candy such as M&Ms as the markers for students to cover their boards. I dispense the M&Ms to each student team in cupcake holders, warning them not to eat too many of their markers until after the review.

Valuable prizes are important, but they can be as simple as assorted fun-sized candy bars that the students select after their team yells, "Quizo!"

Conduct of the Review

On the night of the review, I arrive at the session with the file folders containing the Visible Quiz cards, a Quizo marker board, and any additional needed materials, such as a present value table. Finally, I place five copies of a "final exam anti-stress kit" (Figure 2.5) into the folders to ease student tension. I also bring the questions I have written and a way to project them to the class. Because my university's classrooms are networked, projection simply means accessing the network drive. Before we had that capability, I used an overhead projector.

As the students enter the classroom, I quickly assign them to groups of four and give the group a file folder and a cupcake holder filled with M&Ms, instructing them to sit close together.

Because my final examination reviews are extremely informal, students know that they can come late or leave early. This means that group membership is fluid. I have learned to back off my normally structured approach for the review sessions.

To begin the review sessions, I give detailed instructions to the students, including the criteria for "winning" the Quizo game: five squares in a row, in a column, or diagonally, covered by the M&Ms. The students locate the

Final Examination
Anti-Stress Kit

Bang
Head
Here

Directions:
1. Place on firm surface.
2. Follow directions in circle.
3. Repeat until stress is gone or you are unconscious.
4. Perform procedure again as necessary, not to exceed four times during finals week.
5. If circle turns red, consult a physician.

Figure 2.5

needed materials in the folder in preparation for the multiple-choice questions I will project on the screen.

In their groups, they discuss the question and quickly come to consensus about the right answer. Then, at my signal, a group member holds up the colored card containing the letter that corresponds to the right answer. I then draw a card from the deck: those groups with correct answers place an M&M on the designated square. Groups with five covered squares in a row shout "Quizo!" to get their valuable prize.

My review focuses on learning. If most teams hold up the colored card with the right answer, I decide that the class got it and announce the square to be covered. If a "rainbow" appears with multiple answers, I consider this a "teachable moment." I usually call on students to determine how their groups determined their answer (right or wrong). Often, misconceptions emerge. When the majority of students arrive at incorrect answers in their teams, I know I need to review the accounting concept addressed by the question.

After asking the students if they have questions, I proceed to the next review question and continue this sequence until a group announces "Quizo!" Students in that group select their valuable prize. (This is when they discover what the prize is. I am asked often if they can substitute a higher grade.)

The members of the winning group are told to clear their board, and the game continues. Usually, by the end of the review, all the groups have been able to announce "Quizo!" The review ends when I have exhausted the questions that I have brought. Most students find the final exam review an enjoyable and worthwhile experience. I have received favorable feedback about it over the years.

QUALITY CONTROL CIRCLE

Because cooperative learning and PBL are new to most students, I like to use a classroom assessment technique (CAT) suggested by Angelo and Cross (1993) to keep myself informed about the progress of student learning during the semester. This CAT was originally adapted from industry. In that setting, production-line employees work closely with managers to solve manufacturing problems.

Each of my sections elects two members to the quality control circle. I encourage all students to take any course-related suggestions, complaints, or compliments to their representative on the quality control circle. To elicit frank assessments, I assure students that I will not request—nor will the quality control circle representatives reveal—the names of students who provide feedback. I meet frequently with the quality control circle throughout the semester. I schedule a formal conference room for these meetings to communicate to its members the importance that I attach to the quality control circle.

Over the years, the information that I have gleaned from the quality control circle has been marvelous. For example, one day I walked out of a class convinced I had thoroughly confused students with an example I had used to explain the difference between construction costs and construction expenses when using the percentage-of-completion method. That same evening, coincidentally, I met with the quality control circle. Two members reported that several students had made complimentary remarks about the clarity of the example covered in class. Because of this feedback, I have kept an example in my teaching repertoire that I would otherwise have discarded.

I establish trust with my quality control circles by being careful never to react negatively to information that they bring to me and never to probe for the source of comments. I have to exercise restraint sometimes because comments sometimes seem trivial and even immature. One comment in particular always makes me bite my tongue: "Your method differs from the book's."

My best tactic is simply to write down all comments and assure students that I will take them under consideration, rather than react in the moment. In the main, comments from my quality control circles have been helpful, enabling me to make rapid, positive adjustments to my teaching.

The quality control circle has been particularly useful to me in keeping the pulse on cooperative learning and PBL. Many students resist these approaches because they represent change. Through the quality control circle, I have been able to assess how the attitude of the class changes over the semester. I can also find out what troubles the students and then meet these concerns head-on or make adjustments before it is too late.

SOME FINAL THOUGHTS

Cooperative learning is a pedagogy that I recommend to everyone in the teaching profession. In my experience, it enhances not only student learning, but also student confidence in their ability to learn. Nonetheless, its chief benefit is a selfish one. Cooperative learning keeps the teaching experience alive and fresh for the teacher. It has greatly added to both my effectiveness and my enjoyment of the craft of teaching.

References

Angelo, T. A., & Cross, K. P. (1993). *Classroom assessment techniques* (2nd ed.). San Francisco: Jossey-Bass.

Bellas, C. J., Marshall, J., Reed, M. M., Venable, J. M., & Whelan-Berry, K. S. (2000, October). *PBL in business—understanding Problem-Based Learning and trying*

PBL in your business discipline: An interactive approach. Paper presented at PBL 2000, Birmingham, AL.

Bransford, J. D., Brown, A. L., & Cocking, R. R. (Eds.) (2000). *How people learn: Brain, mind, experience, and school.* Commission on Behavioral and Social Sciences and Education National Research Council. Washington, DC: National Academy Press.

Cottell, P. G., & Millis, B. J. (1993, Spring). Cooperative learning structures in the instruction of accounting. *Issues in Accounting Education, 8*(1), 40–59.

Cooper, J. (1990, May). Cooperative learning and college teaching: Tips from the trenches. *The Teaching Professor, 4*(5), 1–2.

Duch, B. J. (2001). Writing problems for deeper understanding. In B. J. Duch, S. E. Groh, & D. E. Allen (Eds.), *The power of problem-based learning: A practical "how to" for reaching undergraduate courses in any discipline* (pp. 47–53). Sterling, VA: Stylus.

Duch, B. J., Groh, S. E., & Allen, D. E. (Eds.) (2001). *The power of problem-based learning: A practical "how to" for reaching undergraduate courses in any discipline.* Sterling, VA: Stylus.

Johnson, R. T., Johnson, D. W., & Smith, K. A. (n.d.) *Cooperative learning.* Minneapolis: Cooperative Learning Center. Retrieved February 13, 2010, from http://www.ce.umn.edu/~smith/docs/CL%20College-604.doc.

Johnson, D. R., Johnson, E. J., & Smith, K. A. (1991). *Cooperative learning: Increasing college faculty instructional productivity.* ASHE-ERIC Higher Education Report No. 4. Washington, DC: The George Washington University School of Education and Human Development.

Johnstone, K. M., & Biggs, S. F. (1998). Problem-based learning: Introduction, analysis, and accounting curricula implications. *Journal of Accounting Education, 16*(3/4), 407–427.

Millis, B. J., & Cottell, P. G. (1998). *Cooperative learning for higher education faculty.* Phoenix, AZ: American Council on Education/Oryx Press.

Staley, C. C. (2003). *Fifty ways to leave your lectern.* Belmont, CA: Wadsworth/Thompson.

Sugar, S. (n.d.). Quizo Game System. Retrieved February 2, 2010, from www.thegamegroup.com.

3

Cooperative Learning in General Chemistry Through Process-Oriented Guided Inquiry Learning

Susan E. Shadle

A colleague of mine in engineering overheard a student in my course explain to a peer how his chemistry course worked. His comment went something like this: "She doesn't really teach you anything, but you do these activities and, you know, at the end, you have really learned it."

When I tell people that I teach my general chemistry course at Boise State University using cooperative learning techniques and largely without lecturing, I am often greeted with suspicion: "How can that work? After all, general chemistry is 'hard.'"

Chemistry is one of those content-rich classes in which students need to master a new language replete with abstract vocabulary words that no one uses in real life. After all, most of us have no experience "seeing" at the molecular level. Complicating the challenges, students must master all the course content in order to continue to the next course, the one after that, and the one after that: nearly all the chemistry, biology, and engineering majors in my course take multiple sequenced courses in our department.

General chemistry is heavily dependent on mathematical problem solving—full of dreaded "word problems." Students with weak algebra skills often get stuck on the math, depend only on algorithmic problem solving, and never get to engage in the content that fascinates us as chemists. Don't these challenges require an instructor to provide extensive lectures to define vocabulary, introduce concepts, and provide numerous problems that are worked on the board? The answer is no.

A number of years ago, drawing upon educational research and the best practice of others in chemical education, chemists at several different institutions devised a framework for engaging students in cooperative learning and authentic inquiry—as a way to guide them through the content and problem-solving skills needed in the discipline. The approach I use in my course is built upon their models for Process-Oriented Guided Inquiry Learning (POGIL). Moog and Spencer (2008) have recently reviewed the genesis of this approach. Significant numbers of faculty in chemistry now use this approach and other cooperative learning strategies in classes of all sizes (e.g., Cooper, 1995; Cooper, 2005; Straumanis & Simons, 2008; Yezierski et al.).

Because each teacher's context is different, each implementation of this Process-Oriented Guided Inquiry approach is unique (e.g., Farrell, Moog, & Spencer, 1999; Hanson & Wolfskill, 2000; Lewis & Lewis, 2005; Ruder & Hunnicutt, 2008). However, in all contexts, a key component of this approach has students working cooperatively to explore data or models, solve problems, think critically about new information, share questions, and articulate their emerging understanding to one another (Hanson, 2006). Additional information about the POGIL approach can be accessed at http://www.pogil.org; this chapter focuses specifically on how I use a cooperative learning-based version of POGIL approaches in my chemistry classroom to facilitate student learning.

OVERVIEW

My general chemistry course meets for three 50-minute periods each week. In a typical class meeting, the 48 students sit at tables in assigned groups of four. The student I designate as the manager assigns the other roles for the day. Students bring a book of inquiry-based class activities to class each day; I assign the day's activity and tell the students which components of their work to hand in at the end of the class period using their preassigned group folders. Students then proceed to work through the activity as a group.

I introduce and reinforce—through their group work—definitions, concepts, problem-solving processes, and the cooperative development of inquiry skills. In fact, I introduce very little content in the course by any other mechanism. Along with several undergraduate peer teachers, I circulate from group to group, asking questions about their work, providing clarifying explanations, and keeping students on task. On some days, I may interrupt the group work to provide some clarification or illustration to the class as a whole.

I often give a 5-minute mini-lecture near the end of class to wrap up the concepts and applications in which they were engaged. I dismiss the students with instructions to finish whatever parts of the activity they did not complete in class. On most days, I give a follow-up quiz to keep students individually accountable for this work. Sometimes, it is a quick online quiz, and other times the quiz takes the first few minutes of the next class. Over the course of the semester, my students take four hour-long exams. The semester ends with a cumulative final exam.

The success of this approach rests on several crucial components that are solidly grounded in the principles of cooperative learning (Millis & Cottell, 1998). First, the structure of the course encourages students to interact effectively with others, to understand what to expect, to hold themselves accountable for their own learning even as they help others learn, and to feel confident that their learning is well supported.

Second, I design the classroom activities to foster student interactions, through which understandings of new content emerge. Each activity incorporates elements of authentic inquiry. Students engage in a scaffolded approach to concept building and the analysis of data that is characteristic of the work that chemists actually do.

Third, students are supported in developing good cooperative learning skills. As students work effectively with others, their explanations to each other draw upon evidence and their emerging conceptual understanding of the content. Students working cooperatively as a group are thus more likely to arrive at consensus-based answers to guiding questions. Students who articulate their understanding to others—translating meaning and debating their new ideas about how it all works—build deep understandings of the course material, as well as valuable analytical and communication skills.

In addition to these essential elements, two other factors contribute to the success of my course. First, using cooperative learning has transformed my role as the course instructor. I do not provide definitions, conceptual explanations, or prepackaged models of the work that I want students to do. Instead, I am a facilitator in an environment that is designed to challenge students to work cooperatively and engage deeply and directly with the content and concepts of chemistry.

Finally, I have found that I must explicitly address student concerns that cooperative interactions do not effectively support their learning—my course differs from others they have taken. The remainder of this chapter describes the ways in which these various course components work together to support student learning.

STRUCTURING COOPERATIVE LEARNING

Consistent with other chapters in this volume (see chapters 2, 5, 6, and 7), the cooperative learning in my course must be well-structured (Millis & Cottell, 1998). Students need to know what to expect during class time; they also need an understanding of the boundaries around the content and skills that

I expect them to master in my course. I work intentionally to have the groups and their activities provide the structure that students need to have confidence in the course.

On the first day of class, students sit at tables of four; those sitting together become the first groups. As students complete an activity designed to explore the syllabus, they see right away that the class will use groups. By the second day of class, I have assigned students to permanent groups, using the rationale described by cooperative learning experts.

Millis and Cottell (1998) note that "most cooperative learning theorists and practitioners advocate instructor-selected teams." Further, they recommend that groups be created to "build on students' varied strengths" (p. 51). Thus, I deliberately construct heterogeneous groups. I have observed that stronger students benefit from having to teach those for whom understanding of the material comes more slowly. Weaker students, or students who have less background, benefit from being able to ask questions of peers, which, despite all my efforts to be open and welcoming to questions, is still less risky than their asking the professor.

In general chemistry, students' prior learning in the subject has a huge impact on their ability to be successful. Thus, on the first day of class, I ask students to provide pertinent information on an index card: their major, their last chemistry class and the year they took it, and their grade in that chemistry class. I use this information to create groups with diverse backgrounds in chemistry and in majors.

In creating these heterogeneous groups, I also try to form groups in which people don't feel isolated (Felder & Brent, 1994). For example, because women are a minority in most of my classes, I avoid putting one woman with three men. As much as possible, I also try to identify other ways in which a student might feel isolated in a group (e.g., nontraditional student status), and I use that information when forming the groups.

On the second day of class, students find a handout at each table, listing their names and their group number. Each table has a "table tent" (a folded-over index card) showing the table number. They quickly identify where they need to be and sit with their new groups. Most of the time, these groups work quite well, and, in some semesters, I have left the groups intact for the rest of the semester, moving only a few students to compensate for those who've dropped the class or to break up a group that is not working well.

In other cases, I've moved everyone after the first exam. This change usually occurs to address differences in communication or learning styles. For example, I have observed that four strong introverts can struggle with the kind of verbal communication that this approach encourages. I usually try to connect those students with other students who are skilled at interacting with people. Some students provide help to other students more generously than others. Once I know their attributes, I can arrange groups to meet the needs of as many students as possible.

Each student group has a numbered folder. At the beginning of each class period, I hand out the 12 folders that contain anything I'm returning (folded to preserve grading confidentiality) and any handouts they need for that day's work. At the end of the class period, I collect those 12 folders, which now contain any homework that they were to complete and written records of the day's work. I review the folder contents to identify or grade student work.

My electronic grade books are organized according to groups, so it is easy to enter grades—no alphabetizing. I have students record their group number on anything that gets handed in (including exams), which makes sorting papers by group straightforward and saves time in class returning papers.

Each day, students take on specific roles in their groups (Hanson, 2006; Johnson, Johnson, & Smith, 2006; Millis & Cottell, 1998). This saves the group from having to negotiate who does what, it ensures accountability because all group members have jobs to do, and it gives students the opportunity to develop skills working in different roles.

Within each group of four, students have an assigned letter, A, B, C, or D. These letter assignments are recorded on a group list that remains in the group folder in case they forget their letter. Before class, I assign the manager of each group by specifying the letter of the student who will manage that day. I put each group's folder on the table, and the manager reviews it to identify any feedback on the previous day's work that must be shared with the group. At the end of the class period, the manager hands in the folder.

During class, it is the manager's job to balance the need to keep the group moving and the need for each member to understand the work before the group moves on. He or she also invites participation from all group members and determines when the group needs assistance and asks for it. Finally, the manager assigns any other roles that are important that day. The regular rotation of roles promotes positive interdependence in the group, an important component of cooperatively learning (Hanson, 2006; Millis & Cottell, 1998).

Every day there is a need for two different recorders. The "activity recorder" records answers to selected questions from the routine activities in class. These are consensus answers that have been drawn from the interaction of group members as they discuss each question in the activity. The "activity recorder" writes the answers on a form I put in each folder.

After class, I check the group's work and provide any necessary feedback. Because the student teaching assistants and I monitor student work during class, there is rarely a need for any feedback on these reports. The "big idea recorder" keeps track of those "big ideas" that come up as students are working. These might be things such as "a large equilibrium constant indicates that the products in the reaction are highly favored" or "an anion is negatively charged because it has fewer protons than electrons." After each class, the big ideas are collected, typed, and posted on Blackboard for students to use as a study guide. Once the course is underway, it is not unusual for a student in the group to exclaim to the big idea recorder, "Hey, I think that is a big idea! Did you get that down?"

The opportunity for reflection on group processes is important to the success of cooperative approaches (Millis & Cottell, 1998). Thus, another role I use is that of "reflector"; that student's job is to note how the group is working and reflect back, either to the group or to me or to the whole class about what seems to be going on to make the group work well or what could improve the group's work.

The reflector's role can be difficult. Students are, understandably, reluctant to be critical of their peers, especially peers they've just met—but with whom they need to work throughout the semester. Students sometimes don't feel qualified at first to judge how well the group is working. I am therefore careful about how I organize their reports.

The first time I use reflectors, I might only ask them to notice a strength of their group or to identify an insight—something interesting they noticed that happens when people are working in groups. The next time I might ask them to identify things they noticed that would improve the effectiveness of their group. I often do this early reporting out as a whole class, inviting students to think about this as feedback about the way the class is going, not as a focus on their particular group.

Later, I invite the reflector to give his or her group direct feedback. I also introduce a rubric for group work (included as an Appendix to this chapter) that not only makes my expectations explicit, but also gives the reflectors some language to use in describing their group's work. Once the students begin to understand how to work effectively in cooperative learning groups, I tend to use the reflector less often.

In addition to rotating group roles, positive interdependence is supported by an incentive for everyone in the group to do well on regular quizzes. If everyone in the group does well on a quiz (e.g., 8 out of 10 or better), everyone in the group gets an additional point. This practice means that everyone has a vested interest in seeing that all group members "get it."

Positive interdependence is further fostered through the use of activities that require students to work together. The questions that students must address during our in-class activities are challenging. Very few students in my class, even in an Honors College section, are able to work through the inquiry-based activities independently, at least not quickly or with confidence. This level of challenge motivates students to work with others.

INQUIRY-BASED ACTIVITIES

In my classroom, I am still responsible for delivering content, but that work no longer consists of preparing notes and examples for face-to-face lectures. Now, I deliver the content by choosing or writing well-constructed activities for the students to do during class. These essential activities contribute to the course's effectiveness because they both frame the content and allow for valuable cooperative interactions between students. Similar to the problem-based learning activities previously described (chapter 2), the activities in my course are structured intentionally to help students achieve the learning goals in the course.

I have written some of the course activities; others come from a textbook (Moog & Farrell, 2008). All of them engage students in the analysis of models and data, and, through that analysis, they introduce the course content. Each activity leads students through a Learning Cycle approach (Lawson, Abraham, & Renner, 1989), in which students are prompted by questions to examine tables of data or features of a model very closely. This is the exploration phase of the learning cycle.

Additional questions prompt students to generalize principles that may be illustrated by the model or the data. Frequently at this stage the questions that the students focus on introduce new terms. This is the concept invention or term introduction phase.

Next, students apply these newly formed concepts in contexts that are similar to the ones in the model they've studied, a phase aptly named "application." Eventually, the activity presents problems that pose more complex applications of the new material.

As an example, the following synopsis describes a classroom activity that (1) guides students to an understanding of the components of an atom, and (2) helps them use the periodic table to identify certain characteristics of an atom:

> Typically, a lecturer would tell the students that the constituents of atoms are protons, neutrons, and electrons, and that the number of protons in the atom is known as the "atomic number" that determines the atom's identity. In the POGIL activity, the approach to this content is markedly different. The activity begins

with a series of diagrams providing examples of a number of atoms and ions, with the corresponding element identified along with the number and location of the protons, neutrons, and electrons in each. Through a series of guiding questions, the students are led to recognize that all of the atoms with the same number of protons are identified as the same element. They also are asked to determine the significance of this number (6) with the number on the periodic table that identifies carbon and are able to conclude that they are the same. Only at this point, as this concept is developed, is the term "atomic number" used to describe the number of protons in one atom of a given element. Thus, an "exploration" of the information presented in the diagrams allows each student to develop the concept that the number of protons determines the identity of an element; the term "atomic number" is introduced following this construction. The "application" of this concept entails using the periodic table to identify the number of protons in other elements. (Moog & Spencer, 2008, p. 4)

Because writing good activities takes time, the best ones are those that have been classroom tested with input from multiple instructors. POGIL instructors have developed several rubrics to help colleagues create high-quality activities that follow the Learning Cycle, support inquiry and critical thinking skills, and engage students in interactions with each other and in self-assessment of their learning. They are available at http://www.pogil.org/resources/implementation/writing. Additionally, example activities are available at http://www.pogil.org/resources/curriculum-materials.

DEVELOPING COOPERATIVE LEARNING SKILLS AND HOLDING STUDENTS ACCOUNTABLE

Several of the conditions needed for effective cooperative learning have already been described, such as appropriate grouping, the promotion of positive interdependence, and the opportunity for group processing. Other important elements include the need for individual accountability and cooperative social skills (Millis & Cottell, 1998, p. 11)

As noted by Cohen (chapter 5), cooperative learning skills are not innate. Simply putting students in groups does not result in cooperative learning. Left alone, students in my course generally choose to work independently, using their group members only to check answers. It takes time and coaching to help students develop the skills to work well with others.

To encourage students to develop and use cooperative skills, I regularly emphasize that having to explain one's ideas or questions to other people is a valuable skill that can lead to a deeper understanding of material (just ask a teacher!). Johnson, Johnson, and Smith (1991) note that a student giving an oral explanation "benefits from the cognitive organizing and processing, higher level reasoning, insights and personal commitment to achieving the groups goals" and the receiver "benefits from the opportunity to utilize others' resources" (p. 2:6).

In addition, I have observed that it is valuable for students to articulate the nature of their incomplete understandings when forming questions for their peers. On the second day of class, I introduce both the group roles and a "group work" rubric that identifies what good group work looks like. Included as an Appendix to this chapter, it outlines exemplary work with respect to a variety of criteria, including attendance, discussion skills and active listening, contributions and participation, on-task behavior and time management, overall group effectiveness, and their effectiveness at various roles within the group.

We discuss, for example, what it "looks like" to be listening to someone else. This discussion allows students to begin to model cooperative behavior in their groups. Periodically throughout the semester, I return to the rubric and use the student reflector in each group to remind students of the expectations. This approach echoes strategies described by Cohen (chapter 5) that are aimed at engaging students in reflection about successful cooperative learning behaviors.

The literature is clear about the need for individual accountability within a cooperative learning setting (Johnson et al., 2006; Millis & Cottell, 1998). In addition to assigned student roles—which help discourage individuals from "checking out" for the day—the quizzes, homework, and exams in my course are graded on an individual basis.

The in-class activities generally build upon understandings students were to have constructed during the previous class. Thus, for students to tackle new class activities, they must have mastered (or at least digested) the last class period's material. Further, for groups to work well, all group members need to come to class ready to move on.

To motivate my students to stay on top of the material, I require them to do something individually to demonstrate their understanding. I've tried a variety of strategies including in-class quizzes administered at the beginning of the class period, take-home quizzes, a short homework assignment that is due during class, and online quizzes administered the day before class. Generally, I use a combination of two or more of these approaches. The important idea is that students must demonstrate their individual readiness to move to new material each day.

Of course, just because I've asked students to be responsible for material doesn't mean they always come prepared. To balance the need for everyone to be ready to move on with the need for individual accountability, I occasionally administer a quiz, collect their individual work, and then let the group take the quiz again, together. Students get the average of the score between the attempts; everyone in the group is then primed to move on to new material. I don't generally announce this in advance, and I tend to do it for topics that I know students either didn't review or struggled with in the first place.

FACILITATION OF COOPERATIVE LEARNING

Moving to a cooperative-learning, inquiry-based approach in my class has radically changed my role in the course. I now facilitate students working in groups (Hanson, 2006). This responsibility takes a variety of forms. Sometimes it is coaching, both about content and about working with others. Sometimes it looks like tutoring when I ask questions and provide input to one group at a time. It also involves finding ways to help groups and individuals work together at a reasonable pace.

Most of my class time is still spent working with students on course content. However, instead of providing students with information (delivering the content), I spend time working with students on the process of understanding the content (see, for example, Hanson, 2006, p. 27). The carefully constructed class activities allow me to ask students to defend their reasoning, to explain how they know something, or to generalize their understanding.

When a group is stuck, I ask questions such as, "What do you already know?" "How far have you taken this question?" "Why do you think you are stumped?" After encouraging this reflection, I can point them to their answer for a previous question or to data or models they have explored; I can ask them related questions to help lead them to an answer. Frequently, once one student figures it out, I leave the group and let that person teach the rest of the group members.

The practice of inquiry built into my course tends to de-emphasize rote memorization and algorithmic problem solving. It also makes it easier to move students away from depending on me for the answers. Not only do the activities themselves require students to use data and models, but I also emphasize to students that the work they are doing is analogous to the kind of thinking scientists do. When students ask me, "Is this answer right?" I counter by asking them to tell me how they arrived at the answer. I then ask them if their approach makes sense to them. Did they all agree on the approach? If they are able to say yes to these questions, I say, "Well, what do you think?"

Of course, most of the questions in the activities have correct and incorrect answers; my questions tend to help an off-track group find its own errors.

By focusing on the students' process, rather than their answers, I keep the responsibility for understanding the material squarely on their shoulders. Sometimes, however, I'll invoke the power of peer consensus by pointing at an answer and telling them that other groups of scientists in the room have arrived at a different answer and that they might want to reconsider their approach. I sometimes suggest they send an "ambassador" to another group (one that I know is on the right track) to compare conclusions or to discuss strategies.

I occasionally stop the group work to offer a brief example or a clarification to the entire class. Sometimes I review a question or problem that they've all completed and provide a more complete context for their work.

In addition to focusing on students' understanding of the content, I also focus on their team's problem-solving pace. Because within a week of the course's start students learn what will happen each day, they are able to move into the work quickly. Sometimes, however, certain groups take extra time to get started, or they get distracted in the middle of their work. They may discuss class-related issues (e.g., the previous day's Blackboard quiz), but sometimes their conversations are irrelevant (e.g., their other classes or the upcoming football game).

Generally, the teams get back on task when the student assistants or I remind them that they need to be working. Sometimes, I shift this responsibility to the manager by asking, "Who is manager today? OK, Sharon, please work to get your group started on the activity." If teams have gotten off task in the middle of the class, a simple question such as "What kind of answer to question 10 has your group arrived at?" refocuses their work.

Groups talking about the chemistry content but spending an unnecessary amount of time on given problems pose particular challenges. They sometimes do this because the group is really stuck on how to answer a question. In other cases, groups get involved in discussions of real-world applications of the content.

In an ideal world, we would give students unlimited time to struggle with questions, applications, and ideas beyond the scope of the given activity. After all, who wants to interrupt students who are working hard to understand and synthesize knowledge? In practical terms, however, just as is the case in a lecture-based course, the need to move through material ("cover content") must be balanced with the need to have everyone in the class "get it" before moving on.

In my cooperative learning POGIL classroom, I try to address this tension by having a general sense of how long various questions should take and by paying attention to how different groups are moving through material. If a group seems stuck, I work hard to ask the students in the group targeted questions to focus their thinking. This approach is usually enough to lift them over whatever hurdle is slowing them down. In some cases, when a single group member is stuck, I and the other group members work together to focus questions or explanations that help that person "get it" so that the team can move forward.

As mentioned earlier, when multiple groups have similar roadblocks, I stop to offer a whole-class clarification. After having taught in this way for several years, I can now anticipate the topics that need well-timed interventions. At other times, these clarification opportunities are completely spontaneous. I also use specific strategies to help the class as a whole with pacing. For example, I might announce, "Most groups are now done with question 5. In a few minutes I will ask you all to move to the next section."

Some students need more time than others to come to an understanding of this difficult material either because their prior knowledge of chemistry or math is weak or because they process information at a slower rate than other classmates. In a lecture course, students who need more processing time are invisible and often become "throw-away students" who drop out or fail. They rarely ask questions because they haven't had time to think about what questions to ask.

In my cooperative learning class, however, these students' need for more time becomes obvious and can lead to frustrations for them and for their group members. Although there is no perfect solution to this challenge, I have used two strategies with good success. First, I try to put these students in groups with patient people who genuinely enjoy helping others and are good at it. Second, I work with these students outside of class to help them identify when it is really important for the group to wait for them to settle all their questions and when they can proceed with some questions still unresolved.

With some practice, they begin to see that in many activities the concepts needed to answer one question are revisited later in the activity if they move forward with the group. I have also suggested to these students that they make a copy of the activity and work on it independently in advance. Even though I generally discourage this independent work, it gives slower students the chance to think about the concepts and questions in an activity before class. I ask them to bring their unmarked original activity to class and work on it with their group. This advance preparation is often enough to allow them to keep pace and contribute substantively to the group discussion.

My classroom is generally full of people who are talking, making it difficult to grab students' attention when I need to gain it periodically—probably twice per class period. On the first day, I introduce a quiet signal to get their attention. When I raise my hand, I want each of them to raise one of theirs and to stop what they are doing.

A part of me hates this approach—it feels as though I'm treating my students as if they were in grade school. However, I continue to use this approach because it works—no other approach I've used gets students' attention as quickly. Students who are already focused on listening to their peers can still see my hand go up, and this signal requires a response from them. The kinesthetic motion of raising their hand helps them stop what they are doing.

When I've taught using this method with a small group of students (24 people) enrolled in our Honors College, I have been able to manage the classroom by myself. However, when I teach a section of 48 students, it is crucial to have some help in the classroom.

Each semester, I recruit two to four undergraduate students to act as peer teaching assistants in the course. In some cases, I've been able to pay them; at other times, I've been able to offer them credit for independent study. In some cases, these students have previously been students in my course, but that hasn't been necessary as long as they have a strong background in chemistry.

Before the semester begins, I hold a meeting with these assistants to lay out my expectations. I expect them to review the activity in advance and contact me with questions ahead of time. Their role, like mine, is to help groups balance the pace at which they move, to offer clarification, and to ask questions, but to avoid providing direct answers.

Within about two weeks, once students know how the class works, I sometimes feel that the classes could proceed productively without me. I can certainly walk out of the room for several minutes and not have anyone notice. Despite this, knowing when and how to intervene—and having a good sense of when to tell students "You can figure this out" and when they need a boost or explanation—makes a huge difference in student confidence and their motivation to continue. I have a different but essential role to play.

STUDENT RESPONSE

Although many cooperative learning approaches involve a partial move away from lecture (Robinson and Cooper, chapter 7), this approach, as I have implemented it, has involved an almost complete departure from prepared lectures. As noted by several others in this volume, many students, particularly at first, are resistant to the idea that this approach effectively supports their learning.

They insist that they learn best when the instructor is teaching and that having to work with others does not help them learn. I suspect that their negative perspective also comes from previous bad experiences with group work. It is also possible that some of my students have a learning style that is more reflective (Kolb, 1984), so having to talk about their ideas and questions on the spot may not be comfortable for them. However, other students resist the approach simply because it is different and demands a great deal of them as learners. In fact, they are often convinced that they know what a chemistry course is like, and this is not it.

Several authors in this volume (chapters 10 and 11) have noted that cooperative pedagogies can be used to move students to more sophisticated levels of understanding within a framework for student development. In a similar vein, I have found these models (Hofer & Pintrich, 1997; Perry, 1999) to be helpful in understanding and moving beyond student resistance to cooperative learning.

Many students begin their college careers viewing knowledge as a collection of facts to be known. Broadly speaking, these students believe that teaching is the delivery of those facts by an authority, and their learning means reproducing correct answers on an exam. For students in these early stages of development, my approach is understandably disconcerting. They can't see that I am indeed teaching, and thus they can't understand how they can be learning.

Regardless of the source and degree of student resistance, student anxiety runs high in the first few weeks of my course. I address this student anxiety in two ways. First, I am explicit about the way the class will work. I talk about the reasons I've chosen to teach in this manner. I explain my role in the course and how my approach benefits both their learning of chemistry and their development of other useful skills.

Later, when I see good things happening in class, I point them out as evidence that the approach is working. For example, often when a group that is stuck calls me over, although I do nothing but listen, they figure out the answer to their question. I don't hesitate to point out this breakthrough to them.

Although I work to reduce student resistance, I simultaneously aim to move students in the direction of a more complex view of knowledge. I do this both by expanding their awareness of what is going on during class time and by working to develop their metacognition—their ability to "self-manage," "self-assess," and "reflect on [their own] learning" (Hanson, 2006, p. 17). As I work with students in the classroom, I talk about the need for them to trust their own judgment and their own constructed knowledge.

To address their anxiety in the short term, I communicate that I'm paying attention to what they are doing and that I'm not going to let anyone get off track. This is, in fact, the reason I collect the activity recorder's reports. I also emphasize that I'm interested in their deeper learning, not what they can memorize. I talk frequently with the class about how practicing scientists look at data, formulate ideas, discuss them with others, and compare them with others' answers.

I also discuss their need to develop trust in their ability to figure things out. At some point, they will not have a textbook or a course to support their learning on a new topic or a teacher to tell them if they are "right" or if they "know enough." I underscore the fact that there is no time like the present to learn to make judgments about their own ability to gather and use new information and then assess when they really know it. It is my intention that these conversations—and the in-class experiences—help students to move to more advanced levels of intellectual development.

Generally, once the class has gotten past the first exam, most of their anxiety has subsided. Students realize that they've learned quite a bit that they can demonstrate on an exam, even if I've not done a single problem on the board or defined any terms for them. After several weeks, when I administer a mid-semester survey, 90–100% of students report that the "the group work has been helpful to my learning of chemistry." For the few students who continue to be resistant, I try to be sympathetic, but I remain clear about the expectations for the course and encourage them to find ways to be successful in spite of their discomfort with the approach.

After several weeks, most students are comfortable working cooperatively with their peers and appreciate the way in which this approach facilitates their learning. The following are typical student comments on mid-term and end-of-semester course evaluations.

"Being able to ask frequent questions and discuss chemistry with peers has made learning chemistry easy."

"Not only did I learn chemistry, I also learned how to communicate with my group members."

"If I didn't see something, someone else would. Also, if I did understand something and someone else didn't, it helped me to learn it better when I had to explain it."

"Group work forces you to want to understand the material, especially when you get to know your group better. Much better than boring lectures."

"At first I wasn't sure that group work would be effective, but now that I have seen it, I am totally for it. The biggest reason I like it is because it forces you to put effort in and learn."

"I have found the work with others has really solidified my knowledge of subject matter both by me explaining topics to others and also them taking time to help me get that knowledge. With lecture only, I feel like I am slowing down the learning if I keep asking questions until I get it."

Although comments such as these are typical, it is important to note that most students also comment that they find the mini-lectures helpful. Most indicate that their preference is for a course with a mixture of cooperative group work and lecture.

STUDENT RETENTION AND CONTENT COVERAGE

A variety of studies provides compelling evidence that the use of this approach can improve exam performance, attendance, student retention in the course, and student success in future courses, in a variety of contexts (Farrell, et al., 1999; Hanson & Wolfskill, 2000; Lewis & Lewis, 2005; Straumanis & Simon, 2008). In my own context, the number of Ds, Fs, and Ws has decreased from a range of 20–30% to 13–17%.

Consistent with concerns noted for introductory economics (chapter 10), colleagues sometimes question how much content I've had to give up in order to allow students to learn material through cooperative work. Because my course is the beginning of a long sequence of courses, and because my department works collaboratively to identify consistent content-related outcomes across sections of a course, I have not cut any large chunks of material.

Instead, I've streamlined content, primarily by limiting the examples that students study as illustrations of a larger conceptual knowledge base. This means that I often omit explicit discussions of exceptions with the assumption that when students need to know about the exceptions, they will learn about them.

For example, when my students learn about gases, they learn only the relationships governing ideal gases. They do not learn equations that apply to real gases. When they learn about double displacement reactions, we focus on precipitation reactions and not those reactions that produce gases.

Interestingly, my students' conceptual understanding is strong enough that I can ask a conceptual exam question about an example they've not studied explicitly and many of them are able to make a reasonable prediction about, for example, the behavior of a real gas. In the end, I find that I've sacrificed relatively little content by using this cooperative learning and POGIL-based approach.

CONCLUSION

For some students, such as the student whose observation opened this chapter, my course comes as a surprise. Even though I never "taught" him anything, he ended up "learning." I hope that all my students will come to understand that learning is not related to hearing or to taking notes on what I or any other teacher has to say—but is, instead, a function of the work that they do to master knowledge, skills, and understanding, work that is frequently best accomplished by cooperative interactions with others.

References

Cooper, M. M. (1995). Cooperative learning: An approach for large enrollment courses. *Journal of Chemical Education, 72,* 162–164.

Cooper, M. M. (2005). An introduction to small-group learning. In N. J. Pienta, M. M. Cooper, & T. J. Greenbowe (Eds.), *Chemists' guide to effective teaching* (pp. 117–128). Upper Saddle River, NJ: Pearson.

Farrell, J. J., Moog, R. S., & Spencer, J. N. (1999). A guided inquiry general chemistry course. *Journal of Chemical Education, 76,* 570–574.

Felder, R. M., & Brent, R. (1994). *Cooperative learning in technical courses: Procedures, pitfalls, and payoffs.* Eric Document Reproduction Service Report ED 377038. Retrieved February 3, 2010, from http://www4.ncsu.edu/unity/lockers/users/f/felder/public/Papers/Coopreport.html.

Hanson, D. M. (2006). *Instructor's guide to process-oriented guided-inquiry learning.* Lisle, IL: Pacific Crest.

Hanson, D. M., & Wolfskill, T. (2000). Process workshops—A new model for instruction. *Journal of Chemical Education, 77,* 120–130.

Hofer, B. K., & Pintrich, P. R. (1997). The development of epistemological theories. Beliefs about knowledge and knowing and their relation to learning. *Review of Educational Research, 67,* 88–140.

Johnson, D. W., Johnson, R. T., & Smith, K. A. (1991). *Active learning: Cooperation in the college classroom.* Edina, MN: Interaction Book Company.

Johnson, D. W., Johnson, R. T., & Smith, K. A. (2006). *Active learning: Cooperation in the college classroom* (3rd ed.). Edina, MN: Interaction Book Company.

Kolb, D. A. (1984). *Experiential learning: Experience as the source of learning and development.* Upper Saddle River, NJ: Prentice Hall.

Lawson, A. E., Abraham, M. R., & Renner, J. W. (1989). *A theory of instruction: Using the learning cycle to teach science concepts and thinking skills [Monograph number one].* Kansas State University, Manhattan, KS: National Association for Research in Science Teaching.

Lewis, S. E., & Lewis, J. E. (2005). Departing from lectures: An evaluation of a peer-led guided inquiry alternative. *Journal of Chemical Education, 82,* 135–139.

Millis, B. J., & Cottell, P. G., Jr. (1998). *Cooperative learning for higher education faculty.* Phoenix, AZ: American Council on Education/Oryx Press.

Moog, R. S., & Farrell, J. J. (2008). *Chemistry: A guided inquiry* (4th ed.). Hoboken, NJ: John Wiley.

Moog, R. S., & Spencer, J. N. (Eds.) (2008). *Process-Oriented Guided Inquiry Learning,* ACS Symposium Series, No. 994. New York: Oxford University Press.

Perry, W. G., Jr. (1999). *Forms of intellectual and ethical development in the college years: A scheme.* (Reprint of the 1970 edition with a new introduction by L. Knefelkamp.) San Francisco: Jossey-Bass.

Ruder, S. M., & Hunnicutt, S. S. (2008). POGIL in chemistry courses at a large urban university: A case study. In R. S. Moog & J. N. Spencer (Eds.), *Process-Oriented Guided Inquiry Learning.* ACS Symposium Series 994. (pp. 131–145). New York: Oxford University Press.

Straumanis, A., & Simons, E. A. (2008). A multiinstitutional assessment of the use of POGIL in organic chemistry. In R. S. Moog & J. N. Spencer (Eds.), *Process-Oriented Guided Inquiry Learning.* ACS Symposium Series 994. (pp. 224–237). New York: Oxford University Press.

Yezierski, E. J., Bauer, C. F., Hunnicutt, S. S., Hanson, D. M., Amaral, K. E., & Schneider, J. P. (2008). POGIL implementation in large classes: Strategies for planning, teaching, and management. In R. S. Moog & J. N. Spencer (Eds.), *Process-Oriented Guided Inquiry Learning.* ACS Symposium Series 994. (pp. 60–71). New York: Oxford University Press.

Appendix:
Group Work Performance Rubric

Criteria	1	2	3	4
Attendance	Attendance is marked by habitual absence	More than two class sessions are missed during the semester.	Only one or two class sessions are missed during the semester.	Student attends all class sessions
Discussion Skills and Active Listening	Inconsiderate of others' ideas. Frequently interrupts, ignores, dismisses, and/or puts down the views of others. Does not ask questions or clarification of others.	Pays attention to the group discussion. Occasionally asks questions and builds on others' comments or questions. Needs to be encouraged to participate.	Body and/or verbal responses indicate active listening. Often asks questions and builds on others' comments or questions.	Shows respect for and actively encourages the views of others. Listens attentively to others. Consistently asks questions, offers clarification, and builds on others' comments.
Contribution and Participation	Rarely provides useful ideas/questions to the group. May refuse to participate or opt out by noninteraction. Shows no concern for group goals.	Sometimes provides useful ideas/questions when participating in the group and in classroom discussion. A satisfactory group member, who mostly does what is required but sometimes opts out. Occasionally demonstrates effort, sometimes to help the group work together.	Usually provides useful ideas/questions when participating in the group and in classroom. Demonstrates effort to help the group work together.	Routinely provides useful ideas/questions when participating in the group and in classroom discussion. A consistently strong group member, who is concerned that all group members gain from participation in the activity. Actively participates in helping the group work together better.

On-Task Behavior & Time Management	Is always on-task and focused on the group working to complete the day's work.	Exhibits on-task behavior most of the time.	Exhibits on-task behavior some of the time, but is often found to be off-task.	Consistently distracts group work with off-task behavior.
Group Effectiveness	Encourages group members to evaluate how well they are working together.	Participates in group evaluation.	Participates marginally in group evaluation.	Discourages evaluation or is dismissive of how well the group is working.
Roles within the Group	Effectively and enthusiastically performs multiple roles within the group.	Performs some roles very well and needs improvement in others.	When assigned a role, performs only the minimal tasks associated with that role. Tries, but needs improvement in all roles.	Does not engage in the performance of appropriate roles.

Cooperative Learning Structures Help College Students Reduce Math Anxiety and Succeed in Developmental Courses

Theodore Panitz

Higher education faces the growing problem of providing remedial mathematics for incoming first-year students, particularly at community colleges. Despite efforts by the federal government and the states to improve mathematics education through the use of standardized competency tests, more incoming students are placed in developmental math courses over time. These courses may include arithmetic, pre-algebra, algebra, and intermediate algebra.

Offered as standard high school sequences, placement tests, such as Acquplacer, put as many as 95% of Cape Cod Community College's (CCCC's) new students into one of these courses. Not only are more students underprepared in math, but many exhibit strong math anxieties because of previous failures. Their anxiety often prevents them from completing their developmental math courses, and thus their college careers are either substantially lengthened or terminated prematurely.

Many in the college community view developmental mathematics as a gatekeeper course that prevents students from completing their degrees. This chapter describes my approach to helping students overcome their math anxiety through the use of cooperative learning structures, an approach that leads to higher retention rates and success in developmental math courses.

CAUSES OF MATH ANXIETY

Mathematics anxiety has been defined as feelings of tension and anxiety that interfere with the manipulation of numbers and the solving of mathematical problems in a wide variety of ordinary life and academic situations. Math anxiety can cause students to lose self-confidence (Tobias, 1993). Research confirms that the pressure of timed tests and the risk of public embarrassment cause many students unproductive tension. Three specific practices—common in traditional mathematics classrooms—cause enormous anxiety: (1) imposed authority, (2) public exposure, and (3) time deadlines.

Cooperative learning structures address each of these problems and much more by encouraging students to become active learners, to take more responsibility for their learning, and to become more involved in the course procedures. Cooperative learning approaches encourage students not to rely on their instructors for all their learning.

Deborah Russell (2008) has captured the essence of the causes of math anxiety.

> Math anxiety or fear of math is actually quite common. Math anxiety is quite similar to stagefright. . . . Math anxiety conjures up fear of some type. The fear that one won't be able to do the math or the fear that it's too hard or the fear of failure which often stems from having a lack of confidence. For the most part, math anxiety is the fear about doing the math right, our minds draw a blank and we think we'll fail and of course the more frustrated and anxious our minds become, the greater the chance for drawing blanks. [The] added pressure of having time limits on math tests and exams also cause[s] the levels of anxiety [to] grow for many students. (p. 1)

Russell continues with the observation that math anxiety often results from "unpleasant experiences in mathematics." "Math phobics" often have been exposed to math in crippling ways that limited their understanding. She concludes that math anxiety often results from poor teaching, with an emphasis on math procedures rather than actually understanding the mathematical concepts. "When one tries to memorize procedures, rules and routines without much understanding, the math is quickly forgotten, and panic soon sets in."

She cites the division of fractions as a classic case. Typically, the procedures related to reciprocals and inverses are taught without regard for the underlying concepts. In other words, she quips, "It's not yours to reason why, just invert and multiply." Students who memorize the rule, she notes, find that it works. But, do they understand why it works? Did their teachers ever use "pizzas or math manipulatives" to show them why it works?

If not, they simply memorized procedures, a process that worked fine—until they forgot some of them. At that point, they need to understand the underlying concepts. "Once students realize they can do the math because they understand it," they overcome the math anxiety. Both teachers and parents—any "coaches"—must ensure that students truly understand the math being presented to them (Russell, 2008, p. 1).

RECOMMENDATIONS FOR DECREASING STUDENT MATH ANXIETY

Because many students experience math anxiety in traditional classrooms, professors should design their classes to make students feel more successful. Students must have, at best, a high level of success or, at worst, a level of failure that they can tolerate. Therefore, teachers must handle incorrect responses positively to encourage students' participation and enhance their confidence.

Studies have shown that students learn best when they are active rather than passive learners (Spikell, 1993). Additionally, the theory of multiple intelligences addresses the different learning styles. To reach a majority of students, math lessons should be designed to appeal to different modalities: visual/spatial, logical/mathematics, musical, body/kinesthetic, interpersonal/ intrapersonal, and verbal/linguistic. Every student is capable of learning, but each may learn in different ways. Therefore, lessons must be presented in a variety of ways.

For example, new concepts can be introduced by using cooperative groups, visual aids, hands-on activities, and technology. Learners are different than they were forty years ago when students rarely questioned the "why" of math concepts and focused instead on memorizing and mechanically performing the necessary operations. Today's learners are often more demanding, wanting to know why something is done this way or that way.

Because students today need practical math, it needs to be relevant to their everyday lives. Students enjoy experimenting. To learn mathematics deeply, students must be engaged in exploring, conjecturing, and thinking—rather than merely learning by rote the rules and procedures. Cooperative groups give students a chance to exchange ideas, ask questions freely, explain concepts to one another, clarify ideas in meaningful ways, and express feelings about their learning. These critical thinking skills will be beneficial throughout their adult working life.

COOPERATIVE LEARNING METHODOLOGY

To establish a positive tone for each upcoming class, two weeks prior to the start of the semester, I send my students a letter with a humorous introduction to the class and cooperative learning, a course syllabus, and a writing assignment in the form of a mathematical autobiography. I ask them to read the first chapter and start working on the text problems. The first chapter includes review materials from the prerequisite course.

I want to emphasize the students' responsibility in the learning process well before the class starts and to demonstrate my own interest in helping them become independent mathematics learners. I include my home and work phone numbers and e-mail addresses to encourage students to contact me if they have any questions or concerns about working in groups or studying material before class.

Nuhfer (chapter 11) stresses the importance of the first class meeting of the semester by emphasizing that the initial activities that we undertake establish a norm for cooperative learning and help students learn how to learn. This focus must continue throughout the term as we introduce additional cooperative learning exercises, such as the examples that follow.

To establish group work as a norm, during the first class meeting I ask the students, who are seated at tables with four to six to a group, to interview a student they do not know but who is sitting next to them. I want them to begin the process of interacting with other students by using a cooperative structure called Pair Interviews/Introductions.

I suggest that they ask their partners three specific questions: "How do you feel about math and why?" "What concerns do you have about this course?" "Why are you taking this course at this time?" In addition, I ask students to acquire as much biographical information as possible by inquiring about majors, employment, family, pets, hobbies, travel, where their partner has lived, etc. I want the students to discover as many commonalities as possible.

Next, I ask each pair to introduce their new "math buddy" to their table partners in order to practice what they will say to the whole class. Finally, each student introduces his/her partner to the whole class. The students discover a very important affective response. They are not alone in their math anxiety, fear of failure in this course, or concerns about previous bad math experiences. It actually becomes humorous to hear the repeated statements to the effect that students are in the class because they are required to be and not out of choice (given that this course is a prerequisite for many other science and math courses they need to fulfill graduation requirements).

There is a palpable sense of relief when I seem to understand their feelings. I also use this interview process during the semester to help students ascertain how thoroughly they and their partners understand the concepts we are working on.

On the first day of the semester, I distribute a class schedule that specifies which textbook sections students are responsible for on a given day. I encourage students to try to understand the chapter concepts and procedures before coming to class. To accomplish this, I assign worksheets that ask students to write out the chapter section's outcomes, to record crucial vocabulary definitions, and to solve six to ten problems from the section exercises.

I count these pre-class worksheets as extra credit, to reduce the students' anxiety over being asked to study and apply the material before receiving a lecture from me. I also ask the students to attempt to solve as many problems from the section exercises as possible after class. Their student manuals and texts provide worked-out solutions for all the odd-numbered problems, allowing them to check their work. For the even-numbered problems, I encourage students to check their solutions prior to class by going to the mathematics tutorial center or by consulting with classmates.

During class, students sit at tables with four to six to a group. At the beginning of each class, I give a short explanation of the concept or procedure we will work on. I try to keep my lectures under ten minutes, usually targeting five minutes. I distribute worksheets with problems or questions covering the day's topic or cooperative activity.

Students first attempt to complete the worksheet problems in pairs, progressing from simpler problems to more complex ones. Pair work creates an optimal learning environment because one student is explaining while the other is listening. Thus, all the students in the class are participating actively by listening or talking about mathematics.

After the pairs complete the assignment, they share their results with the other pairs of students at their table. This paired sharing provides additional repetition and feedback for the students. As Millis (chapter 9) points out, "Learning is defined as stabilizing, through repeated use, certain appropriate and desirable synapses in the brain" (Leamnson, 2000, p. 5).

Then I place the problems on the board in sequence and ask groups to present their solutions to the class. I also ask students to work directly out of the text together. The text I use has a workbook format that encourages an interactive approach to studying mathematics. When students read the text together and explain sections to their partners, they also have an excellent opportunity to build their mathematics vocabulary.

During each class, I circulate around the room, observing each group's progress. I make suggestions about how they might go about finding the answers to their questions, but, like Cottell (chapter 2) and Shadle (chapter 3), I do not directly answer questions initially. Instead, I encourage the students to use as resources both their texts and any other student or group in the class.

Those who did not do the reading and practice problems beforehand have an opportunity to do so at this point in the class. If most students appear to be having difficulty or are making fundamental mistakes, I ask volunteers to put their solutions on the board while explaining and defending their methodology. With this approach, explanations come from the students' peers, not from an expert speaking "professorese." After the student explanations, the groups return to work and try to resolve whatever questions remain. If they are still confused, I facilitate a whole-class discussion that usually clarifies the source of their confusion.

In addition to the worksheets, I often give group quizzes as a form of review. First, each student works the problems individually. Next, they compare answers within their groups and try to reach agreement. To reduce their sense of threat and to reduce anxiety, I count these quizzes as extra credit.

The quizzes help me identify which students have reached a competency level. I encourage those who need it to get extra help outside of class, stressing again their responsibility for their learning as part of the class philosophy. I recommend the Mathematics Learning Center or other tutorial agencies on campus. I also suggest that they work with their peers in study groups or make arrangements to see me.

Cooperative learning allows for flexibility in content coverage. On occasion, I postpone a test when I see that most students have not mastered the material. With all the outside pressures students face today, they may not be ready to demonstrate their knowledge at the time specified on the syllabus. Putting them through a rigorous test at that point merely raises anxiety and results in multiple failures.

My courses, however, are not open-ended. We continue covering the syllabus while the students review the material they will be tested on. By negotiating test schedules, the students become more involved in establishing the course procedures and thus empowered to control their learning environment.

Finally, I give an individual in-class test to maintain the accountability of each student. I use a mastery approach in which students have an opportunity to correct their mistakes during the exam before a final grade is calculated. While the students work on the exam, I walk around the room, observing their progress. When they have completed their test, I check it immediately and circle any incorrect answers, without, however, indicating what mistake they made.

The students then have an opportunity to make corrections. If they get less than 80% after corrections, they are required to retake a new test outside of class using the same procedure. If they get greater than 80%, I encourage them to continue making corrections until they have completely corrected the test. Their grade is based upon the final corrected test.

Every step of this cooperative learning paradigm is intended to encourage students to take responsibility for their learning. This mind-set creates very high expectations for the students—and for me as the course facilitator. I need to provide materials to guide the students through the process, and I work with them to develop appropriate group interaction skills. I am intensely involved in each class as I circulate around the room, talking to students individually, in pairs, or in larger groups. I also carefully balance the classes between group discussions and individual work.

Students comment that the classes fly by. Even though they are exhausted at the end of class, they feel good about what they have accomplished. By the end of the semester, the better students have learned how to become independent learners, their math phobia has all but disappeared, and they actually begin to like math. The less motivated students have learned more math than they ever expected to master. In class, the students actively work through the content and grow to understand concepts in ways that make sense to them because they have developed their own solutions to problems.

The procedures just described have evolved over a long period through a process of trial and error. I don't recommend that new teachers initiate an extensive cooperative learning system without first participating in training programs and conferences dealing with cooperative learning techniques. It takes time for them to develop a comfort level and gain confidence with cooperative processes. To incorporate cooperative learning in math classes, I recommend that teachers initiate one or two new techniques per semester until they have acquired a full repertoire of activities.

EXAMPLES OF COOPERATIVE ACTIVITIES

To give readers an idea of how cooperative learning is implemented, I describe three activities: Pair-Reading and Math-Olympics, which may be used to cover any content area, and Factoring Jigsaw, which was developed for a specific content area.

Shudle (chapter 3) stresses the need for providing well-structured cooperative learning activities, which she achieves through the groups and their activities, not through passive lecturing.

Pair-Reading

As one might expect, pairs of students work together on the highly structured Pair-Reading exercise. First, both students read the same section of either the text or instructor-provided materials. Next, one student explains a single paragraph or short section of the text to the partner. The partner listens and asks questions if he or she does not understand the explanation. The listener then rephrases what he or she heard. The students alternate roles of "explainer" and "listener" until they complete all the material being studied.

When the entire class has completed the exercise, I ask groups at random to explain the material to the whole class. These explanations serve as a check to make sure the students understand the material they are reading. To prepare the students for this activity, I have the students Pair-Read the syllabus during the second class. The syllabus describes the cooperative nature of the class and the mastery approach to testing, grading, attendance policies, and other topics that are pertinent to the operation of the class.

I have found that students initially read through course materials very casually, often missing key elements of course policies. This Pair-Reading activity causes students to review the syllabus carefully and think critically about each element because they must explain each paragraph to their partners or listen to their explanations. Because this syllabus activity also encourages students to work with their neighbors, it begins the process of training students in cooperative learning.

As Nuhfer (chapter 11) does, Cohen (chapter 5) stresses the value of using the first class period to model, through cooperative learning activities, the collaborative efforts needed for learning. She uses her syllabus and ice-breaking activities during the first week and beyond to reinforce this emphasis.

In my math classes, once we have practiced using the Pair-Reading approach on the syllabus, which is a relatively simple document, I continue to have my students do Pair-Reading in the textbook or with extra handouts that clarify mathematical concepts. Anecdotally, like many other professors, I am observing that more and more students read less, especially when it comes to math textbooks.

In fact, as Hobson notes, "A consistent pattern of research findings has established compliance with course reading at 20–30% for any given day and assignment (Burchfield & Sappington, 2000; Hobson, 2003; Marshall, 1974; Self, 1987). The Pair-Reading exercise helps students overcome their lack of interest in reading and assures me that they have read the material.

Math-Olympics

The second example, the Math-Olympics activity, can be used with any content that involves multiple problems. It is especially useful for chapter reviews or section practice. I use this activity, for instance, to introduce solving equations in elementary algebra classes.

The class is divided into groups of four. Existing groups may be used or new groups formed. I place five questions on the board. I use one more question than there are students in the group, to discourage having the groups simply divide up the questions, one for each student. After five to ten minutes, depending on the complexity of the problems, I ask each group to send one student to the board to record the group's answers on a grid I have drawn.

I check all the answers. This process can be repeated for the duration of the class or for a portion of it only. If I see that groups are having trouble with a set of problems, I stop the activity and facilitate a whole-class discussion or give a mini-lecture on the material. Students are actively involved in solving many problems in a short period during class. I encourage groups to work out their own processes for solving each set of problems. Thus, the students assume some of the responsibility for the class process. I have an opportunity to observe the students solving problems individually and in groups.

Maier, McGoldrick, and Simkins (chapter 10) identify research showing that students working together solve problems more accurately. Research by mathematics educators Vidakovic (1997) and Vidakovic and Martin (2004) also shows that groups are able to solve problems more accurately than individuals working alone. Even when one member is more skilled, the collective group is able to correct errors that remain unnoticed when the skilled problem solver works independently, without explaining his or her procedure.

Factoring-Jigsaw

The third example, the Factoring-Jigsaw activity, is useful whenever material can be segmented into separate components. Each group member becomes an expert on a different concept or procedure and teaches his or her concept to the group. I use this activity when covering factoring of polynomials where the coefficient of the first term is 1. There are four unique cases. The second and third coefficients may be both positive or both negative or have opposite signs.

I form base groups of four students. Students count off from one to four. I distribute a worksheet for each case. The worksheets have five sample polynomials to factor, plus a space for each student to make up five problems of his or her own.

Students reform groups by combining with other students who have been assigned the same case number, again four to a group. The students work together to determine what is unique about their case. They are, in effect, becoming experts in their case.

In the next step, the students develop a teaching strategy to bring back to their base groups. In this stage, they make up their own problems. Each student practices his or her explanation with the case group.

Finally, the students return to their base groups and teach their case. There is no preconceived way in which students must teach their material, so the results are quite varied. In addition to providing an interesting and often entertaining class, this activity helps students understand what teaching mathematics involves. Students learn how to work with different partners and begin to see that they can indeed assume responsibility for their own learning.

Maier et al. (chapter 10) remind us that learners have trouble retaining large amounts of information that has been presented over a short period, as in a straight lecture format. They emphasize that, because cooperative learning techniques such as Think-Pair-Share require equal participation by all students, a cooperative approach "is more likely to actively engage the entire class in the learning process."

STUDENT RESPONSES TO MY COOPERATIVE LEARNING APPROACH

At the end of each semester, I give a writing assignment to get the students to reflect on their performance and behavior in the class. The assignment is also designed to have them think about how they will approach their next math class and about needed changes to ensure their success in future classes.

Some of the questions I ask are the following: "Has your approach to math changed during this course or compared to previous courses? If yes, how?" "Have your attitudes or feelings about math changed?" "How do you feel you performed in this course?" "What would you do differently in this course if you had it to do all over again?" "What would you suggest I do differently in my future classes?" "What else would you like to add that I did not ask?"

The responses are very candid, but not always positive, a result that I attribute to using cooperative learning techniques throughout the semester, which allow me to get to know students and allow them to get to know and trust me. I emphasize that I am never offended by what students write if they are being honest and constructive. Developing this relationship with my students is extremely important to me.

Most of the students' comments about the class and my techniques are positive. I regard this as a testimonial to the nature of cooperative learning, which allows me to show the students my human side at the same time that I get to know them as people, not just as ciphers in my grade book.

Students wrote about their experiences as follows:

In the past as you know, Ted, I have taken a class with you and have enjoyed your approach in learning the material. Before your classes I disliked math. I was always getting aggravated and scared by it. Working together with those around me in a group has been a great help in understanding the material and the many different ways in which a problem can be tackled and solved. For me the beauty was being able to work one on one with someone every day. I was constantly learning something new and leaving class feeling relaxed and in control. On those days I could not understand something, I did not feel half as bad as I normally would have, I knew that if it were something I could not figure out at home or at the next class period I could count on receiving help.

When I re-entered school almost two years ago I was told that I needed to take an algebra course. I panicked. Even though I had taken a large number of math courses in high school I feared that I had forgotten everything I had learned so long ago. It was a pleasure to realize how much I truly enjoy working with numbers once again. The course was presented in a way that made learning and remembering fun. During this semester I have not only learned new tricks for doing algebra but I have also enjoyed the exchange of ideas with other students. Working in groups has been one of the most enlightening aspects of the course since we have each had the opportunity to become teachers as well as students. Each of us brought a different approach to learning and everyone was willing to share. Since my own personal objective in life is to enter the educational field, I hope to bring many of the ideas I have learned here with me to my own students in the future.

Before taking this class I had negative attitudes towards math. I did not understand too much and focused little on learning it. However, my thinking has begun to change. I am able to figure out problems that I once thought were too complicated to complete. You made the atmosphere one in which it was fun to learn. I feel that my performance has improved as a result of this. Students were able to communicate and work through problems together. The grades I received were higher than any other math course I have been in. I was happily surprised.

Overall I would have to say that the laid back, conversational and non-threatening way the course was structured seemed to help me overcome some of my preconceived notions about math. The course was set up in such a way that made learning a little more fun than in previous math classes. Also, being able to converse openly to my neighbor, or the teacher, if I had a problem, certainly helped me feel relaxed, non-threatened, and at ease if I ever had trouble finding an answer to a problem. I had a feeling that if I ever had a problem I could go to the teacher or a student and I could troubleshoot or dig until I got the information I needed.

CONCLUSION

Cooperative learning techniques, when used extensively in mathematics classes, generate many advantages for the students and teachers. Students' critical thinking skills are enhanced. Motivation levels are increased, as students become familiar with working with their peers, leading to a new-found enjoyment of mathematics classes. Achievement levels increase, and thus math anxiety is reduced and student self-esteem is increased.

Professors and students get to know each other better as individuals, increasing motivation for both. Students form lasting relationships among their peers, leading to study groups outside of class and taking follow-up classes together. Professors get to learn about their students' backgrounds, abilities, and learning styles.

Cooperative structures address different student learning styles in every class, including verbal, visual, and kinesthetic. All these benefits improve student math competence and reduce math anxieties, leading to better retention and success in developmental math classes.

References

Burchfield, C. M., & Sappinton, J. (2000). Compliance with required reading assignments. *Teaching of Psychology, 27*(1), 58–60.

Hobson, E. H. (2003, November). Encouraging students to read required course material. Workshop presented at the 28th Annual Conference of the Professional and Organizational Development (POD) Network in Higher Education, Denver, CO.

Hobson, E. H. (2004, July). *Getting students to read: Fourteen tips.* IDEA Paper #40. Kansas State: IDEA Paper Series. Retrieved February 3, 2010, from http://www.theideacenter.org/IDEAPaper40.

Leamnson, R. (2000). *Thinking about teaching and learning: Developing habits of learning with first-year college and university students.* Sterling, VA: Stylus.

Marshall, P. (1974). How much, how often? *College and Research Libraries, 35*(6), 453–456.

Russell, D. (2008). Math Anxiety. About.Com: Mathematics. Retrieved February 3, 2010, from http://math.about.com/od/reference/a/anxiety.htm.

Self, J. (1987). Reserve readings and student grades: Analysis of a case study. *Library & Information Science Research, 9*(1), 29–40.

Spikell, M. (1993). *Teaching mathematics with manipulatives: A resource of activities for the K–12 teacher.* New York: Allyn and Bacon

Tobias, S. (1993). *Overcoming math anxiety.* New York: Norton.

Vidakovic, D. (1997). Learning the concept of inverse functions in a group versus individual environment. In E. Dubinsky, D. M. Mathews, & B. E. Reynolds (Eds.), *Readings in cooperative learning for undergraduate mathematics* (pp. 173–195). Washington, DC: Math Association of America.

Vidakovic, D., & Martin, W. O. (2004). Small group searches for mathematical proofs and individual reconstructions of mathematical concepts. *The Journal of Mathematical Behavior, 23*(4), 465–492.

5

Cooperative Learning in Educational Psychology

Modeling Success for Future Teachers

Margaret W. Cohen

The Psychology of Teaching and Learning (EdPsych 3312) is an undergraduate course offered by the Division of Educational Psychology, Research and Evaluation in the College of Education at the University of Missouri-St. Louis (UMSL). It is designed to deepen preparing teachers' knowledge of the psychological principles, theories, and concepts that they will rely upon as they learn to teach in K–12 classrooms.

The course emphasizes theoretical and practical approaches for analyzing teaching and learning in prekindergarten through secondary school classrooms. The curricular content guides students preparing to become teachers in analyzing and reflecting on how their interaction patterns and instructional processes influence how students behave, develop, and learn. Prerequisites for the course are a series of three foundational courses in education and formal admission to the teacher education program. EdPsych 3312 is a requirement for graduate and undergraduate students seeking to earn state teaching certificates.

Undergraduates usually enroll their junior year in sections with a maximum enrollment of 30–40 students. The course meets twice a week for 75 minutes or once a week for 160 minutes. Because of the campus' exceptionally high transfer rate of 70%, more than two-thirds of the students registered each semester in EdPsych 3312 are taking their first course on campus. Because the average age of students at UMSL is 27.3 years, those enrolled are a diverse group of students with varied life and work experiences.

Many students with years of parenting and teaching experiences enroll so that they can earn the state certification credential that enables them to teach in public schools. Because students are working at a wide range of jobs to earn their college tuition and they are enrolled in 3–15 credits a semester, it is unusual for a cohort of students to progress together through the teacher education program. For the most part, students do not know others in the class and meet for the first time as the term begins.

Course objectives and requirements align with the Missouri Beginning Teacher Quality Indicators. Students become very familiar with these indicators as they progress through the teacher education curriculum and come to understand how course objectives relate to the state standards that provide a framework for the teacher education program. The students' wide range of experiences and perspectives inform reflections on course content and on themselves as learners and as future teachers as they consider how concepts apply to the classroom settings where they observe and, eventually, interact with young learners.

Aside from facing the usual teaching issues posed by teaching nontraditional students who commute to campus from home and work, I face three pressing challenges when teaching these particular students who are preparing to be elementary and secondary education teachers. My first challenge is modeling exemplary teaching, both to meet my own mastery goals (Dweck, 1986) and to respond to a perception that preparing teachers hold their College of Education professors to higher standards of teaching excellence.

A second related challenge is to demonstrate how the literature that informs my course affects how I teach in the higher education classroom because what I model is how my students will one day practice in their own classrooms. The third challenge is to craft effective environments for my students so that their learning experiences in my course strengthen their commitments to adopt effective, validated teaching and learning practices. I try to meet these challenges in many ways, including requiring students to complete a project—described in this chapter—using the pedagogy of cooperative learning.

I regard these challenges as goals that keep me striving to refine my course objectives and to design instructional activities that engage students productively in learning. The educational psychology literature provides the filter that I rely upon for direction. This filter guides my design of instructional activities that require students to use, apply, and write about course concepts.

For example, research on how individuals process information suggests how activity, elaboration, and organization are supports for student learning (Bransford, Brown, & Cocking, 1999). This literature stresses the role of metacognition in problem solving and steers me to show preparing teachers how to conceptualize a situation or problem before reviewing and selecting strategies to master or solve it (Brown, Campion, & Day, 1981).

The educational psychology literature affirms the importance of the social context to learning by exploring the role of the teacher and the influence of one's peers on the process of learning (Vygotsky, 1978). As my students come to appreciate what they learn from their peers and the social context of our classroom, my intent is that they will create classrooms where such interdependence is also valued.

The concepts central to the motivation literature—relevance, choice, goal setting, self-assessment, self-regulation—apply as readily to the K–12 setting as they do to learning in higher education (Dembo, 2004; Svinicki, 2004). Likewise, the research about cooperative learning—derived from analyses of goal structures (Ames & Ames, 1981), the social psychology of small groups (Johnson & Johnson, 1975), and informed by the prosocial outcomes that result when working in heterogeneous groups (Slavin, 1995)—offers wisdom and application to learning in college classrooms.

Viewed holistically, the educational psychology literature is foundational to how learning-centered teaching is understood in higher education (Weimer, 2002). Our responsibility as professors is not only to teach our disciplines to our students, but also to teach our students the strategies and skills that lead to a successful learning experience. This evolving imperative is due, in part, to changes in our national and cultural norms. Shifting demographic patterns steer an increasingly diverse group of students to higher education (Association of American Colleges and Universities, 2002).

Although many of these students have technology skills that are more sophisticated than those of their professors (Oblinger & Oblinger, 2005), they also bring to campus and the classroom the unsophisticated but demanding consumer attitudes that they use in the marketplace (Levine & Cureton, 1998). Those attitudes are reflected in how they engage with one another, their professors, and the campus community (Kuh, 2003; Kuh, Kinzie, Schuh, Whitt, & Associates, 2005).

In response to these changing norms and demanding attitudes, I endeavor to send a firm message that my classes are designed for effortful activity and learning. Even though I recognize that some students arrive with the consumer expectation that they can purchase course credits, my strategy is to steer them, gradually, to accept the challenge to learn. The syllabus sends the first message about this by including objectives and expectations about attitudes and behaviors. I refer to these in class throughout the term and spend the early weeks of the term establishing related classroom norms with my students.

As the term begins, I expect to hear a few complaints about assignments that require students to work in pairs or in small groups. What I hear in those disdain-filled messages is that many students have not yet had successful cooperative learning experiences. They will have successful experiences this term, I explain, as I refer them to the course objective stating that they will "develop and practice using effective interpersonal skills in a group setting."

To justify why such an objective is included in the curriculum, I convey the serious responsibilities to society that preparing teachers have. Students must not only master a complex curriculum, but they must also develop a sophisticated set of behaviors to be successful practicing teachers. The research literatures from both education and psychology provide the foundations for teaching and learning in school settings from preschool through higher education. My intent is to draw from these literatures to offer students the supports they can use to achieve academic success in my course and, eventually, to help their future students be successful.

In fact, long before the learning-centered teaching concepts were adapted and applied to higher education, elementary and secondary teacher educators recognized the importance of also supporting students' social and developmental growth (Johnson, Johnson, & Holubec, 1987; McCombs & Whisler, 1997). I offer these explanations in class and include them in a section of the syllabus under "expectations" where I introduce my philosophy for teaching educational psychology. When someone questions a strategy or rationale for an assignment or activity, I refer to the statement.

Although I repeat these messages as needed—orally, personally, and intermittently—from the start of the semester, I have less need to do so as the term gets underway. The messages become internalized as students contribute to setting and enforcing the behavioral norms for the term. As the semester begins, I provide the structures to help students learn the interpersonal skills and pedagogical strategies they need to approach and tackle the group projects that will be due later in the semester.

We start early with short exercises and assignments and incrementally build to a large group project. Although the interpersonal and social skills are integrated with course activities and assignments, they are presented separately in the sections that follow.

FOCUSING STUDENTS ON INTERPERSONAL AND SOCIAL SKILLS

Reviewing and Using Social Skills

The heterogeneity of the UMSL student body easily justifies focusing in class on social and interpersonal skills. Students need these skills to complete course assignments and class activities successfully. In addition, students will be able to use the course as a model for structuring group activities when they student-teach, intern, and later have responsibility for their own classrooms.

On the first day of the term, students are surprised to learn that I will keep them the entire class session and that I will expect each person to contribute verbally before we adjourn. During the first week, I want students to get to know me, one another, and the structure, expectations, and broad concepts of the course. Discussing the syllabus only partially sets the stage for learning. I also intend to reinforce the printed messages experientially. When a show of hands indicates that more than two-thirds of the class are new to campus, students begin to appreciate my efforts to help them meet each other.

Working in Dyads

During the first class, students meet those sitting close to them. They exchange names and contact information so that if they miss a class, they can contact at least two other students to learn about the class session, related activities, and assignments. Why two others? Answering that question affords me an opportunity to preview course content by questioning the reliability of a single source of information and commenting on how individuals process information in different ways.

In addition, course success is related to attendance and participation. Students are responsible for arriving in class prepared to work even if that entails conferring with two other students about the work they missed and how they should prepare for the next class. Knowing others in class helps many students feel comfortable enough to question or respond. Finally, allocating time for introductions on the first day of class creates students' first opportunity to meet potential group members. I point this out, assuring them that they will have additional opportunities to meet other classmates.

Other opportunities during the first week of the term allow students to turn to a neighbor to share perceptions or review knowledge from prerequisite courses. After asking a question or providing direction, I suggest that pairs of students introduce themselves, talk about their individual responses, and plan to volunteer an answer to the class. After accepting responses from several pairs of students, I label this Think-Pair-Share strategy as one that I will use during the semester.

Next, we analyze the partners' interactions for foundational interpersonal skills. I ask if they looked one another in the eye when they exchanged ideas. Establishing the importance of this nonverbal behavior creates discussion related to comfort levels, preferences, cultural norms, and possible clues about disabilities, all topics relevant to EdPsych 3312 and other teacher preparation courses. We discuss whether each person contributed equally to the discussion and how turn-taking is an essential communication tool for productive work in small groups.

Working in Triads and Small Groups

Before the first week of the term concludes, students work in groups of three and in small groups of seven and eight. They analyze each opportunity in two ways, by looking critically at both the content and the group processes. With each opportunity, students are able to attend to and practice the social skills introduced earlier, and they have an opportunity to add a new behavior, skill, or process to their developing repertoire of interpersonal skills.

Working in triads, for example, requires a designated leader who ensures that each person contributes to the group, perhaps by inviting a quiet group member to contribute or by coaxing an uninvolved member to participate. Some small group assignments require that participants agree on a response. Others require that one person observe the group dynamics and offer feedback to the group members about their use of names, eye contact, turn-taking, and the roles of leader and participants.

Working in dyads or triads raises the noise level in the classroom. This noisiness creates an opportunity to agree upon a signal we can use during the term to reconvene as a large classroom group. The class might suggest a hand signal, blinking the lights, or designating someone to whistle. It is important that the suggestion come from someone in the group and be acceptable to others. After using my own signal for one class, nontraditional students complained that they felt that my blinking the lights treated them as children. Since that revelation, I am careful to allow students to voice opinions and reach consensus.

Working Effectively in Small Groups

As the semester progresses, I encourage students to meet others in class and to take the in-class opportunities to work briefly with as many people in the class as possible. I want students to know one another before they have to align for the group project. The vehicles for creating these opportunities are short homework exercises that are reviewed in-class in small groups and short essays that require peer reviews and revisions. Each activity offers a chance to gather data about class members' work habits (preparation, depth, completeness), reasoning and problem-solving skills, and interpersonal strengths and weaknesses as they consider which behaviors support exemplary group experiences.

Over time, students practice a variety of roles as they work together in small groups on course content. They take turns suggesting how to select the leader, lead the group, energize it, summarize progress, mediate differences, take notes, and evaluate group members' behaviors. They learn to agree upon and practice enforcing a set of ground rules for the group. They learn to monitor and offer feedback on group members' contributions.

Occasionally, an ambiguous discussion point in an exercise stumps more than one small group, and they try to default on that item by arguing that the problem has no solution. When this occurs, I engage the entire class in a discussion of whether the group members consulted every resource available to them. Resources include their textbook and other members of their group, but they are always surprised to learn that they can consult another group as a resource. This realization results from my deliberate strategy of moving from an individualistic goal structure to a cooperative goal structure: the students learn that a behavior that was previously considered dishonest (conferring with a fellow student on homework) is not only permitted, but desirable.

When students subdivide into small groups for these tasks, we create teams based on variables that are unique to higher education (the type of teaching certificate each student is pursuing, the neighborhood where each lives, current work experiences) or variables that they could use in their future classrooms (last green vegetable consumed, counting off in fives, suits in a deck of playing cards, last movie attended). My plan is that students meet and experience working with others so that they will choose carefully those with whom to complete the joint project that synthesizes the content of the first half of the term.

Organizing Cooperative Teams

When it is time to subdivide the class into teams for the group project, I provide a moderate amount of structure in the description of the developmental case study project. Students select their own groups, but I recommend groups of five persons. Class time is allotted regularly to group work so that students can work, share with other groups, and seek feedback on the tasks that they are designing to assess a youngster's developmental maturity.

I request project updates at unannounced intervals. I urge students to select their group members carefully, taking into account their campus and work schedules; how close they live to one another; whether they are preparing to teach in early childhood, elementary, middle, or high school settings; and what they have learned to date about one another's work habits, interpersonal skills, and creativity and conceptual reasoning. The project is complex and multifaceted, one that benefits from group members' critical thinking skills—and one, I caution, that would be an enormous undertaking to do singlehandedly.

I upload to the EdPsych 3312 campus course management system sample cooperative group agreements, guidelines, descriptions of roles and responsibilities, and monitoring sheets. These have already been used for small group work in other classes. The project groups have the responsibility to negotiate their own cooperative group agreements and figure out which roles will best serve their groups. One strongly recommended guideline is to rotate roles each time they meet to work on the project.

Cottell (chapter 2) and Shadle (chapter 3) comment on using and rotating roles within small groups. Shadle offers detailed strategies for helping students master and use roles in small chemistry groups; Cottell explains his reservations and solutions for assigning roles.

I require them to monitor group behaviors at each meeting. Members sign the monitoring form and submit these completed forms with the final project. Ten percent of the project grade is based on each member's contributions to the group project as corroborated by his or her team members on a rating form completed after the project is submitted. Using the form, each person assesses on a 10-point scale his or her own and each group member's participation, effort, and contributions to the group. Students submit these independent ratings after the project is submitted and after they have had some time to step back and reflect on the group processes and experiences. These data determine what portion of the 10% each person earns on the project. Samples of these guidelines and forms are included in the chapter appendix.

STRUCTURING COURSE ACTIVITIES AND ASSIGNMENTS FOR COOPERATIVE LEARNING

Attendance, Participation, Professionalism (APP)

The patterns used to introduce interpersonal skills also support students as I ease them into the course requirements. From the first day of class, we take small deliberate steps that slowly and gradually steer students to buy into an assignment or activity and to do so with the goal of learning as an outcome.

To reinforce the course objectives of adopting the skills of the profession throughout the semester, students break into small groups to define what behaviors will be valued during the term with a focus on attending class, participating fully during class, and exhibiting the behaviors of a professional. Because 10% of the semester's grade is based on how I and the students assess themselves on these three dimensions, it is important to devote time as the semester begins to agreeing upon their behavioral definitions.

I divide the class quickly by signaling small clusters of five or six students sitting in close proximity to move their chairs into small circles. One-third of the groups define attendance, one-third define participation, and one-third define professionalism. The group selects the concept that interests them. They have 10 minutes to arrive at a list of the behaviors that define the concept.

I prompt their thinking by reminding them that they have responsibilities during the term to partners, to small groups, and to the class. I suggest that they consider the behaviors that qualify a group member as a responsible citizen in each of these situations and that they draw their lists from memories of their own positive or disappointing experiences.

I ask that everyone contribute and that only one person talk at a time, and I explain that the lists will not be finalized until the second week of the term. A volunteer in each group records the list, projects it visually, and presents it orally when the class reconvenes.

This activity gives students their first opportunity to note the basics of effective presentation skills and to offer constructive ways to provide feedback to one's peers. When students present their lists for each concept, they also solicit additional suggestions from the class. We discuss the appropriateness of assigning the same behaviors to more than one category.

The lists, which are posted on the course management system, are available for review and for online or printed additions as students arrive for the next class session. We spend time discussing how these behavioral lists will become the class code of conduct for the semester and how important it is for each person to offer his or her input. This includes the professor.

If no one has mentioned how unprofessional it is to gripe and complain, I add "No whining" to the list when it is in my possession. The lists are combined into one document defining three categories of behaviors and posted on the course management system. Students can review and discuss each category before the class decides at the end of the second week of the term to accept these behaviors as the class code of conduct.

I remind students that the syllabus requires them to submit a self-assessment on their class attendance, participation, and professionalism at midterm and at the end of the term. This exercise removes any mystery from the APP grade because it is based on how the class defined the three categories. As a result of completing this exercise early in the semester, students are present for class, and they accept opportunities to be active participants while learning to take responsibility for their professional behaviors.

Interdependence develops as each class member becomes responsible for making and enforcing the code of conduct. This approach is reinforced later in the semester when the curriculum focuses on models of classroom management. Students send messages in advance if they will be late or unable to attend class; they know what they have to do to be prepared for the next class they attend, and they encourage similar behaviors in one another. Valuing and adopting these behaviors are essential for successful learning experiences in EdPsych 3312.

When students submit their midterm self-assessments and set a goal for the remainder of the term, I either agree with their assessment or take the opportunity to remind individuals of their responsibilities to the class and possible goals they might set for the remainder of the semester.

This activity works early in the semester because everyone has attended university classes prior to this one and has experiences to bring to the task. It sets the stage for conduct during the term, creates an opportunity for students to provide input, and leads small groups to productive ends that benefit the class over the term. It enables me as the professor to lead class participants in creating their own ground rules, thereby avoiding the need for an authoritative mandate that could provoke more resistance than acceptance.

Critical Response Journals (CRJ)

Although defining the APP behaviors was a low-risk activity that relied completely on the prior knowledge of class members, the essays written as Critical Response Journal entries are designed to challenge students to apply to themselves, as preparing teachers, what they are learning. Students will be peer reviewing one another's essays. This feedback process adds an element of risk to the writing and reviewing process, although students do not know this when I make the assignment.

I provide structure by limiting the essays to three double-spaced pages. Four essay topics during the semester require students to construct an essay about themselves by demonstrating their comprehension of key concepts. As an example, the first essay, "How are you smart?" requires students to reflect about themselves using Gardner's (1993) theory of multiple intelligences.

The second essay, on professional objectivity, requires students to recognize and write about personal expectations and beliefs that may interfere with their maintaining a professional and objective attitude toward others, including future students.

Each essay requires students to be introspective and self-reflective and to show competence in applying course concepts. These essays model future teaching practices that emphasize writing as a process and revision as a tool to challenge students to construct stronger products. I accomplish this with a peer review process. Peer review and revision establish the value of collaborative learning processes early in the semester so that students learn that both processes are instrumental to completing the developmental case study successfully as a group.

The routine for accomplishing peer review and revision is initiated during the fourth week of the term when the first essay assignment is due on the first meeting day of the week. Students arrive in class expecting me to collect their papers. Instead, I ask them to take a few minutes to review their essays using the five criteria outlined in the essay assignment. I distribute a scoring guide that lists the five criteria as rows on a chart with three empty columns. They are to include a score from 1 (low) to 5 (high) on the chart for each criterion.

When we discuss this exercise, students realize which criteria they did not address in the essay or notice that they had neglected to proofread their work. Then I ask them to exchange essays with someone in class so that each person becomes a peer reviewer. I acknowledge that some essays may contain information that they may not want a peer to read and ask them to select from their essays a few paragraphs that they are willing to exchange. They may also select a specific class member as a reviewer. Then, they apply the same criteria to a peer's essay and assign 1 to 5 points to each criterion.

A practice exercise on giving feedback that is honest, diplomatic, and informative follows this first peer review. Students practice offering feedback that points out strengths in the essay as well as areas where further work is needed. They write their feedback on the scoring guide, and they communicate it orally.

I explain that students can earn full credit on their essays only if each is peer reviewed, and, usually before I mention it, someone in the class asks if they may use the feedback to rewrite the essay before submitting it. This activity begins a new habit for the class: essays that are due, for example, on Monday are self-assessed before class, peer reviewed for 15 minutes during class, and revised for submission to the instructor on Wednesday.

We introduce new quality standards, and students accept the challenge to use the feedback to improve their essays. On Wednesdays, they submit the original essay, the revised essay, and the scoring guide with columns for self-assessment, peer review, and instructor review. Space is available for each reviewer to offer written comments about the essay. If the class meets only once weekly, this pattern is adapted for that schedule.

What transpires is evidence that students respect and want to use the process: they exchange papers for peer review electronically and arrange to meet each other for lengthier peer review sessions before or after the class meets. Robinson and Cooper (chapter 7) describe alternatives for introducing and sustaining a peer review process.

Group Project: The Developmental Case Study

Setting the stage for a complex group project—gradually and deliberately from the beginning of the term—helps students anticipate and learn to use the interpersonal skills and organizational processes that are integral to completing the Developmental Case Study. When we discuss this requirement, I explain that this project must be successful because they want to engage their elementary and secondary students with meaningful cooperative learning experiences.

Further, I suggest, none of us arrived in the world knowing how to work in groups: this is something we all learn and something they will teach their future students. This message is one of many that I send to help students see the parallels between our work together and their future work in elementary and secondary classrooms.

Although many sources recommend that cooperative learning groups should be randomly or teacher-assigned from the beginning of the term to ensure heterogeneity within each group, students in EdPsych 3312 create their groups for this project. This is due to the heterogeneity of the UMSL student body and to the students' insistence that groups cannot meet successfully when everyone's course schedule, work, and living arrangements are scattered over a large metropolitan area.

From the beginning of the term, students have learned about one another's strengths, creativity, interests, personalities, and work habits. Rather than electing to work with others just like themselves, more often, students form groups based on other factors such as the proximity of their homes or the convergence of their available free time.

Traditional-age college students often figure out that nontraditional students who are parents bring a unique and valued dimension to their group. Someone returning to school from the corporate setting may bring organizational experience that is regarded as helpful wisdom. Those who have taught previously in private or parochial schools bring skill sets that facilitate the tasks of the case study.

Because I encourage students from the first day of class to get to know their classmates, I trust that this attention pays off in their team selections. I hope that the attention paid since the beginning of the term to acquiring interpersonal and group skills has provided the experiential base that students use to identify those with whom they will complete this project.

I emphasize that the group functions much as a care team operates in a school setting, when a team of professionals with varying expertise and multiple perspectives meet to plan the most appropriate and balanced response to a youngster's Individualized Education Plan. The child benefits from the multiple lenses that each person brings to the team. A commitment to heterogeneity among team members strengthens the case study product.

The project description provides a structure that guides the students to develop hands-on, interactive activities that they use to assess the developmental maturity and individuality of one pupil between the ages of 9 and 14. To create the assessments, students must probe their comprehension of five broad theoretical approaches explored in class: cognitive development; socioemotional and moral development; individual differences in intelligences; learning and cognitive style; and motivation.

Based on the students' original assessments, completed projects describe the pupil's interests, motivations, and learning styles and how the pupil thinks, processes information, reasons, and justifies choices. Each group makes curricular and instructional recommendations about the student to a hypothetical teacher.

It is not expected, nor desired, that the group use formal tests and instruments to assess the child's progress. EdPsych 3312 does not offer the specialized training required to administer and interpret such products. In fact, their use detracts from the project's evaluation. Instead, groups are assessed on the originality and practicality of the strategies that they devise.

I stress using the interactive and thinking tools that are naturally available to a teacher as he or she works with a child. Many examples and suggestions are in the textbook. I create class exercises to illustrate various assessment strategies. I devote group time during class to demonstrate the interactive activities that each is creating on a classmate who is acting, for example, as a pupil with a specific learning style or at a certain developmental stage. Feedback follows each demonstration, with attention to how a child would respond at varying places of development on different stage theories.

One intentionally ill-defined (Davidson & Sternberg, 2003) feature of the project is how the group members divide the work and collaborate on the product. The group is responsible for figuring this out. Some groups regard the project as a Jigsaw and assign one theoretical approach to each team member, making that person responsible for researching the concept and figuring out its assessment. The assessments are complete when these contributions are compiled.

Other groups assign individuals to devise the assessments, others to administer them, and others to analyze and interpret the results. Among other required tasks, the project includes identifying a pupil, finding a location to interact with him or her, obtaining permission to participate from the pupil and his or her parents, recording and transcribing the interview, and constructing recommendations based on the results.

Mastering the project's complexity—by identifying the tasks, dividing them among team members, and negotiating their completion to everyone's satisfaction—is an important part of the process. When groups realize that each member has multiple responsibilities and when they decide to separate the content tasks from the process tasks, they work more efficiently. This project cannot be completed without each team member developing a richer understanding of the major concepts in the course curriculum. At its conclusion, group members report on and justify the ratings they give to the quality of the group's work and their own and their teammates' contributions.

CONCLUSIONS

The strategies used in EdPsych 3312 developed over 25 years of teaching the course at three universities. As my own comprehension of the content deepened, I increasingly tried to apply to my own students the theories and concepts that I was teaching them to apply to their future students. I carefully consider the success of a class activity or assignment, wondering more about why it didn't work for certain students than whether it was successful for others. Focusing on the students whom I did not reach keeps me thinking and wondering about how to refine an experience or innovation so that it will work for more of my students. This focus on learning is a helpful obsession. I often ask a student directly to tell me whether an exercise or discussion was helpful or to explain to me what he or she learned in class that day.

I rely on students' feedback to guide changes that I make to specific class activities or to the overall structure of the course. The changes are small steps that evolve gradually into a revised product or process that I implement. The feedback is both informal and formal.

Students' nonverbal or verbal expressions and behaviors during or after class convey a great deal. I also seek formal, more structured feedback. In addition to the department's required course evaluation, I always include my own course evaluation. Students complete both under the guidance of a student proctor who turns the evaluations in to the department office.

As EdPsych 3312 evolved to include its major emphasis on cooperative learning, I began asking students in this course evaluation to reflect retrospectively on their interpersonal and group skills at the beginning of the term and at its conclusion. Using a 5-point scale, students rate themselves on the same set of behaviors—first, thinking about their skills as the term began, and, then, thinking about their skills as it concluded. (This customized course evaluation is also included in the chapter appendix.)

I learned from students' responses to the evaluation that they were able to separate the course content from the group processes. They recognize and value how the focus on process enhanced the learning they did in the course. Unfortunately, I have not yet compiled the responses into one data set, but I have used it each term to provide evidence that the course was working and to learn what students thought was successful. Their comments confirm that the strategies are working and keep me thinking about ways to ensure that each student's experience is as productive as those reflected in these comments:

"At the beginning of the term I did not have the confidence to achieve group consensus, taking the initiative, and rotating group roles. At the end of the term I have improved in all areas. With the experience of cooperative projects, my learning has taken a new perspective."

"I have learned more about myself as an individual regarding issues in teaching. I have become a better public speaker and a better professional. I work better with a group and I have been exposed to many aspects of teaching."

References

Ames, C., & Ames, R. (1981). Competitive versus individualistic goal structures: The salience of past performance information for causal attributions and affect. *Journal of Educational Psychology, 73,* 411–418.

Association of American Colleges and Universities (2002). *Greater expectations: A new vision for learning as a nation goes to college.* Washington, DC: Author. Retrieved February 3, 2010, from http://www.greaterexpectations.org/.

Bransford, J., Brown, A. L., & Cocking, R. (Eds.) (1999). *How people learn: Brain, mind, experience, and school.* Washington, DC: National Academy Press.

Brown, A. L., Campion, J., & Day, J. (1981). Learning to learn: On training students to learn from texts. *Educational Researcher, 10*(2), 14–21.

Davidson, J. E., & Sternberg, R. (2003). *The psychology of problem solving.* Cambridge, UK: Cambridge University Press.

Dembo, M. H. (2004). *Motivation and learning strategies for college success: A self-management approach.* Mahwah, NJ: Lawrence Erlbaum.

Dweck, C. S. (1986). Motivational processes affecting learning. *American Psychologist, 41,* 1040–1048.

Gardner, H. (1993). *Multiple intelligences: The theory in practice.* New York: Basic Books.

Johnson, D. W., & Johnson, R. T. (1975). *Learning together and alone: Cooperation, competition, and individualization.* Englewood Cliffs, NJ: Prentice Hall.

Johnson, R. T., Johnson, D. W., & Holubec, E. J. (Eds.) (1987). *Structuring cooperative learning: Lesson plans for teachers.* Edina, MN: Interaction Book Company.

Kuh, G. D. (2003). What we're learning about engagement from NSSE: Bookmarks for effective educational practices. *Change, 35*(2), 24–32.

Kuh, G. D., Kinzie, J., Schuh, J. H., Whitt, E. J., & Associates (2005). *Student success in college: Creating conditions that matter.* San Francisco: Jossey-Bass.

Levine, A., & Cureton, J. S. (1998). Collegiate life: An obituary. *Change, 30*(3), 14.

McCombs, B. L., & Whisler, J. S. (1997). *The learner-centered classroom and school: Strategies for increasing student motivation and achievement.* San Francisco: Jossey-Bass.

Oblinger, D. G., & Oblinger, J. L. (Eds.) (2005). *Educating the net generation.* Boulder, CO: Educause.

Perry, W. G., Jr. (1999). *Forms of intellectual and ethical development in the college years: A scheme.* (Reprint of the 1970 edition with a new introduction by L. Knefelkamp.) San Francisco: Jossey-Bass.

Slavin, R. E. (1995). Cooperative learning and intergroup relations. In J. A. Banks & M. Banks (Eds.), *Handbook of research on multicultural education* (pp. 628–634). New York: Macmillan.

Svinicki, M. D. (2004). *Learning and motivation in the postsecondary classroom.* Bolton, MA: Anker Press.

Vygotsky, L. (1978). *Mind in society: The development of higher psychological processes.* Cambridge, MA: Harvard University Press.

Weimer, M. E. (2002). *Learner-centered teaching: Five key changes to practice.* San Francisco: Jossey-Bass.

Appendix

I. Guidelines for a Cooperative Group Agreement in EdPsych 3312
   - Roles are rotated for each assignment and project meeting.
   - Assignment work is divided evenly among group members.
   - All members are team players—by being prepared, participating, and attending.
   - All differences are resolved through constructive criticism using non-judgmental language.
   - The group is responsible for being sure that all members understand the assignment and content.
   - The group monitors and maintains feedback on how it functioned at each meeting.
   - Look and listen: use appropriate eye contact and refer to each group member by name.

II. Group Roles and Responsibilities in EdPsych 3312
   - *Facilitator/leader:* directs group work on the assignment; ensures that the work is equally divided; encourages all to participate; sets schedules and time frames as needed; facilitates members carrying out their respective roles.
   - *Recorder/evaluator:* documents group's discussions by recording contributions/ideas, suggestions, and decisions made at the meeting; attaches meeting notes and monitoring sheet for the meeting; maintains a file of these records until a new monitor assumes the role.
   - *Elaborator(s)/energizer(s):* asks questions, seeks elaboration or extension on others' contributions; serves as devil's advocate to encourage multiple perspectives before decisions are made.
   - *Summarizer/mediator:* integrates and verbally summarizes ideas; checks for understanding by all members; helps resolve differences; asks for clarification when it is needed.
   - *Monitor:* observes and completes monitoring charts while participating in meetings; offers objective feedback to each member on the role

each assumed at the meeting; obtains signatures of those participating at each meeting.

III. Cooperative Groups: Monitoring Roles and Skills

Assignment _____   Date _____

	Role	Who (list names)?
Facilitator/leader	
Recorder/evaluator	
Elaborator(s)/energizer(s)	
Summarizer/mediator	
Monitor	

Group Process Skills

Group Members' Names					
attend meeting					
look and listen					
participate/present ideas					
use nonjudgmental language					
check for understanding					
work to achieve consensus					
use role responsibilities					

Comments on process:

Signatures:

IV. Self and Peer Ratings on Contributions to the Group Project

Self and Peer Evaluation Form: Developmental Case Study Group Project

Name: _____ Date: _____

Please use the following scale to indicate the extent to which each of the members of your case study group performed the indicated activities. You are to base your evaluation on **EFFORT**, not the quality of the results. Circle the appropriate number for each item.

Completely Unsatisfactory Effort   Completely Satisfactory Effort

1   2   3   4   5   6   7   8   9   10

Insert the name of each group member. The final block is for your self-evaluation.

1. _____
   a. Attended all group meetings   1 2 3 4 5 6 7 8 9 10
   b. Completed all assigned tasks   1 2 3 4 5 6 7 8 9 10
   c. Was prepared for all group meetings   1 2 3 4 5 6 7 8 9 10
   d. Overall effort to contribute   1 2 3 4 5 6 7 8 9 10

2. _____
   a. Attended all group meetings   1 2 3 4 5 6 7 8 9 10
   b. Completed all assigned tasks   1 2 3 4 5 6 7 8 9 10
   c. Was prepared for all group meetings   1 2 3 4 5 6 7 8 9 10
   d. Overall effort to contribute   1 2 3 4 5 6 7 8 9 10

3. _____
   a. Attended all group meetings   1 2 3 4 5 6 7 8 9 10
   b. Completed all assigned tasks   1 2 3 4 5 6 7 8 9 10
   c. Was prepared for all group meetings   1 2 3 4 5 6 7 8 9 10
   d. Overall effort to contribute   1 2 3 4 5 6 7 8 9 10

4. _____
   a. Attended all group meetings   1 2 3 4 5 6 7 8 9 10
   b. Completed all assigned tasks   1 2 3 4 5 6 7 8 9 10
   c. Was prepared for all group meetings   1 2 3 4 5 6 7 8 9 10
   d. Overall effort to contribute   1 2 3 4 5 6 7 8 9 10

5. Your name _____
   a. Attended all group meetings   1 2 3 4 5 6 7 8 9 10
   b. Completed all assigned tasks   1 2 3 4 5 6 7 8 9 10
   c. Was prepared for all group meetings 1 2 3 4 5 6 7 8 9 10
   d. Overall effort to contribute   1 2 3 4 5 6 7 8 9 10

V. Supplemental course evaluation customized for EdPsych 3312

This semester activities and assignments were structured using a cooperative learning model. For each role or skill, indicate how competent you were before the semester began. Then, rate your present competence. Rate yourself by circling a letter grade of A (very high) to E (very low).

Role or Skill	Before this term	As the term concludes
1. Facilitator/leader	A B C D E	A B C D E
2. Recorder/evaluator	A B C D E	A B C D E
3. Notetaker	A B C D E	A B C D E
4. Elaborator/energizer	A B C D E	A B C D E
5. Summarizer/mediator	A B C D E	A B C D E
6. attending to group members	A B C D E	A B C D E
7. having eye contact with others	A B C D E	A B C D E
8. taking the initiative in small groups	A B C D E	A B C D E
9. using nonjudgmental language	A B C D E	A B C D E
10. checking with others for understanding	A B C D E	A B C D E
11. achieving group consensus	A B C D E	A B C D E
12. rotating responsibilities when working in a group	A B C D E	A B C D E

13. Would you enroll in another course that relied on cooperative learning skills?

    Yes   No

14. Would you encourage a friend to enroll in this section of EdPsych 3312?

    Yes   No

15. Suppose that, in a future term, you have a choice to enroll in a course section that relies on cooperative and collaborative goal structures [C] or a section that relies on an individual goal structure [I]. Which would you choose?

    C   I

6

Preparing the Next Generation of Engineering Educators and Researchers

Cooperative Learning in the Purdue University School of Engineering Education PhD Program

Karl A. Smith, Holly Matusovich,
Kerry Meyers, and Llewellyn Mann

Cooperative learning has been part of the landscape of engineering education for almost thirty years. The conceptual cooperative learning model was introduced to the engineering education community in 1981 (Smith, Johnson, & Johnson, 1981a; Smith, Johnson, & Johnson, 1981b) and was continually refined and elaborated for engineering educators (Felder, 1995; Prince, 2004; Smith, 1995; Smith, Sheppard, Johnson, & Johnson, 2005) and higher education faculty in general (Johnson, Johnson, & Smith, 1991, 1998, 2000, 2006, 2007; MacGregor, Cooper, Smith, & Robinson, 2000; Millis & Cottell, 1998; Smith, 1996, 1998; Smith, Cox, & Douglas, 2009).

The influence of foundational work on cooperative learning can be seen in the University of Delaware Problem-Based Learning model (Allen, Duch, & Groh, 1996; Duch, Groh, & Allen, 2001), the SCALE-UP model at North Carolina State (Beichner, Saul, Allain, Deardorff, & Abbot, 2000), and the Technology Enhanced Active Learning (TEAL) model (Dori & Belcher, 2005; Dori, et al., 2003), as well as many others.

Cooperative learning, as well as other forms of active student engagement, has received lots of attention in undergraduate STEM (Science, Technology, Engineering, and Mathematics) programs. Because these approaches are less common in graduate programs in engineering and other STEM disciplines, this volume presents an opportunity for a unique contribution.

Numerous studies and reports claim that a different type of engineering graduate is needed, one with a much broader range of professional skills in addition to the widely sought technical skills. The principal question addressed in this chapter is "Can we increase the rate of development of the theory and practice needed to prepare engineering graduates for twenty-first century opportunities and challenges through the use of cooperative learning strategies such as Constructive Controversy?" The context is an engineering education PhD course, History and Philosophy of Engineering Education, in the School of Engineering Education (ENE), College of Engineering, Purdue University. We used the instructional strategy of Constructive Academic Controversy, a formal cooperative learning strategy.

BACKGROUND, CONTEXT, AND URGENCY

A growing number of national reports argue that a different type of engineer is needed to practice effectively in the twenty-first century (Duderstadt, 2008; Galloway, 2007; Lynn & Salzman, 2006, 2007; NAE, 2004, 2005; Redish & Smith, 2009). These reports also emphasize that the approach to preparing these students needs to be different, i.e., better matched to developing the knowledge, skills, and habits of mind or modes of thinking that are required.

For example, engineers in practice must be skillful at representing and managing trade-offs, such as this one: thicker metal in automobiles makes them safer (they can absorb more energy in a crash) versus thinner metal, which makes the automobile more fuel efficient (lighter weight). This specific example focuses on trade-offs at a technical level. Many of the decisions facing engineers involve multiple perspectives, including not only technical, but also social, economic, environmental, global, and so forth; thus, the trade-offs are more complex and difficult to represent and manage. Effectively managing trade-offs requires that engineers understand multiple perspectives and make persuasive and compelling arguments based on evidence.

We claim that modeling and coaching graduate students in the use of cooperative learning better prepares future faculty and researchers for educating the new engineer. Also, the ENE PhD students learn a mode of inquiry that helps them craft compelling arguments and assists them in becoming effective researchers.

The engineering education PhD program at Purdue is a competency-based program focused on (1) developing engineering education research practitioners, and (2) modeling, coaching, and preparing ENE PhD students to use modern empirically and theoretically grounded pedagogical practices such as the conceptual cooperative learning model.

Several courses within the ENE at Purdue focus on an argument-claim-evidence-method model (Booth, Colomb, & Williams, 2008; Lunsford,

Ruszkiewicz, & Walters, 2004), including three foundation courses: Engineering Education Inquiry; History and Philosophy of Engineering Education; and Content, Assessment, and Pedagogy: An Integrated Design Approach. These courses—as well as most courses in the program—use aspects of cooperative learning, including Think-Pair-Share, cooperative Jigsaw, cooperative projects, and Constructive Controversy. The key elements of well-structured cooperative learning—positive interdependence, individual and group accountability, promotive interaction, teamwork skills, and group processing—are emphasized (Johnson et al., 2006).

HISTORY AND PHILOSOPHY OF ENGINEERING EDUCATION

The specific course selected for this chapter is History and Philosophy of Engineering Education. This course was selected for a variety of reasons: (1) it is a new course and the instructors tried to be as transparent as possible with the students in the course development process, with an emphasis on learning pedagogy, not just content; and (2) the course featured the Constructive Controversy formal cooperative learning strategy. History and Philosophy of Engineering Education is one of six core courses taken by engineering education PhD students within ENE.

We put a lot of effort into planning the course. Like Robinson and Cooper (chapter 7) and Cohen (chapter 5), we believe in a mastery-oriented classroom where outcomes are identified, modeled by faculty, and practiced by students with peer and faculty feedback. The student learning outcomes for the course were the following:

1. Understand the history of engineering education and how that shapes our collective role as constructor or participant in this emerging field (Felder, Sheppard, & Smith, 2005; Steering Committee, 2006).
2. Critically describe the forces influencing past, present, and future scenarios of engineering education.
3. Describe how personal past experiences within engineering connect with future roles in engineering education.
4. Develop and articulate a personal philosophy on engineering education.
5. Construct arguments about the similarities and differences between the constructs of engineering, science, art, and design.
6. Participate in a "community of practice" culture through formation of our own community and participation in the broader community of engineering education.

7. Use reflection as a tool of self-discovery for shaping and refining personal philosophies.

8. Articulate personal perspectives on foundational topics within engineering education by engaging in and leading thoughtful and critical discussions.

Three themes were repeated throughout the course: What is engineering? Who gets to be an engineer? Who decides? We encouraged students to keep these questions in mind as they read the course materials as well as during their discussions and writing. Assessment feedback at the end of the semester indicated that the objectives were met, and more than a semester later, we still hear students echoing the three theme questions.

The class met twice per week for 75 minutes over a 15-week semester. Eight students were enrolled in the course, including five women and three men. The normal flow for the class included assigned readings for each class period. We expected the students to complete the readings prior to class and to come to class prepared to engage in discussion or a discussion-based activity.

CONSTRUCTIVE CONTROVERSY

Constructive Controversy is a good pedagogical choice for the course because of the link between forming and articulating good arguments—claim-reason-evidence—and the format of the Constructive Controversy approach, which provides students with structure and practice in providing evidence and rationale to support their positions. The specific application had the following features:

1. Students have the opportunity to craft arguments with a partner and verbally try out the claim:
   - Students' short arguments must be laden with reasons and evidence.
   - Students have opportunities to reshape arguments during conversation.
   - Students actively see the importance of evidence in convincing peers of their position.
   - Students also have the opportunity to argue for other positions, which helps them see what evidence is needed to change their own minds.

2. Students examine a question such as "What is engineering?" by analyzing the activities of people actually doing design work.

3. Students have the opportunity to grapple with the importance of representing and managing trade-offs in engineering and to practice arguing from evidence.

Constructive Academic Controversy

Constructive Academic Controversy (sometimes referred to as Structured Controversy) is a formal cooperative learning approach that emerged from the Johnson and Johnson cooperative learning group at University of Minnesota in the late 1970s and early 1980s. The approach has been studied extensively and has excellent theoretical, empirical, and practical support (Johnson & Johnson, 1987, 2007, 2009; Johnson, Johnson, & Smith, 1997, 2000). Structured Controversy was introduced to the engineering education community in the 1980s (Smith, Johnson & Johnson, 1982; Smith, 1984), and although it was received with some interest, this approach didn't resonate with the community as much as cooperative project-based or problem-based learning did.

Re-engaging students and faculty with Constructive Controversy is important and timely for numerous reasons, including Daniel Pink's (2005, 2006) argument about our current era, the importance of mastery learning, and the role of complexity in decision making.

Pink claims in his book, *A Whole New Mind*, and his DVD that we are moving from the knowledge age to the conceptual age. He argues that artists and empathizers will rule. Pink emphasizes the importance of the "right brain" senses, particularly the idea of empathy (perspective taking), symphony (connecting many ideas together), story (the ability to develop an argument rather than rely on facts), meaning (developing a greater understanding of the issues within context) and play (to a certain extent, the open discussion and flow of ideas seen as a form of play through language), and design (designing an argument and then a counterargument). Pink's ideas get at the heart of the kinds of thinking and the essential attributes—creativity and empathy— needed by future engineers.

Peter Block (2002) makes similar arguments and offers a creative synthesis. Block argues that a synthesis is needed among the engineer, economist, and artist archetypes. He suggests that the architect provides an image that integrates the polarized worlds of the engineer, the economist, and the artist. Furthermore, he notes that the "task of the social architect is to design and bring into being organizations that serve both the marketplace and the soul of the people who work within them" (p. 171).

Constructive Controversy is aligned with promoting an environment with a mastery learning orientation because each group has a cooperative goal of ensuring that all members understand and are able to articulate the best arguments on all sides. This is similar to Robinson and Cooper's (chapter 7) goal of using discussion to strengthen understanding through explanation.

In a mastery-oriented environment, learning is of primary importance over end performance. Constructive Academic Controversy is not about winning or losing the argument, or even who has the best argument; it is about finding the best solution that is agreeable to all participants. Learning environments can influence the learner's approach (Pintrich, Marx, & Boyle, 1993). Mastery learning orientations promote deeper understanding and greater self-regulated learning (Dweck & Leggett, 1988; Pintrich & De Groot, 1990; Pintrich et al., 1993).

Researchers examining complexity and complex adaptive systems provide lots of evidence for the difficulty of prediction (Axelrod & Cohen, 2001; Miller & Page, 2007). Page (2007) provides detailed support for the claim, "Diverse perspectives and tools enable collections of people to find more and better solutions and contribute to overall productivity" (p. 13). The importance of articulating and representing diverse perspectives is another central feature of the Constructive Academic Controversy model.

We have presented a compelling argument for using Constructive Controversy:

1. National reports call for change in the way we educate our students, so the timing is right.
2. Constructive Controversy is in line with best teaching practices related to active and mastery-oriented learning and new ways of thinking about knowledge and knowing.
3. Constructive Controversy promotes the types of skills we want future engineers to have.

This argument prompted our own use of Constructive Controversy, and the outcomes support the argument. The details of our use of Constructive Academic Controversy in the History and Philosophy of Engineering Education PhD course are summarized in the next section.

IMPLEMENTATION OF CONSTRUCTIVE CONTROVERSY IN THE HISTORY AND PHILOSOPHY OF ENGINEERING EDUCATION

Although we tried to integrate Constructive Academic Controversy throughout the course, one specific session that worked well was assigning viewing perspectives for a video of engineers at work. Like Robinson and Cooper (chapter 7) and Cottell (chapter 2), we believe that the clarity of assignments is critical and therefore put effort into introducing and guiding the activity so that our expectations were clear.

In the class period prior to conducting the Constructive Controversy, students received a brief overview of the activity and a reading assignment by Rowland (2004) describing a philosophy of engineering. Based on previous activities, we found that students tend to be more mentally and emotionally prepared to engage in class if they know what is expected of them; Panitz (chapter 4) and Cohen (chapter 5) also emphasize setting expectations for students' responsibility for learning.

It is also helpful if students understand how assigned readings connect to those class activities. We explained to students that the activity involved thinking about ways that design is represented and that Rowland's article "Shall We Dance? A Design Epistemology for Organizational Learning and Performance" would help them think creatively about the philosophy of engineering.

Our overview of the procedure was based on an assigned reading (Johnson et al., 2000), and we used a set of PowerPoint slides developed by Smith and Matusovich to guide the students. The slides are posted to www.ce.umn.edu/~smith/links.html (scroll down to presentations). Several students had experienced this approach in prior courses such as Leadership, Policy, and Change, another ENE foundation course.

Three factors made this activity easy to facilitate: (1) some of the students had prior experience with Structured Controversy, (2) most students were familiar with cooperative learning, and (3) the students generally wanted to learn to use best teaching practices.

Similar to the novice geology students described by Nuhfer (chapter 11), ENE graduate students are often used to the large lecture-style courses that they experienced as undergraduate engineering students. Unlike Nuhfer's geology students, the ENE graduate students focus on the faults they see in how they were educated and want to make changes for coming generations of engineers.

Where students are less familiar with cooperative learning practices, content appropriate exercises similar to Nuhfer's (chapter 11) Unique Earth Brainstorming Posters or Panitz's (chapter 4) pre-semester letter introducing cooperative learning might help facilitate the transition to cooperative learning activities.

We introduced Constructive Controversy with the following paraphrased quote from Helen and Alexander Astin (Astin & Astin, 1996):

Controversy with Civility: recognize that differences of viewpoint are inevitable and that such differences must be aired openly, but with civility. Civility implies respect for others, a willingness to hear about each other's viewpoints, and the exercise of restraint in criticizing the views and actions of others. Controversy can often lead to new creative solutions to problems, especially when it occurs in an atmosphere of civility, collaboration, and common purpose. (p. 59)

On the day of the activity, we had approximately 75 minutes to introduce, complete, and reflect on the Constructive Academic Controversy activity. The overall plan for the class session was the following:

1. Brief introduction to Constructive Controversy as an activity and as a teaching tool.
2. Details on mechanics of activity.
3. Assignment of pairs.
4. Watching of video.
5. Constructive Controversy discussion with their partner.
6. Entire class discussion.

The introduction and supporting slides emphasized the importance of understanding the best arguments on all sides (goal interdependence), highlighted the steps in the controversy process shown in Figure 6.1, and reminded the students of the features of skilled disagreement and helpful rules.

Constructive Controversy Procedure

Step	Typical Phrase
Prepare	Our best case Is . . .
Present	The answer Is . . . because . . .
Open Discussion	Your Position is Inadequate because . . .
	My position is better because . . .
Perspective Reversal	Your position Is . . .because . . .
Synthesis	Our best reasoned Judgment is . . .

Figure 6.1 Constructive Controversy Procedure

Skilled Disagreement

1. Define "decision" as a mutual problem, not as a win-lose situation.
2. Be critical of ideas, not people. (Confirm others' competence while disagreeing with their positions.)

3. Separate one's personal worth from others' reactions to one's ideas.
4. Differentiate before trying to integrate.
5. Take others' perspectives before refuting their ideas.
6. Give everyone a fair hearing.
7. Follow the canons of rational argument.

Rules for Constructive Controversy

1. I am critical of ideas, not people. I challenge and refute the ideas of the opposing group, but I do not indicate that I personally reject them.
2. I remember that we are all in this together, sink or swim. I focus on coming to the best decision possible, not on winning.
3. I encourage everyone to participate and to master all the relevant information.
4. I listen to everyone's ideas, even if I don't agree.
5. I restate what someone has said if it is not clear.
6. I first try to bring out all the ideas and facts supporting both sides, and then I try to put them together in a way that makes sense.
7. I try to understand all sides of the issue.
8. I change my mind when the evidence clearly indicates that I should do so.

The remainder of the slides guided students through the controversy process. As noted previously, the entire set may be downloaded.

With a program goal of creating the next generation of teachers and a class design philosophy of being transparent in all teaching methods and activities, we gave the students a brief introduction to Constructive Controversy as a teaching and learning tool. After explaining the mechanics, we put students into pairs and gave them their primary argument roles.

Students then watched the video that was based on their initial argument perspective. Following the video, the students engaged in Constructive Controversy. The final aspect of the activity was a reflection and discussion with the entire class on the content and process.

Initially, the instructors were concerned that students would not find enough controversial material to engage in a meaningful discussion or that students might struggle to accept their assigned roles over their preferred side of the argument.

Our fears were immediately dispelled in the few moments after the video ended: students spontaneously leaped into the point of the activity. One student called out, "How can we have an argument when the answer is so obvious: the video displayed design work!" Then the student explained why she felt this way, giving a clear reason. A second student immediately responded that it was not design and offered a reason. The first student seemed to become aware of the rigidity of her own thinking and the purpose of the entire activity. We all agreed that this learning activity could not have been better!

Feedback during the reflection portion of the activity suggested that students generally enjoyed the Constructive Controversy as a way to explore a discussion topic and to practice crafting arguments. The students in the ENE PhD program play dual roles as students and future teachers, so their feedback from both perspectives is important. As potential future instructors, the students in our class also saw Constructive Controversy as an important teaching tool.

Students engaged in the activity with different levels of vigor. Some students, particularly those who seem to enjoy a good argument as a means of discussion, latched right on to their assigned roles and argued passionately for their positions. Other students found accepting a role that might not match their personal position to be slightly more challenging.

However, these engagement patterns were similar to those observed in the previously referenced Leadership, Policy, and Change course where students had more choices and preparation time in the controversy activity. In the Leadership, Policy, and Change graduate level ENE course, Constructive Controversy was used to explore policy initiatives in STEM education.

In this application, students could select their own topics of argument from a given list and select their own side of the argument. In this course, students also did most of their preparation work outside of class and brought the final arguments to class. Both classes incorporated structures that encouraged regular engagement of the students with their peers, so the Constructive Controversy activity was familiar in that regard.

In both applications all class members participated, although we observed varying levels of passion. This suggests that flexibility in structuring the activity is possible without sacrificing participation, perhaps with the caveat that students need to be familiar with peer engagement.

Further, although we did not use such an approach, Constructive Academic Controversy could be paired with Quick-Thinks (chapter 7), either in individual groups or as a whole class, to spark deeper thinking and enhanced participation.

Based on our experience in the History and Philosophy of Engineering Education course, we believe that future uses of Constructive Controversy could be enhanced by adding an opportunity for reflection, specifically on the aspect of supporting claims with evidence. Such an opportunity, combined with coaching on meta-reflection, would help students better connect their Constructive Controversy experience to the importance of supporting claims with reasons and evidence. We agree with Panitz (chapter 4) and Nuhfer (chapter 11) that reflection is an important part of the cooperative learning process. It helps students develop an appreciation for cooperative learning, increases students' awareness of changes in personal learning strategies, reinforces the content learning, and emphasizes course learning objectives.

For this activity and as a whole, students generally responded positively to our transparent approach to teaching, i.e., they appreciated the modeling of tools that they could practice and incorporate into their own teaching toolboxes.

CONCLUSION

The principal question addressed in this chapter is "Can we increase the rate of development of the theory and practice needed to prepare engineering graduates for twenty-first century opportunities and challenges through the use of cooperative learning strategies such as Constructive Controversy?" Through application of Constructive Controversy in the context of a PhD-level engineering education course where students are preparing to become future educators of engineering students, we argue that we can. Our evidence is the response of the students, both in seeing the importance of differing perspectives on arguments and in their embracing Constructive Controversy as a teaching and learning tool.

References

Allen, D. E., Duch, B. E., & Groh, S. E. (1996). The power of problem-based learning in teaching introductory science courses: New directions for teaching and learning. In L. Wilkerson & W. H. Gijselaers (Eds.), *Bringing problem-based learning to higher education: Theory and practice* (pp. 43–52). San Francisco: Jossey-Bass.

Astin, H. S., & Astin, A. W. (1996). *A social change model of leadership development.* Los Angeles, CA: Regents of the University of California.

Axelrod, R., & Cohen, M. D. (2001). *Harnessing complexity: Organizational implications of a scientific frontier.* New York: Simon & Schuster.

Beichner, R. J., Saul, J. M., Allain, R. J., Deardorff, D. L., & Abbot, D. S. (2000). *Introduction to SCALE-Up: Student-centered activities for large enrollment university physics.* Paper presented at the Annual Meeting of the American Society for Engineering Education, St. Louis.

Block, P. (2002). *The answer to how is yes.* San Francisco: Berrett-Koehler.

Booth, W. C., Colomb, G. G., & Williams, J. M. (2008). *The craft of research* (3rd ed.). Chicago: University of Chicago Press.

Dori, Y. J., & Belcher, J. (2005). How does technology-enabled active learning affect undergraduate students' understanding of electromagnetism concepts? *The Journal of the Learning Sciences, 14*(2), 243–279.

Dori, Y. J., Belcher, J., Bessette, M., Danzinger, M., McKinney, A., & Hult, E. (2003). Technology for active learning. *Materials Today, 6*(12), 44–49.

Duch, B. J., Groh, S. E., & Allen, D. E. (2001). *The power of problem-based learning: A practical "how to" for teaching undergraduate courses in any discipline.* Sterling, VA: Stylus.

Duderstadt, J. J. (2008). *Engineering for a changing world.* Ann Arbor: The University of Michigan.

Dweck, C. S., & Leggett, E. L. (1988). A social cognitive approach to motivation and personality. *Psychological Review, 95*(2), 256–273.

Felder, R. M. (1995). A longitudinal study of engineering student performance and retention. IV. Instructional methods and student responses to them. *Journal of Engineering Education, 84*(4), 361–367.

Felder, R. M., Sheppard, S. D., & Smith, K. A. (2005). A new journal for a field in transition. *Journal of Engineering Education, 94*(1), 7–10.

Galloway, P. D. (2007). *The 21st-century engineer: A proposal for engineering education reform.* Reston, VA: American Society for Civil Engineers.

Johnson, D. W., & Johnson, R. T. (1987). *Creative controversy: Intellectual challenge in the classroom.* Edina, MN: Interaction Book Company.

Johnson, D. W., & Johnson, R. T. (2007). *Creative controversy: Intellectual challenge in the classroom* (4th ed.). Edina, MN: Interaction Book Company.

Johnson, D. W., & Johnson, R. T. (2009). Energizing learning: The instructional power of conflict. *Educational Researcher, 38*(1), 37–51.

Johnson, D. W., Johnson, R. T, & Smith, K. A. (1991). *Cooperative learning: Increasing college faculty instructional productivity.* ASHE-ERIC Higher Education Report No. 4. Washington, DC: The George Washington University School of Education and Human Development.

Johnson, D. W., Johnson, R. T., & Smith, K. A. (1997). *Academic controversy: Enriching college instruction with Constructive Controversy.* Washington, DC: The George Washington University Press.

Johnson, D. W., Johnson, R. T., & Smith, K. A. (1998). Cooperative learning returns to college: What evidence is there that it works? *Change: The Magazine of Higher Learning 30*(4), 26–35. Retrieved February 3, 2010, from http://www.laspositascollege.edu/facultystaff/documents/CooperativeLearning.pdf.

Johnson, D. W., Johnson, R. T., & Smith, K. A. (2000). Constructive Controversy: The power of intellectual conflict. *Change: The Magazine of Higher Learning 32*(1), 28–37.

Johnson, D. W., Johnson, R. T., & Smith, K. A. (2006). *Active learning: Cooperation in the college classroom* (3rd ed.). Edina, MN: Interaction Book Company.

Johnson, D. W., Johnson, R. T., & Smith, K. A. (2007). The state of cooperative learning in postsecondary and professional settings. *Educational Psychology Review, 19*(1), 15–29.

Lunsford, A. A., Ruszkiewicz, J. J., & Walters, K. (2004). *Everything's an argument: With readings.* Boston: Bedford Books.

Lynn, L., & Salzman, H. (2006). Collaborative advantage: New horizons for a flat world. *Issues in Science and Technology, Winter 22*(2), 74–82.

Lynn, L., & Salzman, H. (2007). The real global technology challenge. *Change: The Magazine of Higher Learning, 39*(4), 8–13.

MacGregor, J., Cooper, J., Smith, K., & Robinson, P. (2000). *Strategies for energizing large classes: From small groups to learning communities.* San Francisco: Jossey-Bass.

Miller, J. H., & Page, S. E. (2007). *Complex adaptive social systems: An introduction to computational models of social life.* Princeton, NJ: Princeton University Press.

Millis, B. J., & Cottell, P. G. (1998). *Cooperative learning for higher education faculty.* Phoenix: American Council on Education/Oryx Press.

NAE. (2004). *The Engineer of 2020: Visions of engineering in the new century.* Washington, DC: National Academies Press.

NAE. (2005). *Educating the engineer of 2020: Adapting engineering education to the new century committee on the engineer of 2020.* Washington, DC: National Academies Press.

Page, S. E. (2007). *The difference: How the power of diversity creates better groups, teams, schools, and societies.* Princeton, NJ: Princeton University Press.

Pink, D. H. (2005). *A whole new mind.* Riverhead, NY: Riverhead Books.

Pink, D. H. (2006). *A whole new mind: Or why the right-brainers will rule the future* [DVD].

Pintrich, P. R., & De Groot, E. (1990). Motivational and self-regulated learning components of classroom academic performance. *Journal of Educational Psychology, 83,* 33–40.

Pintrich, P. R., Marx, R. W., & Boyle, R. A. (1993). Beyond cold conceptual change: The role of motivational beliefs and classroom contextual factors in the process of conceptual change. *Review of Educational Research, 63*(2), 167–199.

Prince, M. (2004). Does active learning work? A review of the research. *Journal of Engineering Education, July 2004,* 1–10.

Redish, E. F., & Smith, K. A. (2008). Looking beyond content: Skill development for engineers. *Journal of Engineering Education Special Issue, 97*(3), 295–307.

Rowland, G. (2004). Shall we dance? A design epistemology for organizational learning and performance. *Educational Technology Research and Development, 52*(1), 33–48.

Smith, K. A. (1984). Structured controversy. *Journal of Engineering Education, 74*(5), 306–309.

Smith, K. A. (1995, March). Cooperative learning: Effective teamwork for engineering classrooms. *IEEE Education Society/ASEE Electrical Engineering Division Newsletter,* pp. 1–6.

Smith, K. A. (1996). Cooperative learning: Making "groupwork" work. In C. Bonwell & T. Sutherlund (Eds.), *Active learning: Lessons from practice and emerging issues* (pp. 67, 71–82). San Francisco: Jossey-Bass.

Smith, K. A. (1998). Grading cooperative projects. In B. Anderson & B. W. Speck (Eds.), *Changing the way we grade student performance: Classroom assessment and the new learning paradigm. New directions for teaching and learning* (pp. 78, 59–67). San Francisco: Jossey-Bass.

Smith, K. A., Johnson, D. W., & Johnson, R. T. (1982). Study of Controversy in Cooperative Learning Groups. Proceedings—Frontiers in Education Conference, Columbia, SC.

Smith, K. A., Cox, M., & Douglas, T. C. (2009). Supportive teaching and learning strategies in STEM education. In R. Baldwin (Ed.), *Improving the climate for undergraduate teaching in STEM fields. New directions for teaching and learning,* No. 117 (pp. 19–32). San Francisco: Jossey-Bass.

Smith, K. A., Johnson, D. W., & Johnson, R. T. (1981a). Structuring learning goals to meet the goals of engineering education. *Journal of Engineering Education, 72*(3), 221–226.

Smith, K. A., Johnson, D. W., & Johnson, R. T. (1981b). *The use of cooperative learning groups in engineering education.* Paper presented at the Eleventh Annual Frontiers in Education Conference, Rapid City, SD.

Smith, K. A., Sheppard, S. D., Johnson, D. W., & Johnson, R. T. (2005). Pedagogies of engagement: Classroom-based practices. *Journal of Engineering Education Special Issue on the State of the Art and Practice of Engineering Education Research, 94*(1), 87–102.

Steering Committee (2006). The research agenda for the new discipline of engineering education. *Journal of Engineering Education, 95*(4), 257–261.

7

The Interactive Lecture in a Research Methods and Statistics Class

Pamela Robinson and James L. Cooper

Because cooperative learning lends itself to a variety of approaches, we use it with a number of instructional procedures that have proved successful in our classes in research methods and statistics. We have also implemented techniques drawn from the active learning literature, classroom assessment procedures popularized by Angelo and Cross (1993), and from other research-based principles of teaching and learning.

In this chapter we propose to do three things: (1) offer a definition of the Interactive Lecture and explain how we use several procedures during lectures, including Quick-Thinks and cognitive scaffolds, to make traditional instructional formats more engaging; (2) describe a number of additional procedures that we have found to be effective in fostering deeper processing of course content, in managing course pedagogy to improve student time on task, and in facilitating teaching; and (3) express thoughts on the instructional process based on our collective fifty years of teaching at the college level.

THE INTERACTIVE LECTURE

The Interactive Lecture embeds active learning, group learning, and classroom assessment strategies at frequent intervals in traditional lectures to foster deeper processing of course content. The Johnson brothers at the University of Minnesota have used the term "interactive lecture" for over a decade when referring to procedures in which cooperative learning exercises occur within the lecture at regular intervals. Donald Bligh (1972), University of Exeter, in his classic text *What's the Use of Lectures?*, newly updated in a U.S. version (2000), has been making a case for more interactive lectures for decades. Dean Osterman (1985) and his colleagues at Oregon State University used the term "feedback lecture" in referring to comparable procedures. Graham Gibbs and Alan Jenkins (1992) in England used the term "structured lecturing" to describe a similar strategy in the late 1970s and early 1980s.

Although differing in detail, each of these approaches involves breaking lectures into segments and asking students to reflect on problems or issues at regular intervals. Empirical documentation of the impact of Interactive Lecture techniques can be found in Johnston and Cooper (1997). We have focused on two procedures to make lectures more interactive: Quick-Thinks[1] and scaffolding. These procedures are effective in most instructional formats, including lecture-discussion, laboratories, and distance learning.

QUICK-THINKS

Quick-Thinks are classroom assessment procedures in which the instructor stops the presentation every 10–20 minutes and poses a question or issue to students that requires them to process information individually or collaboratively. Examples of Quick-Thinks have been described in previous work (Johnston & Cooper, 1997, 2007) and include the following activities:

Select the Best Response

This Quick-Think involves using a multiple-choice item. For example, after explaining measures of central tendency, we pose a question, such as: "What is the most sensitive measure of central tendency? A. Mean; B. Median; C. Mode." After students think about this for a brief time, we have students pair for a 30-second conversation before reporting their responses to the whole class. This procedure in the cooperative learning literature is called Think-Pair-Share.

The enthusiasm and interest level of the class is exciting for students and gratifying for us; often, we have to remind our students not to shout out the answer. The look of surprise, chagrin, and then laughter on the students' faces when doing so is infectious. The whole class gets caught up in sharing and enjoying the learning.

---

[1] Editor's note: Quick-Thinks are totally compatible with the use of Personal Response Systems (clickers) and with the use of Visible Quiz cards mentioned by Cottell (chapter 2). The research suggests that the peer interactions (PI) are responsible for the learning gains, not the modality used. Lasry (2008) concludes: "From a learning perspective, using PI with clickers does not provide any significant *learning* advantage over low-tech flashcards. PI is an approach that engages students and challenges them to commit to a point of view that they can defend" (p. 244).

Correct the Error

The students must find the error in a statement, such as "The advantage of 'random assignment' is that it ensures a representative sample of the population."

Complete a Sentence Starter

Students complete a sentence begun by the instructor. For example, "The benefit of using random assignment in a group research design is. . . ."

Compare or Contrast

Students must indicate how two things are the same or how they are different. This is an especially effective way of making sure students understand the differences between scatter plots and frequency polygons, which may confuse them.

Support a Statement

Students are asked to support an assertion such as "Randomized designs are considered the 'gold standard' in evaluations of reading programs."

Reorder the Steps

This procedure is often helpful in laboratory or clinic settings where procedures must be followed in a precise order, such as giving an injection or setting up a classical conditioning experiment. Students are given elements or steps of a procedure in a random order and must arrange them in the proper order.

Reach a Conclusion

This task requires students to make a logical inference about the implications of facts, concepts, or principles they just learned. For example, when teaching group designs, we might say, "Researchers randomly assigned two groups of two hundred students to receive either an active learning or a lecture method of instruction in research methods, and then tested the two groups on a common final exam. If the group taught using active learning performed better on the exam, what is the most likely cause of that difference? Explain your answer."

Paraphrase the Idea

Students are asked to explain something to another person in their own words. For example, "As a teacher, how would you explain to a parent how her child's score of the 50th percentile on the CAT 6 reading test should be interpreted? Be sure to include the idea of a norm group."

Implementation of Quick-Thinks

In our research methods classes, we often lecture on three of nine sampling procedures (e.g., random, stratified, and systematic) and then give students a Select the Best Response item, such as: "A researcher has a school that is 45% Black, 30% Latino, and 25% White (non-Latino), so she draws a sample that ensures that she has these three groups represented in the same numbers as the school population." Then we ask: "Is this an example of: A. Stratified; B. Random; or C. Systematic?"

After introducing three more sampling procedures, we might ask another Quick-Think, such as Compare or Contrast: "How does stratified sampling differ from purposive sampling?" After presenting a total of nine sampling techniques, we might ask a Support a Statement item, such as: "If you were interested in identifying who citizens were likely to vote for in the next presidential election, why would a random sample of registered voters be better than a sampling of people who contributed $10,000 to the Republican Party?" Then we break the class into formal cooperative learning teams of four and present many additional items to ensure automaticity (fluency) on sampling concepts before moving to the next unit of instruction.

Each three-hour class meeting ends with formal cooperative learning work for an hour or more, when students work problems not just from that class meeting but from all previous class meetings for that four-week unit. We often have students start with recognition tasks such as Select the Best Response, and then have them do construction tasks where they have to produce their own original examples of, say, nine sampling procedures. Construction requires much deeper processing of content than does recognition. By the time of the unit exam, students often have had 40 or more practice items on sampling, central tendency, variability, and group research designs.

SCAFFOLDING

As Susan Prescott Johnston and Jim Cooper (1999, 2008) have noted, powerful instructional techniques known as *scaffolds* are available to college faculty in all disciplines (King, 1995; Rosenshine & Meister, 1995). These are forms of support that are temporarily provided by instructors when introducing new content and making assignments. "Novice learners, like construction workers, use structures of temporary support during their efforts to build something new; once the initial phase of construction is in place, the scaffolds can be withdrawn" (Johnston & Cooper, 2008, p. 1).

Johnston and Cooper (1999, 2008) have described five scaffolding procedures, while acknowledging that many more exist. The five they delineated were the following:

Procedural Guidelines

For tasks requiring a number of steps, often ones requiring sequential implementation, procedural guidelines are a good idea. For example, because Pamela has a number of requirements for her qualitative research proposal, she requires that students "check off" that they have completed each requirement before handing in their papers. She has students staple the checked-off guideline form to the front of their papers.

Partial Solutions

This technique is appropriate when the faculty member wants to focus on just one element of a complicated problem. For example, when Jim models how to compute a Pearson correlation on the board, he does a problem in which the means and standard deviations have already been computed so he can focus just on the feature of Pearson computation that he chooses for that day.

To have students compute means and standard deviations, skills they had just learned but not mastered, takes valuable class time. After Jim models the partially worked problem on the board, he has students do the entire computation in their formal cooperative groups of four.

Think-Alouds

In the Think-Aloud procedure, an expert models how to address a problem so that novice students can "overhear" a skilled response to a sometimes complicated solution. For example, when lecturing on random, systematic, and purposive sampling procedures, we might say to our classes, "A researcher was interested in doing a study of anorexia in middle school girls, so she selected just the girls who were more than 20% below their recommended body weight. Which of the three techniques would be most likely here? . . . Well, we said that purposive sampling was when, for example, one was interested in a homogeneous group who shared a common property. . . . It looks as if the researcher just wanted the most underweight girls, so it seems to be a purposive sample. If it were systematic sampling, the researcher would have picked every nth girl, and if it were random, names would have been picked from a set of random numbers." This Think-Aloud provides some scaffolding for sampling after the lecture, but before students work the problems on their own, in pairs, or in teams.

Anticipate Student Errors

Jim teaches correlation scatter plots right after frequency polygons. So, just before he starts drawing a scatter plot, he notes how polygons are labeled on the X and Y axes and then demonstrates how to draw another statistical "picture" that superficially looks similar but actually presents very different information.

Comprehension Checks

These are assessments of student learning that are similar to Quick-Thinks. Probably the best-known comprehension check is the "Minute Paper," often given at the end of class, which asks students to identify the most important and the "muddiest" points they learned in class that day. Comprehension Checks are featured in Angelo and Cross's (1993) *Classroom Assessment Techniques*, approaches they call "CATs" for short.

ADDITIONAL INSTRUCTIONAL PROCEDURES

In addition to the Interactive Lecture approach, we have also developed a number of other cooperative-learning-based procedures that we have found to be instructionally helpful. In this section, we describe them and how they are used.

Scaffolding and Rubrics for Student Papers

We both have our students write qualitative research proposals at the end of a unit on qualitative research. Before students begin to write their own proposals, Jim has students read three samples of other students' work from previous classes and critique them using a grading rubric containing items dealing with clarity, methodology, and appropriateness of the goal statement and research questions.

After each student reads a former student's proposal and individually completes the rubric, formal cooperative teams discuss the ratings made by each team member and then form a team rating for each item. Finally, teams report their ratings to the class, and Jim uses this report-out to discuss each rubric item and advise students on good practice when writing research questions, developing their methodology based on the research questions and other considerations.

Jim finds that making explicit the criteria he uses to evaluate qualitative proposals and having his students use those criteria prior to submitting their own work substantially improves the quality of their papers. Too often, students are given little guidance in completing complex tasks such as term papers and lab assignments. And rarely do they receive models of professional discourse and writing, with which most of our students have little experience and skill.

We both have our students use grading rubrics in doing peer reviews of each other's grant writing efforts. These rubrics are used as teams evaluate other teams' proposals, thus simulating actual peer reviews used in a grant selection processes. We have found that having students use rubrics with complicated assignments is a valuable exercise. Our rubrics are a kind of Think-Aloud, in the sense that we make explicit our grading criteria in analyzing a qualitative paper or a grant proposal. They also help focus our students on a limited number of important ideas. When paired with peer editing, these activities gain particular power in engaging students and thus increasing their learning.

Workbook

When Jim moved from the traditional lecture approach to the Interactive Lecture in the late 1980s, he needed to provide many more problems and exercises for students to complete in informal pair work and in formal cooperative learning teams. Because he had been constructing tests for research methods since 1974, he began by simply providing old tests to students for this work. Then he formalized these tests into a workbook, which was initially 25 pages in length and is now well over 100 pages.

Once he'd written several tests over a given topic, it was easy to develop an unlimited set of test items. The more items that he wrote, the better able he was to write items that were meaningful to the various master's program students in his School of Education (special education students, curriculum students, educational administration students, and so on).

This practical approach made the course more meaningful for his students, who often feared the class at the beginning of the term and did not see how it related to their lives as teachers, counselors, school principals, and other educators. He was also able to slip in occasional popular culture figures and humorous anecdotes to lighten the work being done by his students. Later, he added rubrics for the major assignments, including the qualitative term paper and an in-class grant writing exercise.

Pamela took the workbook and shaped it to her needs and assignments when she started teaching the class over 15 years ago. On the first day of class, students receive the workbook, which also includes the syllabus. Both Pamela and Jim tell them to bring this document to every class meeting. Research indicates that students need many more iterations of problems to develop fluency in a given skill than are offered in most classes (Rosenshine & Meister, 1995). The workbook provides multiple problems over each concept, and students receive fast descriptive feedback from other students and from us at each class meeting. Students who want more practice as they prepare for tests use the problems that have not been completed in class.

Team Folders

Our use of formal cooperative learning teams to increase student interaction in class is fundamental to our teaching. Pamela increases the team-building of her students and manages paperwork in her classes through the use of team folders. Her colleague, Susan Johnston, introduced her to folders during her first year of teaching.

Each permanent team of four students receives a folder with two sheets of paper stapled inside; on one side is a list of team roles with short explanations of duties and a place for students to write their names next to the roles they play. Because the roles (i.e., spokesperson, timekeeper, monitor, recorder) are rotated every 3–4 weeks, this sheet is a handy place to remind students about who is supposed to do what at each class meeting.

Facing the team roles sheet is a page where students take attendance in their teams with a grid for them to keep track of their homework (when they've turned it in, when it's returned, and whether or not they have to redo and resubmit it).

Students write their names on the outside of the folders; we encourage them to come up with a team name. A few years ago, a team getting to know each other discovered that all four had recently gotten married or were planning weddings; they named themselves *Three Brides and a Groom*. Several team members brought in pictures of brides and grooms to paste on their team folder.

Pamela supplies markers, glue, and scissors, telling students they can be as creative as they like in decorating their folders as long at their names are clearly written on the outside so she can easily match graded papers to the folders for return. Susan Johnson showed Pamela the pictures she took of each team and glued to the folder covers, which is another good idea for making each folder unique and also for learning student names.

Because we do not bring our grade books to class, team folders are a great way for students to take responsibility for keeping track of their work rather than having us remind them of missing assignments. Pamela uses the team folders to collect assignments and to return all papers, including exams.

Rather than going over an entire exam when it is returned, Pamela has her students meet in teams to discuss each exam. Although she writes the correct answers directly on graded exams, students are often unclear about why those are the correct answers. She has them first seek help from each other in understanding wrong answers; then they are to check their notes; finally, they see her for explanations if they are still unclear.

The time needed to go over exams in class has been cut drastically since she began doing this; what took an hour ten years ago, now takes 15–20 minutes. The power of this group-based approach, however, is what Spencer Kagan (2009) calls the "principle of simultaneity." Instead of one person in class receiving an explanation from the teacher, all around the class students are teaching and coaching one another in their teams.

Checklists

In addition to the qualitative proposal instructions that we include in our workbook, Pamela has developed a checklist for students to use before they turn in their qualitative research proposals. This checklist simply lists the 15 most common errors that students make when writing their proposals. Each error has a box next to it that students check off after they've rechecked their papers before handing them in (e.g., ☐ only 1" margins were used).

She found that—even though the instructions were in the workbook she'd carefully gone over in class, the students had read and critiqued sample papers, and she'd verbally warned them of common errors the students still made the same errors, semester after semester.

Since she developed the checklist and required that students not only use it but also staple it to the front of their papers as a cover sheet, far fewer students make those mistakes. In addition, students really like using the checklist. For the past three years, she has had students complete anonymous questionnaires asking about the usefulness of the checklist and the peer editing activities that she uses. The responses (both quantitative and qualitative) have been overwhelmingly positive. Students who have taken her research methods class and then enroll in her educational psychology class invariably ask if there is a workbook and if she has a checklist for the paper.

Peer Editing

We both strongly believe that peer editing is a way to help students increase their writing skills. And, although research methods is not a class intended to teach students how to write, many of our students have poor writing skills. Rather than simply lament the fact that they need help, we've each developed peer editing activities to address this issue.

After trying everything from in-team peer editing to whole-class whole-paper peer editing, Pamela has designed an activity that she calls Structured Peer Editing. The week before the final draft of their proposals is due, Pamela has students bring to class drafts that they believe are at least 90% complete. To ensure anonymity, she tells students to replace their names with symbols on the back of the paper that only they recognize.

In her classes of 30 students, she has them sit in six rows of five students. Each row of students edits and checks only one part of each paper. She begins the activity with a brief review of what each row is responsible for checking (e.g., row one is in charge of format: 1" margins, double spacing, correct headings and subheadings, etc.). She then collects and hands out the papers randomly. If during the activity students receive their own paper, she tells them to pass it on to someone else.

Pamela likens this activity to an assembly line in a factory: as students edit their sections, they pass the papers to the person in the next row, who checks a different section. Pamela roams the room, answering questions and making sure that papers don't sit on one student's desk while another student waits for a paper to check. As the papers complete the assembly line, they are placed on a table at the front of the room where students retrieve them at the end of the class. They then take their papers home and rewrite them, using the indications of errors that were found during this editing activity.

Pamela's Structured Peer Editing activity serves several purposes:

1. Students who previously felt that they didn't have the skills to help someone else no longer feel overwhelmed because they are responsible for only one part of the papers they are handed, and they can easily compare the proposal requirements in the workbook as they critique.
2. Students receive at least six other students' reactions to their writing. That means they can no longer complain that "the person who read

my paper didn't know what she was doing," because now there are six editors.

3. Reading even one portion of thirty or so papers is a powerful way for students to see how issues (such as which sampling method is best to use) can be addressed.

4. Many errors that would have appeared on the final drafts that Pamela receives are caught and corrected; the quality of students' papers is much better than it was before the peer editing activity.

GENERAL INSTRUCTIONAL ISSUES: SOME FINAL THOUGHTS

We have observed the Interactive Lecture format used in many disciplines, and both of us have used it in courses such as research methods, curriculum and instruction, educational psychology, and social-cultural issues. Our classes are taught in 16-week semesters with classes meeting once a week for close to three hours in the late afternoon or evening. At times, we have taught intensive classes of six hours per day.

The interactive strategies identified here are important in all formats, but we find them particularly valuable for classes that meet for extended periods, contain dense content, and face enrollments of 30 to 100 or more students. Our usual format in a three-hour class is to lecture for 75 to 90 minutes with Think-Pair-Share problems presented every 15 minutes or so. We then conduct team-learning exercises during the second half of the class.

As described earlier, Think-Pair-Share involves presenting Quick-Thinks, or other problems, to our students in whole-group lectures and having them think about the resolution individually before sharing with a neighbor and then reporting out to the class.

After the lecture, we move the class into formal cooperative learning teams of four for additional practice. Finally, we go over the answers to the problems given to the teams, often reteaching skills that have not been mastered.

This use of pair work and formal team work offers fast and descriptive feedback from other students and from us and ensures that students have a sense of their mastery of course content at very frequent intervals within a class meeting and semester. Astin (1993) reports that frequency and quality of student-student and student-faculty interaction are the best predictors of a host of cognitive and attitudinal outcomes in the college experience, far surpassing curricular interventions. And prompt and descriptive feedback is empirically linked to high level of achievement, particularly when skills are complicated (Marzano, Pickering, Norford, & Paynter, 2001).

We also feel that the mastery learning approach is essential in cooperative classrooms (versus grading on the curve). In mastery learning, a limited set of outcomes is identified, and the environment is structured so students see models of how to achieve those outcomes; they then practice those skills on multiple occasions and receive feedback from one another and from the teacher.

The following are some final thoughts concerning things that we've learned over the years that have made our teaching much better, our students happier, and life in the cooperative classroom much easier.

Clarity Is Essential

When cooperative learning fails, the failure can often be linked to lack of clarity in the assignment. It is not enough to just have students work in groups, especially when asking them to do complicated tasks such as those taught in research methods and statistics. Rather than saying, "Get in groups and help each other understand the sampling procedures we just discussed," it's much better to say, "Working with a partner, make up original examples of random, stratified, and systematic sampling; then select the best example to share with the class." Note that the latter gives specific instructions regarding the nature of the product expected and how the product will be shared with the larger group.

Grading

Clarity in grading is also essential. Undifferentiated group grades, when everyone gets the same grade for a group project, rarely work and contradict basic premises of cooperative learning related to individual accountability. The literature on teacher characteristics that predict student success suggests that clarity is usually among the top predictors (Pascarella & Terenzini, 2005). Jim's experience in more than 30 years of reading files for tenure and promotion reinforces this. Students need to understand what a teacher is saying in class, the nature of the assignments, how they will be graded, and the feedback on the assignments. You can never be too explicit in your teaching.

Put it in Writing

Oral descriptions of tasks are often misunderstood. We put formal cooperative learning tasks in writing and then have students practice individual elements of the assignments before linking the elements into more complicated exercises, such as critiquing quantitative journal articles. Thus, students complete many examples of sampling, group research designs, confoundings, and so forth before they have to apply these concepts in analyzing journal articles on their own.

In-Class Group Work Is Better Than Out-of-Class

Within five minutes of giving an in-class exercise such as a Quick-Think, we can detect when it is working and when it is not, and we can then clarify the assignment quickly and reteach if necessary. Out-of-class group work has many pitfalls, including the dominator or sandbagger effect, the possibility that students will practice incorrect procedures, and the issue of nonattendance (particularly on commuter campuses, where students live far apart and have competing demands on their time—usually family and work). Teachers are unable to monitor out-of-class meetings.

Need for Structure

At the beginning of the semester, students need more structure for their assignments. Toward the end, students can make more decisions. For example, before students have to identify independent and dependent variables in journal articles, they have multiple Quick-Think examples in their pair work and formal cooperative learning examples. Only then do they have to identify these concepts in research articles, which are often more complex than the initial problems given in the workbook.

By the end of the semester, students have more freedom to decide how to do a qualitative proposal or write an evaluation plan for an intervention in a grant proposal. As noted previously, recognition tasks are easier than construction tasks so we often have students do many recognition problems before they have to give their own, original examples of, say, sampling problems.

Interaction

In planning classes, we build in time for student-student and student-faculty interaction. As a rule of thumb, we don't go more than 15 minutes without having students process lecture content in some way.

We have developed and field-tested these procedures over years of teaching and reading the literature on teaching. Many readers may not be ready to implement a system as multifaceted as the one we have described in this chapter. We recommend trying one or two of the techniques described in a familiar class and then expanding to include other classes and techniques over time, as Cottell (chapter 2) also recommends. The rewards for doing this are well worth the occasional lesson that does not go well because you will be teaching within the framework of a coherent, research-based model developed over decades.

References

Angelo, T., & Cross, P. (1993). *Classroom assessment techniques: A handbook for college teachers* (2nd ed.). San Francisco: Jossey-Bass.

Astin, A. (1993). *What matters in college? Four critical years revisited.* San Francisco: Jossey-Bass.

Bligh, D. A. (1972). *What's the use of lectures?* London: Penguin Books.

Bligh, D. A. (2000). *What's the use of lectures?* New York: John Wiley.

Gibbs, G., & Jenkins, A. (1992). *Teaching large classes in higher education: Maintaining quality with reduced resources.* London: Kogan Page.

Johnston, S., & Cooper, J. (1997). Quick-thinks: Active thinking in lecture classes and televised instruction. *Cooperative Learning and College Teaching, 8*(1), 2–6.

Johnston, S., & Cooper, J. (1999). Supporting student success through scaffolding. *Cooperative Learning and College Teaching, 9*(3), 3–6.

Johnston, S., & Cooper, J. (2007). Quick-thinks: The interactive lecture. *Tomorrow's Professor, Msg. #818.* Retrieved March 9, 2010, from http://cgi.stanford.edu/~dept-ctl/cgi-bin/tomprof/posting.php.

Johnston, S., & Cooper, J. (2008). Supporting student success through scaffolding. *Tomorrow's Professor, Msg. #849.* Retrieved March 9, 2010, from http://cgi.stanford.edu/~dept-ctl/cgi-bin/tomprof/posting.php.

Kagan, S. (2009). *Cooperative learning.* San Juan Capistrano, CA: Resources for Teachers.

King, A. (1995, Winter). Guided peer questioning: A cooperative learning approach to critical thinking. *Cooperative Learning and College Teaching, 5*(2), pp. 15–19.

Lasry, N. (April, 2008). Clickers or flashcards: Is there really a difference? *Physics Teacher, 46,* 242–244.

Marzano, R., Pickering, D., Norford, J., & Paynter, D. (2001). *Handbook for classroom instruction that works.* Alexandria, VA: Association for Supervision and Curriculum Development.

Osterman, D. N. (1985). *The feedback lecture.* (Idea Paper No. 13). Manhattan, KS: Center for Faculty Development and Evaluation, Kansas State University.

Pascarella, E., & Terenzini, P. (2005) *How college affects students: A third decade of research* (vol. 2). San Francisco: Jossey-Bass.

Rosenshine, B., & Meister, C. (1995). Scaffolds for teaching higher-order cognitive strategies. In A. C. Ornstein (Ed.), *Teaching: Theory into practice* (pp. 134–153). Boston: Allyn & Bacon.

8

Want Brighter, Harder Working Students? Change Pedagogies!

Some Examples, Mainly from Biology

Craig E. Nelson

Teaching is great fun when it works. To really make it work, faculty members need a deep understanding of their higher-level goals, a set of effective pedagogical techniques for fostering the goals and the content learning that supports them, and a way of combining the goals and techniques within the time that both faculty and students can reasonably devote to the course.

In my case, serendipitous early exposure to Perry's (1968, 1970, 1999) study of students' intellectual development in college was a great boost. Perry helped me understand the tasks that students must master in order to retain the content, to understand scientific thinking and the nature of science, and to use critical thinking generally (Nelson, 1999). Equally important was an early exposure to cooperative learning techniques. My introduction to these techniques included ways of eliciting considerable student effort with minimal marking and an emphasis on including credit sufficient to make the students feel that the assignments were worth doing.

In talking with other faculty, I have found that they often need reassurance that adopting cooperative learning does not require inordinate amounts of time. The examples in the various chapters in this volume allow efficient implementation of cooperative learning. Nelson (2008a) lists books and websites with techniques that are appropriate to biology, as well as websites and review articles on the scholarship of teaching and learning in science.

Another faculty concern focuses on the apparent loss of content coverage that they fear might ensue with alternative pedagogies. Indeed, reducing coverage in order to foster better learning was quite challenging for me (Nelson, 2001). Good examples from biology courses show that reducing coverage increases learning. Sundberg and Dini (1993) showed for introductory-level biology that a course for non-majors taught as much content as a more content-dense course designed for majors, even when both approaches used only traditional methods (see also Sundberg, Dini, & Li, 1994).

Russell, Hendricson, and Herbert (1984) used different lecture content densities in the same medical school course. Students in the lowest density treatment learned and retained the content best. Maier, McGoldrick, and Simkins (chapter 10), Robinson and Cooper (chapter 7), and Smith, Matusovich, Myers, and Mann (chapter 6) highlight further evidence that the approaches advocated in this book increase learning.

In this chapter, I specify the course and level from which each example is drawn. However, I have found that similar techniques and goals can be used in courses ranging from first-year general education and introductory biology to graduate courses. I urge readers to consider seriously how these approaches might work in courses they teach, whatever the level and content. For more on my uses of collaborative approaches, especially for critical thinking, see Nelson (1994, 1996).

I present the examples largely in the framework of my personal history as a way of showing how I moved from simpler applications to more significant ones. I hope that this approach encourages some readers to start small, as advocated by Cottell (chapter 2). Sometimes, however, larger-scale course transformation seems clearly preferable. Two examples where large-scale change is essential are process-oriented guided inquiry (Shadle, chapter 3) and the extensive use of cases (Herreid, 2004).

Most of my examples illustrate the outcomes-focused "backwards design" approach: i.e., start with higher-level learning goals, decide what learning experiences seem most likely to achieve these goals, and only then select the content. Ebert-May and Hodder (2008) explicitly advocate this approach for science and provide extended examples for large biology classes. Cohen (chapter 2) explains how larger contexts can shape the desired outcomes and shows how the educational psychology literature can provide a powerful "filter" to use in designing activities in any course.

COOPERATIVE LEARNING IS ESSENTIAL TO MAXIMIZING LEARNING IN SCIENCE

Much of science teaching focuses on straightforward understanding, we hope as a prerequisite to more advanced goals ranging from right-answer problem solving to critical thinking. Faculty may believe that cooperative learning is not necessary for understanding basic concepts. However, very strong evidence shows that cooperative learning and other active learning approaches are essential even for fostering basic conceptual understanding. These approaches also foster higher-level goals, such as application, and more complicated forms of critical thinking.

Hake (1998a, b; 2002) has assembled the most impressive data set assessing the effectiveness of alternative pedagogical strategies in science. Prior work (Halloun & Hestenes 1985a, b) had produced sets of concept-focused, qualitative pretests and posttests that cover central concepts from introductory physics—tests on which the wrong answers are based on common student misconceptions. One can construct such a measure for other courses as well. To do so, give students short-answer questions that assess understanding and applications of key concepts. Then use common wrong answers to generate multiple-choice questions for pretests and posttests. The wrong answers also provide a guide for more focused instruction. Even better assessments and teaching strategies can be designed by considering prior research on misconceptions (Duit, 2009).

Hake (1998a) compares traditionally taught courses with those taught with cooperative learning ("interactive engagement") approaches. Traditional courses rely "primarily on passive-student lectures, recipe labs, and algorithmic problem exams." Interactive engagement courses promote conceptual understanding through heads-on and, often, hands-on activities that yield immediate feedback through discussion. These range from inquiry labs without lectures to large classes in which short segments of lecture alternate with structured discussion (Crouch & Mazur, 2001).

Four key components of many of the cooperative learning approaches are (1) extensive structuring of the learning tasks by the teacher; (2) strongly interactive student-student execution of the tasks; (3) immediate debriefing or other assessments to provide the teacher and students with prompt feedback about the success of the intended learning; and, importantly, (4) instructional modifications by the teacher that take account of this feedback.

The results for physics are given in Figure 8.1. The horizontal axis is the class average for the percent correct on the pretest, %<pretest>. The vertical axis ("gain") is the difference between class averages as percents on the pretest and the posttest. The measure of teaching effectiveness asks: How much of the total possible improvement in conceptual understanding did the class achieve? This "average normalized gain," <g>, is defined as the ratio of the actual gain in the class average (%<post> – %<pre>) to the maximum possible gain (100 – %<pre>). Here %<pre> is the class average (as a percent) on the pretest and %<post> is the class average on the posttest (Hake, 1998a). This measure gives the instruction credit only for net improvements in the average scores for students' conceptual understanding.

Each symbol on the graph in Figure 8.1 is typically for one physics course. If every student had mastered each of the core concepts by the posttest, the

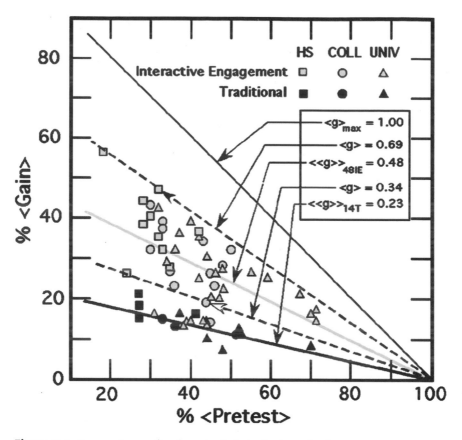

Figure 8.1 Comparisons of pedagogies in introductory physics.
Figure provided by R. R. Hake and used with his permission.

average posttest score (100%) would yield a gain that placed the class on the upper dark diagonal line. No class came close. The gains for traditionally taught (lecture) courses cluster tightly across the lower portion of the graph (darker symbols), with an overall mean or $<<g>>$ of 23% of possible (0.23 ± 0.04, mean ± standard deviation) and a regression shown by the lower solid line (Hake, 1998a). The gains for courses with an important component of cooperative learning ("interactive engagement") spread across much of the graph (lighter symbols), with an overall mean or $<<g>>$ of 48% (0.48 ± 0.14) and a regression shown by the middle solid line.

Quantitatively, the average student taught cooperatively learned twice as much as the average student taught with traditional lectures. The most successful cooperative learning approaches taught almost three times as much as the average lecture course (upper dashed line). Qualitatively, no traditionally taught course came close to the regression line for the gains for courses with an important component of cooperative learning (indeed, none were above the lower dashed line).

Further, only a few cooperative learning sections had gains so low as to fall within the cluster for lectures, and none were below this range. The worst outcomes realized by any teacher who used the cooperative learning approach was a gain no lower than those characteristic of lectures. Moreover, these low scores for interactive approaches were largely from classes in which the teacher knew that the method had been defeated (for example, by interrupting the exercises to provide the teacher's answers) (Hake, 1998b).

Some results from biology courses are even more distressing. For an understanding of natural selection, Sundberg (2003) found very little (2 sections) or no (15 sections) pretest to posttest gain in class average when traditional pedagogy was used. However, the average normalized gain was over 25% for each of three interactive engagement sections. The Conceptual Inventory of Natural Selection (Anderson, Fisher, & Norman, 2002) could be used as a pretest and posttest for similar studies.

Large improvements with no reduction of rigor have been shown in chemistry for students with low math SAT scores (Jacobs, 2000) and for talented African Americans studying calculus (Fullilove & Treisman, 1990; Treisman, 1992). More extensive reviews of the effects of cooperative learning in science were given by Handelsman, Ebert-May, Beichner, Bruns, Chang, and DeHann (2004); Smith, Sheppard, Johnson, and Johnson (2005; chapter 6); and, in a formal meta-analysis, by Springer, Stanne, and Donovan (1997).

The conclusion is clear. Effort spent improving lectures is wasted unless the pedagogy already has been transformed to use effective cooperative learning. This can be rather distressing initially for those of us who have spent a lot of time trying to improve lectures. Fortunately, it is easy to implement basic cooperative learning, even in large classes.

USING IN-CLASS EXAMPLES AND COOPERATIVE LEARNING TO INCREASE LEARNING IN LECTURE COURSES, LARGE OR SMALL

Mazur's "Peer Instruction" technique for large classes has six parts: (1) a short lecture segment; (2) a multiple-choice question that is answered individually by the student; (3) a 2-minute discussion of the question in groups of two or three; (4) a second try by the student on the same question; (5) feedback to the faculty member on the results (originally by show of hands, now often by using clickers); and (6) reinstruction if needed (Crouch & Mazur, 2001). The 2-minute discussion reduces wrong answers by an average of about 50% in 2 minutes and reinforces the learning of right answers. Pretest to posttest gain for the course as a whole doubles or even nearly triples.

I independently developed a similar approach. I needed to teach 350 students in an introductory biology course to do some kinds of multiple-choice questions. Students who had not had AP Biology in high school tended to do poorly on questions that required concept recognition, as well as on those that required higher-level skills such as application or synthesis. I decided to break the lecture into short segments (of no more than about 10 minutes) followed by a multiple-choice question presented on the screen.

The question typically had eight to ten answers, of which usually two or more were right. Sometimes only one was right, and, more rarely, none was right. The students were asked to select the right answers, if any, and then discuss the question with their neighbors in groups of two or three. This usually took 3 to 5 minutes total.

I debriefed the class either by asking for a show of hands or by taking a microphone up and down the aisles and asking individuals what answers their group had chosen and why. In doing this, I also emphasized why some answers were better and what was wrong with the others.

I found a substantial improvement in the students' ability to deal with similar questions on the exams. Sadly, I developed this approach largely in ignorance of the abundant literature on cooperative learning (e.g., Bonwell & Eison, 1991; Millis & Cottell, 1998).

USING PRE-CLASS WORKSHEETS AND WHOLE-PERIOD COOPERATIVE LEARNING TO FOSTER CRITICAL THINKING IN COURSES, LARGE OR SMALL

My first attempts at cooperative learning were inspired by Judith Hanson. In a traditional lecture room with 150 students, she and one graduate assistant gave each student a preparation grade (based on a pre-class worksheet) and a participation grade (based on the roles they manifested, not on the details of what they said). Students liked these discussions, which lasted the entire period. When I combined this worksheet-structured discussion technique with approaches based on Perry's (1968, 1970, 1999) scheme, the students liked the changes so much that they secretly arranged for me to receive a campus-wide teaching award.

Four aspects of my approach now seem central. I assigned cognitively complex material for pre-class reading, material for which cooperative learning would noticeably advance most students' understanding. The worksheet required step-by-step analysis of the assigned material using a specified critical thinking framework. In class, I assigned the students to groups of about five, usually by having them count off (see Cottell, chapter 2, for similar methods). I used different ways of grouping on different days so that the students couldn't predict what group they would be in. And I marked the worksheets on preparation effort, not on having the material completely correct. Indeed, if most students are likely to get the material essentially correct on the worksheets, it may be a bad idea to use extended discussion techniques.

The minimal-effort marking requires explanation. Pre-class papers or in-class quiz answers were written in any color except red or pink. As the students arrived, I handed them a cheap red pen with no cap (not a good thing to put in a purse, pocket, or briefcase). Pens were handed back at the end of class. Students were responsible for changing their own papers, in red, to reflect any improvements or clarifications that arose during the discussion. I then graded only on whether or not the initial answers (the ones before the red pens) showed sufficient effort in preparation. Grading was credit or no credit and required a fraction of a minute per paper, even on a complex worksheet.

Marking for participation was done while I was observing the groups in class and focused on having each student participate usefully but not necessarily equally. A key move was making participation a group responsibility. Every student in the group and I could tell at a glance whether each student had filled out the worksheet. If a student's paper showed that the work was done but the student was not participating usefully, everyone in the group lost points unless they were collectively asking that person what she or he had written down. Prepared students invariably participated when asked.

Marking for participation required knowing the students' names. In larger classes, I took the students' pictures and used the photos as flashcards until I knew the names and faces. I also practiced names in the classroom while the students were writing or discussing. I have found this practice to be essential in large classes.

The structure of the worksheet was important for supporting the students' learning of critical thinking. The critical page had four columns that guided the student through an elementary decision theory analysis of the reading (it took most students several tries to learn to do this analysis successfully):

1. **Summarize the author's argument.** List each main point separately. State it as if you were the author (not "the author thinks. . . ." or "she says. . . ."). Use complete sentences.

2. **Evaluate the strength of evidence.** A. List the factual claims relevant to each main point separately. Evaluate each (very solid, solid = normal science, suggestive, plausible, improbable, or very improbable). Explain (Quality and quantity of data? Other support?) B. Evaluate the strength of the overall argument (Internal consistency? Alternative hypotheses addressed? Overall probability?)

3. **For each main point and for the overall argument: Burden of Proof.** Accept until shown to be probably false? Or reject until shown to be probably true? Why? (Positive and negative consequences? Applications and societal impacts?) **And Level of Proof:** Normal as in basic science (5%), Stronger or Weaker? Why?

4. **Decisions (for each main point and for the overall argument).** Compare the strength of evidence to the level of proof to decide whether you should accept or reject.

At the end of the period, the students marked on a checklist the roles (positive and negative) that they had played individually and the ones they had observed in their small group. To help them remember and use the positive roles, a header on each worksheet page focused attention on key positive roles: "Try: Encouraging, Stating Uncertainties, Pausing, Listening, Contrasting, Summarizing, or Timekeeping."

AN ALTERNATIVE CRITICAL THINKING APPROACH USING MULTIPLE MODES OF COOPERATIVE LEARNING

As I came to understand more deeply the importance of teaching how each discipline approaches critical thinking (Nelson, 1996), I searched for a set of criteria that I could apply across multiple examples in teaching biology, especially in the evolution course. I then developed these criteria in lecture with extensive cooperative learning.

For example, a key way of comparing ideas in science is what I call a "fair test." I defined this in about 5 minutes using an example as I went. Specifically, a fair test is a way of comparing competing hypotheses: (1) using a new kind of evidence (i.e., the new test is not based on a kind of evidence that led to any of the alternatives now being compared), and (2) where the evidence is not biased (i.e., it could have, in principle, supported any of the alternatives being compared). As an example, radioactive dating was a totally new kind of evidence unrelated to that for any prior claims for the age of the earth, and radioactive dating could have supported any age from very young to immensely old.

I then used a multiple-choice question that was first discussed with neighbors and then debriefed in the whole group to reinforce and clarify the concept:

> Scientists think that a *fair test* is one that: (a) could have shown any of the alternatives to be either probably correct or probably wrong; (b) is based on a line of data or reasoning independent of those on which each alternative is based; (c) yields a lot of data; (d) contradicts popular ideas; (e) supports their own preferred answers; (f) none of the above, all of the above, or only two of the above.

I presented a series of criteria in this same pattern of mini-lectures alternating with bursts of cooperative learning. Using the same pedagogy, I applied each criterion as appropriate to five or six major examples. Essay questions for each example were coupled together and discussed in a whole-period session. Students were then asked to propose examples showing how each criterion could be applied in real life. These examples could be drawn from any nonscientific area. The students then compared and refined these examples in another whole-period discussion. Students frequently commented that it was only during this discussion that they fully understood the criteria as used in science.

Importantly, this sequenced approach took at least four rounds of cooperative learning: (1) in "lecture" as the criteria were introduced (multiple, short cooperative learning sessions), (2) in "lecture" as the criteria were applied to different parts of the content (more multiple, short cooperative learning sessions), (3) in whole-period cooperative discussion as the applications to the various course topics were compared, and, finally, (4) in whole-period cooperative discussion to process the student-generated applications. Each of these iterations were quite important to the higher-level outcome that I was focusing on: criteria-governed comparisons as the core of critical thinking.

Another discovery allowed me to free some of the class time from content coverage. This made the focus on critical thinking an even more reasonable investment of class time.

USING COOPERATIVE LEARNING TO REDUCE THE COVERAGE PROBLEM

I have argued elsewhere that the urge to cover the maximal amount of content is perhaps the greatest problem that must be overcome to become an effective teacher (Nelson, 2001). It certainly was for me.

As soon as I began teaching, I told students that I was depending on them to actually read the assignments, stressing that the exams would include a significant number of questions from readings that we did not cover in class.

This approach, combined with my fondness for synthesis questions, produced fairly low exam scores during my initial years of teaching.

Indeed, I soon began to include in my syllabi the statement that a grade of 70% on an exam would be an A. Keeping an A at 90% and flunking perhaps half of the class was not viable because I was teaching senior courses to majors who had already passed several of my colleagues' courses.

Because I did not yet know how to get the students to learn more effectively, I justified this situation to myself by thinking that I was asking for more critical thinking and was spreading out the A students so that they could see what more they could have mastered.

From reading Perry (1970) and related later works, especially *Women's Ways of Knowing* (Belenky, Clinchy, Goldberger, & Tarule, 1986), I gradually came to understand that the crux of teaching higher-level critical thinking was to help students understand explicitly how to do thinking in the discipline. And I came to understand that this, in turn, required teaching them to read and write in the disciple (Nelson, 1996). With considerable reluctance, I decided to prepare study guides over the readings (mostly text chapters) in my senior majors course in evolution.

My past practice had been to go to the chapter as I wrote the exam and find the focus for what I thought was an interesting essay question. Now, I decided the best study guide might be a list of all the reasonable essay questions over each chapter.

The first chapter I tried this on almost killed me. I had written well over fifty essay questions and was only partway through the chapter when two things became evident. First, it was clear that the chapter contained much more material than the students reasonably could be expected to master and, further, that I had been giving them essentially no guidance as to what they should focus on. Second, and more depressing, I realized that I really had not thought very much about my deeper learning goals for the assignments and, consequently, did not have a framework for prioritizing the content.

It took a lot of effort—and time—to go back through the chapter and carefully decide what was most important—and why—and then to construct questions that would help the students understand this. It was also clear to me that what I wanted students to understand required several questions that asked for applications and for syntheses across different parts of the chapter, across different chapters, and among various parts of the course.

I noticed several effects when I distributed these study guides:

1. Students were more likely to do the reading ahead of the exam. The question sets made it clear to them that the amount and difficulty of the required learning was greater than they could undertake in a cram session.

2. Students were working much more extensively in informal cooperative learning groups outside of class. Some of them explained it this way: "In most courses our goal is to figure out what the professor wants and keep that a secret (except from our boyfriends or girlfriends)." The study guides made clear what I wanted. And students could cooperate freely without fear of hurting their own grades because I was not grading on a curve.
3. Students were much more likely to ask me questions about the text in and out of class and even to come to office hours and review sessions, often in small groups—again showing that they were working together. And they usually had specific questions in mind.

I then reinvented another in-class cooperative learning practice. I started by announcing that there would be an in-class quiz over two or three of the most difficult questions. Or I asked students to write the answers out and bring them to class ready to hand in. I carefully picked questions that would enhance the rest of the class period, ones that most students were unlikely to get entirely right by themselves. Once the quiz was finished, or, alternatively, starting with the answers prepared before class, I handed the students red pens, as indicated earlier. They then discussed the answers with their neighbors in small groups.

Grading was credit/no credit, based on preparation effort as manifested on the quiz or in the prepared answers. Grading, again, required only seconds per paper, and I could be certain that most students were actually preparing.

I usually distributed about 150 to 200 essay questions before each exam in the senior evolution class. These summarized and synthesized the readings and linked them to the course themes. I focused on the essential content of the course. I was thus using informal cooperative learning to largely solve the in-class coverage problem. This left me more time to foster critical thinking during the actual class periods.

An additional advantage soon became apparent. Students learned much of the content as well, or even better, from the guided readings than they had when I had lectured on those topics in class. In contrast, there were some key aspects that many could not learn from the text, even when given extensive step-by-step study guides. I could use part of the time I had freed up by using the study guides to teach these aspects more effectively, as in the next example.

FOSTERING AN UNDERSTANDING OF GRAPH-EQUATION-CONCEPT TRANSFORMATIONS

One of the most general problems in teaching science and other quantitative disciplines is getting students to tie concepts accurately to their representations in graphs and equations and vice versa (Arons, 1976, 1997). Grossman (2005) discussed the extent to which we leave these transformations "hidden" in standard presentations. When the faculty presentation goes around the triangle—from verbal expression of a concept to its expression in an equation and then in a graph—the faculty member has shown that he or she understands it deeply. But some of the students are often lost at each transformation, and virtually the entire class may be partially lost by the time all three forms are covered.

With good study questions, students could easily understand a nonquantitative chapter on predator-prey biology. But they would be lost in the chapter on algebraic models of the same ideas, even though they had taken calculus and even if I gave them 50 or 60 questions leading them step-by-step through the models. In many cases, the students' problems appeared to represent math anxiety in science seniors similar to the anxiety that Panitz (chapter 4) addresses for remedial freshmen.

Despite these challenges, I wanted to teach these models for their intrinsic content and for their value as illustrations of the power of mathematical and graphical modeling in science. I decided to do this in small increments with much processing in cooperative groups. I began by saying: "I know that in past classes many of you have found mathematical models to be difficult and fundamentally a waste of time." I assured them that this class was different: "I am going to do the material so slowly that each of you will find it easy." I explained why I thought it was worth spending a significant amount of class time doing this careful analysis.

I then began by plotting a pair of axes, with time on the horizontal axis and population size on the vertical axis. I defined the initial population as N_0 and defined the population at any subsequent time, t, as N_t. I asked each student to sketch and label the axes and to plot the line for $N_t = N_0$ for all t. This is a horizontal line that starts at N_0 on the population axis.

I then asked the students to compare their graphs with those of their neighbors, in groups of two or three, making sure that everyone was included in a group. After a bit, I asked each of several groups to tell us what their graphs looked like. Once we had consensus, I asked each student to write down what the equation and graph told us about the biology.

The students then compared their answers with those of their neighbors. Once we all understood why this was the graph and equation for an unchanging population, we proceeded in small steps to more complicated biology and the corresponding equations and graphs.

Needless to say, this was the most successfully I had ever taught this material. And the students clearly enjoyed the class (to their surprise). Some of these senior science majors even said that this was the first time they had really understood the connections between the three representations.

MULTIPLE APPLICATIONS OF COOPERATIVE LEARNING IN A FIRST-YEAR SEMINAR

I taught a course for students in Indiana University's (IU) Intensive First-Year Seminars program for several summers before I retired. These seminars are 3-credit, 3-week courses offered in August that meet daily for 3 hours. The faculty are allowed to design exciting courses with few constraints. The topics have ranged broadly, from dance productions to personal law. Each course was limited to a maximum of twenty students. My course coupled evolution and creation with an introduction to applying postmodernism across disciplines.

First-year seminars elsewhere often focus on orientation and on fostering close ties among the students, faculty, and upperclass students. The IU program, from its inception, had intellectual excitement as the main goal with orientation and affiliation following in part from co-curricular components. To this, I added the design question: What could I do that would best foster the students' success over the next four years?

I picked two main goals. I wanted the students to have a strong overview of the college experience, a set of "maps" they could use to understand the academic terrain and track their own performance. And I wanted the students to understand fully and accept the importance to their own academic success of working cooperatively in small groups whether or not these were built into the course officially.

I chose three maps: (1) a personally chosen set of goals for four years against which each student could measure her or his own success; (2) an understanding of potential intellectual development during the college years, as laid out by Perry (1968, 1970, 1999) and subsequent work by others, against which they could chart their progress in more normative terms; and (3) an understanding of the academic landscape that they could use to tame more easily the menagerie of academic expectations that they were likely to encounter.

A PERSONAL MAP

The students began work on a personal map before class started by answering two questions: "How is college going to help me earn more money?" "What are the three most important other things that should result from four years of college education?" They then asked the same questions of four college-educated adults and combined their own answers with those of their interviewees.

In class, in small- and whole-group discussions, we generated a set of general alternative goals and, importantly, lists of concrete steps that a student could take in the first two weeks of class to move toward each goal. Each student chose four personal goals and two concrete steps for each goal and summarized these in a short paper.

Students also explained their goals and steps to each other in small groups, thus publicly committing themselves to doing the steps. In retrospect, I should have also organized groups of about three to co-monitor their own progress during the first weeks of the fall semester.

Intellectual Developmental as a Map

Perry (1968, 1970, 1999) found four major modes of thinking among undergraduates: (1) dualism—one authority has the truth (teach me the facts); (2) multiplicity—any view is valid if someone chooses it (listen to me);(3) [contextual] relativism—paradigms and worldviews are ways of choosing better from worse within the context of their scope of expertise (conflicts among these perspectives are still a matter of personal perspective); and, much more rarely, (4) commitment—different worldviews and paradigms, when applied to the real world, have different consequences, often for different groups (seeing these, I can sometimes commit to one as better than the others for addressing particular problems in specific contexts).

We used evolution as a way of understanding how science can tell us that some answers are better than others as science. A consideration of ways of comparing consequences and trade-offs allowed us to understand the wide variety of ways that individuals and religious organizations have chosen to combine science and religion (for details, see Nelson, 2000, 2007, 2008a).

To prepare the students for college-level lectures, I used short segments of lecture interspersed with short answer and multiple-choice questions (such as those discussed previously and used with the same cooperative learning techniques) to help them see what they should have learned from each piece of lecture. My intent was to teach them both the content and how to listen closely to lectures.

The Importance of Learning Cooperatively and a Map of the Academic Landscape

Much discussion in academia and in U.S. politics might be encapsulated by questions such as "How much of what we believe or think is really true?" "How much of it is probably true?" "How much of it is simple social convention?" Freshmen at IU have had little preparation for understanding the constructivist frameworks that faculty in the humanities and social sciences often take as a given. They may do poorly in a course simply because it takes them too long to figure out what the teacher or the texts could possibly mean.

I selected a book that sketches the contrast between modernism and postmodernism across the curriculum, one that takes a constrained constructivist view of postmodernism (not a radical relativist view). The title says it all: *Reality Isn't What It Used to Be: Theatrical Politics, Ready to Wear Religion, Global Myths, Primitive Chic, and Other Wonders of the Postmodern World* (Anderson, 1990).

One example suffices to show how intriguing the book is. Anderson argues that science can be reasonably understood as currently the most fully developed postmodernist field. The book's emphases match several of those that Smith et al. (chapter 6) advocate (following Pink, 2005): the importance of story, the connection of patterns across fields, understanding diverse perspectives, and more. This presents quite a challenge for entering first-year students!

Anderson's book thus was perfect for my purposes. It provided my students with an overview of the academic landscape and of popular culture, too. And it was clearly a book that few of my students could have understood without extensive cooperative learning. Indeed, I had only a couple of students in seven years who seemed ready to understand it on their own.

The first problem was that most students had had no practice in understanding an argument in detail. They could say what a chapter was about, but not what it said or advocated. This clearly required multiple-level cooperative interventions. Usually, part of the day of the first class was cooperative reading of the first two pages of chapter one. These discuss Bloom's (1987) ideas against a heavily structured essay question that "merely" required an accurate summary of the text's argument:

> "The conservative indictment is correct, and yet the strategy that follows from it . . . is doomed to fail." Summarize (i) the indictment, (ii) the strategy, and (iii) the reasons Anderson offers for its inevitable failure. So what, according to Anderson? (Include in your summary of the reasons for failure both diversity and the ultimately self-defeating aspects of the strategy.)

I had the students answer this question in pairs while reading the book. I then had them join with a second group to construct a consensus answer. They wrote these answers on the blackboard and discussed in their small groups the strengths and weaknesses of the answers written by each of the other groups. After listening to the other groups' comments on their own answer and hearing each of the other answers discussed, they rewrote their own consensus answer and again posted it on the board.

Still in their groups of four, they discussed the strengths and weaknesses of the other groups' second answers and of their own answer. By now, they were beginning to see what the answer actually was, and some were beginning to see how to read the book, if given the questions. This exercise took perhaps 90 minutes, but it was clearly essential.

I reassigned the students to new groups of four, taking into account that some appeared to be "getting it" but some still appeared to be clueless. Each student was given a list of about a dozen study questions over the first five or six pages of chapter one. They were assigned to work in groups and had to report on their group efforts with the never-used possibility of voting non-participants out.

The next day, they were given a quiz on which each student in the group of four answered a different question. As soon as the students were done with their own questions, they put their pens away and were given red pens. Students who had finished their own questions exchanged papers within the group and commented on each others' answers in writing—there were no spoken comments of any kind. The marking was largely done for me at this point. After they saw the comments on it, students were free to revise their own answer or not.

Each student received three grades: one was on the unmodified (pre-red ink) answer that the student wrote, one was the average of the grades on the unmodified answers written by their group (but each grade of at least 8/10 was raised by 1/10, up to a maximum of 10/10 before averaging), and one was the average of the grades on the modified answers written by their group. Individual grades below A did not count on the first two or three quizzes because I wanted the students to have a good chance at first understanding the basic themes of the book and to have time to learn how to study cooperatively and how to answer essay questions.

This cooperative practice was repeated almost daily for most of the three weeks using new material. New groups were assigned about once per week. Most of the initial questions simply required deep comprehension of the text (as in the prior example). However, synthesis and application questions became more frequent as we progressed.

With cooperative group learning, almost every student's initial uncorrected answer to a randomly assigned question was at least a B (after the initial two or three practice quizzes). These strong performances were on questions that would have been too difficult for most of the students to master without cooperative learning. The students engaged in active group work almost every afternoon or evening. And the program director commented that my classes were typically the best bonded socially for at least the first half of the session and remained cohesive throughout.

STUDENTS' JOURNALS AS A BASE FOR COOPERATIVE LEARNING IN A GRADUATE BIOLOGY COURSE

I intermittently offered a graduate biology course on "Alternative Approaches for Teaching College Biology" in a science department that has a strong research emphasis (Nelson, 2008b). As Smith et al. (chapter 6) advocate, a key objective was "modeling and coaching graduate students in the use of cooperative learning." In addition, graduate courses on teaching can address both general problems of undergraduate learning and special problems of the field.

The strong persistence of students' alternative conceptions or misconceptions is a general problem in science (Duit, 2009). Similarly, many learning difficulties that limit students' ability to work with equations and models reflect incompletely developed abstract thinking skills (Arons, 1976, 1997). Evolution and other topics with complex real-world applications provide special problems that are difficult to address adequately without simultaneously considering adult cognitive development (Nelson, 2000, 2008a). Such essential topics may be too esoteric for many general courses on college teaching, but they can make a departmentally based course more interesting and important.

In the more recent versions of the class, I used discussions based on structured written journals both as the main class activity and as the major assessments. I required printed copies of the journals 24 to 48 hours before each weekly class. Each journal had to provide the following:

1. A summary of each reading assigned for the week with a consideration of its implications for or applications to undergraduate biology teaching.
2. For the prior week's class meeting, a summary of the key points that emerged with their implications for teaching, especially in biology.
3. A discussion of what did you learn about teaching and learning—from the way the class session was conducted and from the patterns of participation.
4. An evaluation of the class session, both in terms of the value of the material and the way the class played out.
5. A self-evaluation ("What were the strong points in your participation? What were the weaker points? How are these ideas and processes related to the strengths or weaknesses of your past teaching and learning experiences?")

I read the journals before each class session and made quick comments on each one. Class began by the students taking five minutes to read my comments and refresh their memories of their considerations of the articles in preparation for discussion.

Some sessions or pairs of sessions were structured in part as learning cycles (Svinicki & Dixon, 1987). For example, we began a consideration of learning styles by having the students read descriptions of the styles for a couple of tests and decide which one or two seemed to fit them best.

Each student then took the learning styles tests and compared the results with their own assessments. We then tabulated the amount of agreement and the variation across students. I took this to be the "concrete experience" step of the Kolb learning cycle (Svinicki & Dixon, 1987).

Journaling on the class session provided "reflection." Reading a couple of papers on learning styles and their applications provided "abstract conceptualization." Writing on the applications and discussing applications in class provided some elementary "active experimentation."

Overall, this journal and discussion approach was quite successful in producing deep learning as demonstrated in the journals, in the discussions in class, and in the draft teaching philosophies that the students wrote toward the end of the course. A molecular biology professor who audited the class decided to use a similar journal-based cooperative learning approach in her graduate molecular biology courses.

CLOSING OVERVIEW

I have tried to illustrate the deep power of cooperative learning as developed and applied in a succession of increasingly effective strategies for fostering deeper learning. Learning to use cooperative learning for one goal—fostering critical thinking, for example—led to trying it for another.

In my case, I turned to using it to produce a deeper understanding of the text. As I became successful with this, I freed up time that I had previously felt compelled to use in covering content. This, in turn, allowed me to turn to the applications of cooperative learning in teaching material that had previously seemed unlearnable for many students. As refinements within a course became more successful, I had a base for expanding these approaches to other courses and to deeper goals.

In beginning this chapter, I argued that one key component of effective higher education is a deep understanding of the higher-level learning goals that one seeks to advance. As my understanding of higher education and of effective pedagogics matured, I turned, in the first-year seminars, to asking how I could make the biggest difference over the student's entire academic career.

I chose to provide the students, through cooperative learning, with three maps that would help them obtain more deeply meaningful total education and to show the students how to do effective cooperative learning on their own. Cooperative learning had thus become both essential to my goals and part of what I felt was the core of higher education. These foci were, in turn, reflected in my course on teaching for prospective college science faculty.

As change continues to accelerate in the larger world—as issues such as environmental changes, equitable social structures, and geopolitical changes have become ever more important—content, in the traditional sense, has become both more transitory and easier to access. If higher education is to be a major part of the solutions—instead of a distraction or barrier—each faculty member and program needs to look more systematically for more effective ways of fostering deeper learning; faculty also need to think more deeply and systematically about the core goals and values of higher education.

We collectively have a variety of answers, but few curricula and courses survive without substantial change. And, as our goals become clearer and our methods more effective, we improve not only achievement but also retention and equity. This book is one set of maps and tools for helping us on these journeys.

References

Anderson, D. L., Fisher, K. M., & Norman, G. J. (2002). Development and evaluation of the conceptual inventory of natural selection. *Journal of Research in Science Teaching, 39,* 952–978.

Anderson, W. T. (1990). *Reality isn't what it used to be: Theatrical politics, ready to wear religion, global myths, primitive chic, and other wonders of the postmodern world.* San Francisco: Harper and Row.

Arons, A. B. (1976). Cultivating the capacity for formal operations: Objectives and procedures in an introductory physical science course. *American Journal of Physics, 44,* 834–838.

Arons, A. B. (1997). *Teaching introductory physics.* New York: Wiley.

Belenky, M., Clinchy, B., Goldberger, N., & Tarule, J. (1986). *Women's ways of knowing. The development of self, voice, and mind.* New York: Basic Books.

Bloom, A. (1987). *The closing of the American mind.* New York: Simon and Schuster.

Bonwell, C. C., & Eison, J. A. (1991). *Active learning: Creating excitement in the classroom.* Washington, DC: ERIC Clearinghouse on Higher Education, George Washington University.

Crouch, C. H., & Mazur, E. (2001). Peer instruction: Ten years of experience and results. *American Journal of Physics, 69,* 970–977.

Duit, R. (2009). Bibliography—STCSE: Students' and teachers' conceptions and science education. Retrieved February 3, 2010, from www.ipn.uni-kiel.de/aktuell/stcse/bibint.html.

Ebert-May, D., & Hodder, J. (Eds.). (2008). *Pathways to scientific teaching.* Sunderland, MA: Sinauer.

Fullilove, R. E., & Treisman, P. U. (1990). Mathematics achievement among African American undergraduates at the University of California, Berkeley: An evaluation of the Mathematics Workshop Program. *Journal of Negro Education, 59*(3), 463–478.

Grossman, R. W. (2005). Discovering hidden transformations: Making science and other courses more learnable. *College Teaching, 53*(1), 33–40.

Hake, R. R. (1998a). Interactive-engagement vs. traditional methods: A six-thousand-student survey of mechanics test data for introductory physics courses. *American Journal of Physics, 66,* 64–74.

Hake, R. R. (1998b). Interactive-engagement methods in introductory mechanics courses. Retrieved March 9, 2010, from http://www.physics.indiana.edu/~sdi/IEM-2b.pdf.

Hake, R. R. (2002). Lessons from the physics education reform effort. Conservation Ecology, 5(2): 28. Retrieved March 9, 2010, from http://www.consecol.org/vol5/iss2/art28/.

Halloun, I., Hestenes, D. (1985a.) The initial knowledge state of college physics. *American Journal of Physics,* 53, 1043–1055.

Halloun, I., Hestenes, D. (1985b.) Common sense concepts about motion. *American Journal of Physics,* 53, 1056–1065.

Handelsman, J., Ebert-May, D., Beichner, R., Bruns, P., Chang, A., & DeHaan, R. (2004). Scientific Teaching. *Science, 304,* 521–522.

Herreid, C. F. (2004). Using case studies in science—And still "covering the content." In L. K. Michaelsen, A. Bauman Knight, & L. D. Fink (Eds.), (2004). *Team-based learning: A transformative use of small groups in college teaching* (pp. 105–114). Sterling, VA: Stylus.

Jacobs, D. C. (2000). *An alternative approach to general chemistry: Addressing the needs of at-risk students with cooperative learning strategies.* Retrieved March 9, 2010, from http://cms.carnegiefoundation.org/collections/castl_he/djacobs/index.html.

Millis, B. J., & Cottell, P. G. (1998). *Cooperative learning for higher education faculty.* Phoenix, AZ: American Council on Education/Oryx.

Nelson, C. E. (1994). Critical thinking and collaborative learning. In K. Bosworth and S. Hamilton (Eds.), *Collaborative learning and college teaching* (pp. 45–58). San Francisco: Jossey-Bass.

Nelson, C. E. (1996). Student diversity requires different approaches to college teaching, even in math and science. *American Behavioral Scientist, 40,* 165–175.

Nelson, C. E. (1999). On the persistence of unicorns: The trade-off between content and critical thinking revisited. In B. A. Pescosolido and R. Aminzade (Eds.), *The social worlds of higher education: Handbook for teaching in a new century* (pp. 168–184). Thousand Oaks, CA: Pine Forge.

Nelson, C. E. (2000). Effective strategies for teaching evolution and other controversial subjects. In W. James, J. W. Skehan, & C. E. Nelson (Eds.), *The creation controversy and the science classroom* (pp. 19–50). Arlington, VA: National Science Teachers Association.

Nelson, C. E. (2001). What is the most difficult step we must take to become great teachers? *National Teaching and Learning Forum, 10*(4), 10–11.

Nelson, C. E. (2007). Teaching evolution effectively: A central dilemma and alternative strategies. *McGill Journal of Education, 42*(2), 265–283.

Nelson, C. E. (2008a). Teaching evolution (and all of biology) more effectively: Strategies for engagement, critical reasoning, and confronting misconceptions. *Integrative and Comparative Biology, 48*, 213–225.

Nelson, C. E. (2008b). The right start: Reflections on a departmentally based graduate course on teaching. *Essays on Teaching Excellence, 11*(7), 1–4.

Perry, W. G., Jr. (1968). *Forms of intellectual and ethical development in the college years: A scheme.* Cambridge, MA: Bureau of Study Counsel, Harvard University.

Perry, W. G., Jr. (1970). *Forms of intellectual and ethical development in the college years: A scheme.* New York: Holt.

Perry, W. G., Jr. (1999). *Forms of intellectual and ethical development in the college years: A scheme.* (Reprint of the 1970 edition with a new introduction by L. Knefelkamp). San Francisco: Jossey-Bass.

Pink, D. H. (2005). *A whole new mind.* Riverhead, NY: Riverhead Books.

Russell, J., Hendricson, W. D., & Herbert, R. J. (1984). Effects of lecture information density on medical student achievement. *Journal of Medical Education, 59*, 881–889.

Smith, K. A., Sheppard, S. D., Johnson, D. W., & Johnson, R. T. (2005). Pedagogies of engagement: Classroom-based practices. *Journal of Engineering Education: Special Issue on the State of the Art and Practice of Engineering Education Research, 94*(1), 87–102.

Springer, L., Stanne, M. E., & Donovan, S. S. (1997). *Effects of small-group learning on undergraduates in science, mathematics, engineering and technology: A meta-analysis.* Madison: National Institute for Science Education, University of Wisconsin.

Sundberg, M. D. (2003, Mar–Apr). Strategies to help students change naive alternative conceptions about evolution and natural selection. *Reports of the National Center for Science Education, 23*, 23–26.

Sundberg, M. D., & Dini, M. L. (1993). Science majors vs. nonmajors: Is there a difference? *Journal of College Science Teaching, 23*, 299–304.

Sundberg, M. D., Dini, M. L., & Li, E. (1994). Improving student comprehension and attitudes in first-year biology by decreasing course content. *Journal of Research in Science Teaching, 31*, 679–693.

Svinicki, M.D., & Dixon, N. M. (1987). The Kolb Model modified for classroom activities. *College Teaching, 35*, 141–146.

Treisman, U. (1992). Studying students studying calculus: A look at the lives of minority mathematics students in college. *College Mathematics Journal, 23*, 362–372.

9

Sequencing Cooperative Activities in Literature Classes

Barbara J. Millis

I began teaching English courses as a teaching assistant (TA) at Florida State University in 1967. All TAs were required to spend time immersed in a one-month "how-to-teach" course, which was revolutionary for the times, even though it focused primarily on the content, not on the delivery methods. Nonetheless, I must have done a credible job my first year because I was thrilled to receive an "Apple Award" from one of my students in a local sorority.

My teaching approaches—a combination of lecture and whole-class discussion—didn't change much, I am embarrassed to say, until 1988 or so. By that time, as the director of a faculty development center at the University of Maryland University College, I was looking for local talent to offer workshops. Someone told me that a man named Neil Davidson at the University of Maryland, College Park, was "good with groups."

Neil's three-hour workshop changed my teaching and my scholarship—and, in a significant way, my life. Neil introduced me to cooperative learning. I was fortunate that Spencer Kagan offered a two-day workshop in Maryland less than a month later, giving me the confidence to tear up my current children's literature syllabus and radically redesign the course to include structured group work.

Now, nearly 20 years after the cooperative learning epiphany, group work remains at the heart of all my courses. Because of my research and work in faculty development, I have integrated other elements, leading me to teach far more *intentionally*, to borrow a term used by the American Association of Colleges and Universities (2000). I agree with Bransford, Brown, and Cocking (2000) that "The emerging science of learning underscores the importance of rethinking what is taught, how it is taught, and how learning is assessed" (p. 13).

My approach to learning and course design is based on synthesis and integration, drawing on a wide range of practical and theoretical approaches that

141

include cooperative learning, of course, but also the writing across the curriculum literature, research on how people learn, Angelo and Cross's *Classroom Assessment Techniques* (1993), and the international research on deep learning. My teaching odyssey is summarized in a recently published article in the Association of American Colleges and Universities' *Peer Review* (Millis, 2009).

I work hard but, I hope, creatively, to sequence activities—both outside and inside the classroom—to strengthen students' learning and their motivation to learn. This approach emerged (with other influences, of course) from a seminal article by James Rhem (1995) that showed me two things: (1) why cooperative learning works and (2) how sequencing in-class activities to build on homework assignments results in deep learning and critical thinking.

Rhem's summary article suggests that deep learning has four premises: (1) motivation, (2) active learning, (3) interaction with others, and (4) a deep foundational knowledge that is conceptually based. I now try to develop motivating homework assignments that get students into the knowledge base, and then I build on what they have learned through cooperative in-class activities.

To illustrate this approach, this chapter focuses on specific literature examples that model this sequencing process, a process echoed by Walvoord (2010), who discusses moving students' first exposure to material into their study time and requiring them to bring to class written homework that becomes the basis for deeper processing and discussion. Fink (2003) refers to a similar type of sequencing as a "castle top" design.

I use team folders (Cottell, chapter 2, and Shadle, chapter 3) to organize my literature classes, typically composed of 16–20 students. In the larger "Introduction to Literature" classes common on research campuses, team folders can provide a way of facilitating classroom management.

USING A GRAPHIC ORGANIZER CALLED A "DOUBLE ENTRY JOURNAL"

A Double Entry Journal (DEJ) is a graphic organizer (Figure 9.1) in the form of a Microsoft Word table template that is e-mailed or distributed to students directly or through the course management system. It is used to structure the homework assignment. On the left side of a grid, students outline the key points of an article, a chapter, or a guest lecture. On the right side of the grid, opposite the author's point, they make personal comments, linking the point to academic material, to current events, or to their personal experiences and opinions.

Name: Barbara J. Millis
Article: "Investing in Creativity" by Robert Sternberg

Author's Critical Points	Student's Response
Creative thinking is every bit as malleable as critical thinking.	Judging from discussions at my own institution—and elsewhere—critical thinking is not as easy to define, let alone "teach," as some educators would have us believe. I happen to believe that critical thinking is taught by "doing" and doing things specifically within the discipline. Activities such as the Double Entry Journal encourage critical thinking. I don't think you can separate creative from critical thinking.
The investment theory of creativity holds that creatively gifted people share common characteristics.	Do we find gifted people and look for these characteristics or do we find the people who have these characteristics in common and then look for their creativity!?

Figure 9.1 Sample Double Entry Journal (Two Points Cited, Only)

Faculty members should limit either the length of the DEJ or the number of key points to prevent overachievers from "burning out" themselves and the teacher.

The deep learning emerges not just from having students wrestle with the complex material, but also from careful sequencing and repetition. For years, I collected and graded homework, sending a signal to students that their work was merely an artificial exercise intended for evaluation by a bored expert. I now pair students and have them read and comment on each other's DEJs, pointing out relevant passages in the original article.

Unprepared students do not pair: they work on their DEJ at the back of the room. After the paired discussion, students turn in their DEJs, and I mark them rapidly to provide feedback, but I do not assign letter grades. The DEJs receive a pass/fail, "all or nothing" grade with assigned points (usually 10). The pass/fail option allows me to comment quickly and personally rather than agonizing over justifying a letter grade that is based on the nuances between, say, an A– and a B+.

As the final step in this sequence, ostensibly to "coach" students to write better DEJs in the future, I share exemplary student DEJ examples or share a composite DEJ based on excerpts—key points and responses—from a variety of student examples.

A DEJ prepared out of class gets students into the knowledge base prior to class and also motivates them because they know their homework will generate an authentic discussion with another peer. Writing responses is also motivating because they are relevant to the students' own lives and learning.

These reflective responses also promote learning because students who place content knowledge in a personal context are more likely to retain the information and be able to retrieve it—the "self-referral" effect (Rogers, Kuiper, & Kirker, 1977). Similarly, Jensen (2000) advises faculty members to help students "discover their own connections" and "use their own words with regard to new learning" (p. 282).

Two biologists help us appreciate the value of repetition for the "basics" of learning and why sequencing is important. Leamnson (1999) states, "Learning is defined as stabilizing, through repeated use, certain appropriate and desirable synapses in the brain" (p. 5). Zull (2002) defines the art of teaching as "creating conditions that lead to change in a learner's brain" (p. 5).

Repetition is thus a key to learning. Reading the assigned article or hearing the guest lecture gives students their first exposure. Then, crafting the DEJ draws the student back into the material—with personally relevant responses—for another repetition. The paired discussion in class provides a third repetition. Students are likely to review their DEJs, a fourth repetition, when I return them with comments. A fifth repetition occurs when I "coach" students on preparing an ideal DEJ by presenting exemplary examples as an in-class follow-up.

USING A GRAPHIC ORGANIZER WITH JIGSAW

Jigsaw, like a DEJ, relies on a graphic organizer to structure the homework, which is sequenced and "processed" in class to promote deep learning.

Jigsaw works well in literature classes, where a key goal is to develop students' proficiency in close textual reading. After I give a mini-lecture on characterization, I assign the four students in each team one of four characters in the literary work we are examining. Four strong characters are common in many literary works such as *Antigone* (Antigone, Creon, Haemon, and Ismene), *Hamlet* (Gertrude, Claudius, Hamlet, and Laertes), or *Charlotte's Web* (Charlotte, Wilbur, Templeton, and Fern).

Because, like Cottell (chapter 2) and Shadle (chapter 3), I use team folders and playing cards, I can readily assign the characters: hearts work on Charlotte, clubs focus on Templeton, etc. In teams with five members, two students work on a particularly complex character such as Charlotte.

To focus their reading, students receive a graphic organizer (Figure 9.2) on which, as a homework assignment, they list four traits that describe their character in the boxes marked "Trait." In the large boxes below marked "Textual Evidence," they list (with page numbers) each quotation or event that provides evidence for this trait.

To process the homework, I use a cooperative learning structure called Jigsaw (Aronson, Stephan, Sikes, & Snapp, 1978). At the next class meeting, all the students with the same character compare their graphic organizers in expert groups of three to five students.

This expert team—there can be more than one in large classes—discusses the various completed graphic organizers and agrees on the best four traits and the best evidence to support them. Then, each member completes a second graphic organizer, using the best ideas of all members.

Those familiar with the original Bloom's Taxonomy (1956) will recognize that students are engaged in the highest levels of cognitive development because they are making judgments about the "best" traits (evaluation) and determining the most relevant evidence to create a new completed graphic organizer (synthesis).

CHARACTER:

Trait:	Trait:	Trait:	Trait:
Textual Evidence:	Textual Evidence:	Textual Evidence:	Textual Evidence:

Figure 9.2 Character Trait Evidence Grid

In a revised version of Bloom's Taxonomy by Anderson, Krathwohl, Airasian, Cruikshank, Mayer, Pintrich, Raths, & Wittrock, Eds. (2001), students are still working at the highest end of the cognitive process dimension because they are evaluating (making judgments based on criteria and standards) and creating (putting elements together to form a coherent or functional whole and reorganizing elements into a new pattern or structure).

At a signal, the expert members return to the home team where they explain in depth their character's four key traits and the evidence in the text to support this interpretation. They are, in other words, teaching their teammates their portion of the Jigsaw, a practice that capitalizes on the use of peer tutoring advocated by Fantuzzo and other colleagues to enhance learning (Fantuzzo, Dimeff, & Fox, 1989; Fantuzzo, Riggio, Connelly, & Dimeff, 1989).

Students receive pass/fail points for the individually prepared graphic organizer that they bring to share in the expert team. It might be worth seven points, for example, toward the final course point-total. Even though the expert-team graphic organizer receives no additional points, I collect them in the team folders for review.

Bransford, Cocking, and Brown (2000) emphasize the value of feedback based on thinking that is "made visible." Such feedback must "focus on understanding, and not only on memory . . . and does not necessarily require elaborate or complicated assessment procedures" (p. 140). Thus graphic organizers, such as the DEJ and the "trait" diagram, submitted for pass/fail points, can contribute to student learning when they are part of a carefully organized sequence.

SEND-A-PROBLEM

The Send-a-Problem structure (Maier, McGoldrick, and Simkins, chapter 10) requires students to focus on issues or problems within a team setting. The exact source of this structure is unclear, but a version of it was generated by the Howard County, Maryland, Staff Development Center in 1989, inspired by Kagan's (1989) high consensus-oriented Send-a-Problem structure using rotating flashcards for content review.

To initiate Send-a-Problem, I identify (sometimes with student input for more "buy-in") a list of problems or issues. A focus on *Hamlet* might produce questions such as "Why does Hamlet treat Ophelia as he does in Act Two?" "What is the complication in the play and why is it significant?" "How are Hamlet and Laertes different/similar?"

I bring to class file folders (envelopes also work) with one problem identified with a sticky note on the cover of each one. I explain the activity and its time limits and then distribute the folders, one per team. In large classes several teams can work simultaneously on the same problems as long as they are spaced at least three teams apart because of the subsequent "pass" process.

I carefully structure this activity in the following way:

1. Each team discusses its particular problem and generates within the given time frame (usually three to seven minutes depending on the complexity of the problems) as many solutions as possible; the team members place a sheet of paper in the folder with the solutions and the team's name or number.

2. The students pass the folder to the team with the next highest number (aces to twos, threes to fours, etc.), but the folder remains unopened. The new team, seeing only the identified problem on the cover of the folder, follows an identical procedure and brainstorms solutions, placing their recorded conclusions in the folder.

3. The teams pass the folders ahead a third time, but in this case, members of the team open the folder and review the ideas/solutions generated by the other two teams. On a new sheet of paper, they create a synthesis of the best of the ideas from all three teams.

Group reports provide useful closure. After allowing time for peer coaching and review, I identify the reporters through the playing card suits in an approach that is called "Numbered Heads Together" (Kagan, 2009) in the cooperative learning literature. The reporters announce the issue that their team members have discussed and offer their synthesis—referencing, if desired, the teams from which they adapted ideas.

If large classes preclude a report from every team, I use two approaches. The first option is "Luck of the Draw." I announce the color of the folder, if necessary in a large class with multiple colors, and draw a card, such as the five of clubs, asking the person holding this card to offer the team's report. I continue drawing cards and hearing reports until class time is over (or until students tire of the responses).

A second option uses a reporting approach called "Three Stay, One Stray," described by Kagan (2009) and Millis and Cottell (1998). After time for review and peer coaching, I call on a student holding one of the suits, such as diamonds, to serve as the "straying" reporter. The designated student from each group rotates to the adjoining team with the next highest number to give the report.

In large classes, the order of rotation must be clear. Playing cards work particularly well because students rotate to the next highest card: the aces rotate to the twos, the jacks to the queens, and so forth. I use colored tent cards with the team number (twos, threes, etc.) that matches the color of the sets (aces through kings) of folders. The reporter for the kings (with, say, red folders) thus reports to the aces in the next colored folder (say, blue), and the ace reporter with the blue folders then rotates to the blue twos.

Three Stay, One Stray offers a pleasant alternative to the whole-class report (with one quivering student facing a class where only sadists would ask questions). Students have low-threat opportunities to learn by teaching and to respond to authentic questions. Three Stay, One Stray is also remarkably efficient. Instead of, for example, ten sequential five-minute reports to the entire class (50 minutes, plus transition time), individual students simultaneously give five-minute reports throughout the room.

I usually have the students rotate three times, making three reports because teams then get exposure to more ideas, and the reporter has more rehearsal time. As a "sponge activity," when there is extra time, members of the team being visited share with the reporter their problem and solutions. To build in individual accountability, when the reporter/visitor returns to the home team, the remaining three team members share in turn what they learned from the three visitors. This helps their learning through repetition and teaching others. These home-team reports also give the reporters/visitors exposure to the variety of reports they missed as they "strayed."

COOPERATIVE DEBATES

In a literature class studying *Antigone*, I establish teams of four to five students to examine two key questions relevant to the play: "Should Antigone have buried her brother? Pro and Con" and "Should Creon be impeached for poor leadership? Pro and Con." Students draw slips of paper to determine their particular team and debate side. This random approach allows students to interact with a variety of classmates and ensures that the highest achieving students do not self-select, skewing the debate results.

As homework, students read the play closely, gathering support for their team's perspective by close textual reading. Students receive time in class to compare their notes and to work on preparing the best possible arguments. Students can also draw material from their own external research, from class discussions, and from an earlier guest lecturer speaking on justice and legality.

I carefully explain the ground rules to the students, which include the "Numbered Heads"/no pre-identified spokesperson approach, ensuring that everyone knows the debate points after peer coaching. Just before the debate begins, I announce each team's spokesperson, chosen at random. Thus, the teams are potentially only as strong as their weakest member. After the spokespersons present their sides in turn, I allot time for preparation of a rebuttal, this time letting the teams choose their own spokesperson. Then, the students who are observing the debate (the half of the class assigned to the other debate topic), vote to determine which side has made the most convincing argument. The second pair of teams follows the same procedure for their debate on the second question.

GUIDED RECIPROCAL PEER QUESTIONING

Developed and researched by King (1990, 1995), this activity helps students generate task-specific questions that can be answered within a cooperative team. To initiate this activity, I give each student a copy of Alison King's question stems (Appendix A) and ask them to e-mail me three to five authentic questions (ones they truly want to discuss) on a given work of literature such as Ernest Gaines's *A Lesson Before Dying*. These question stems, based on Bloom's Taxonomy, challenge students to move beyond dualistic thinking by forming questions such as "What are the strengths and weaknesses of . . . ?" I coach students, using specific examples, to understand the process of generating effective questions.

Students discuss their questions in class in their cooperative teams, with guidance from a discussion leader, recorder, reporter, and time-keeper assigned via the playing card numbers. Students in turn pose authentic questions that they genuinely want to discuss, preferably using a different stem. The team recorders note the questions posed and the "gist" of the discussion.

About 20 minutes before the close of class, I ask the teams to review their recorders' notes to determine the question and discussion that they found most insightful. This process results in deliberate repetition prior to a report. Because my writing-based literature classes are typically small, I ask each team (usually four to five teams composed of four students each) to share succinctly their best question and discussion.

In larger classes, instructors might want to share a few randomly selected reports (Luck of the Draw) but have all of the reports posted via e-mail, a webpage, or a course management system such as Blackboard or Moodle.

BINGO

I love using Bingo for midterm and final exam preparation, carefully sequencing it to build in student input, actual game play, and feedback. I coach students on how to design and submit appropriate Bingo questions, an ongoing process throughout the semester or half-semester.

Initially, students tend to make their questions too rigid for the Bingo format. They need to allow for some "wiggle room" (e.g., not "Name the characters in Ernest Hemingway's *A Farewell to Arms*," but "Name three important characters in the novel"). I have students submit two types of questions: factual ones, which I can use to speed up play, and open-ended ones that encourage deep learning and in-depth responses. The student who submits the question, not I, becomes the "arbitrator" of acceptable answers. Thus, students post questions to a webpage or a classroom management system in the following format:

Type of question: Factual
The Question: Who is the author of *Maude Martha*?
Student's Name: John Doe

The Answer: Gwendolyn Brooks
Source: Title page, *Maude Martha.*

Type of Question: Open-Ended
The Question: Name two important themes in *A Farewell to Arms.*
Student's Name: Jane Doe

Possible Answers: Humans are powerless against a capricious God or random fate.
Love does not conquer all.

I carefully review all the questions, returning for revision any that are inappropriate. Before the game, I add any significant questions that will help students learn critical material. I then rank order the questions within the two categories (factual and open-ended) so that the most valuable questions occur early in the game. To use the questions during play, I enlarge the fonts to prepare transparencies or to project slides. At the top appears the question and the person submitting it.

I purchase needed supplies: Skittles or M&Ms for the markers (seasonal markers can be candy corn or Valentine hearts), and candy bars—large and snack sizes—for the prizes (healthier prize alternatives are bags of pretzels, cocoa packets, ballpoint pens, etc.).

To play the game, I pair students, or form as trios if there is an uneven number of participants. Although most students know the object of Bingo (five markers in a row in any direction) and the rules of play, it is important to explain the procedures so that anyone unfamiliar with Bingo—such as international students—does not feel compromised or inept. Each pair receives markers and two colored worksheets (as an example, green for the factual; gold for the higher-level, open-ended questions) where they record their answers and whether the answers were right or wrong. They can also note the space where the marker is to go. A worksheet [abbreviated] looks like this:

Factual Questions Pair or Trio (responding to a question about William Faulkner's *A Rose for Emily*):		
Answer	Rt or Wrong?	Space
1. rat poison	Rt	B2
2.		

Pairs with correct answers place a marker on the designated square (e.g., B3 or G1). To make the play rapid, I draw cards with the designated letter and number. Pacing is important. To speed up play, I use the single-answer factual questions. To encourage critical thinking, I include as many open-ended questions as possible during the time frame.

The first pair (often, there are ties) to cover five contiguous squares in any direction declares "Bingo." After the two (or sometimes three) pairs of students select prizes, they clear their board and continue playing until the period ends.

I find Bingo to be a useful teaching tool on a number of levels. It encourages reflection on the material when students submit questions. It has assessment value: the worksheets completed by student pairs during play offer me valuable insights into what students know and don't know, including misconceptions. Bingo games keep students actively engaged with the material, thus increasing the likelihood of their remembering it.

Enthusiastic and energetic, students often "high-five" each other when they get a correct answer. They listen attentively to the answers and suddenly care about the material. Best of all, Bingo games build collegiality. The pairs who work together develop personal bonds, and the whole-group discussions over the open-ended questions allow students to engage in meaningful conversations that would probably not occur in less structured settings.

CONCLUSION

Wiggins and McTighe (1998) discuss at length the important of "sequence in the design of the curriculum" (p. 134). They argue for a "spiral" curriculum where "the same ideas and materials are revisited in more and more complex ways to arrive at sophisticated judgments and products" (p. 135).

Thus, I deliberately use tools such as graphic organizers to focus carefully sequenced in-class activities. I also structure classes to build in effective course management approaches and the attributes of cooperative learning discussed elsewhere, such as positive interdependence. The "secret" for me lies in a deliberately created sequence that promotes student learning by building through in-class active learning and student interactions on material encountered through motivating homework assignments. In other words, in my literature classes I am aiming for deep learning.

References

American Association of Colleges and Universities. (2000). *Greater expectations: The commitment to quality as a nation goes to college.* Washington, DC: American Association of Higher Education.

Anderson, L. W., Krathwohl, D. R., Airasian, P. W., Cruikshank, K. A., Mayer, R. E., Pintrich, P. R., Raths, J., & Wittrock, M. C. (Eds.) (2001). *A taxonomy for learning, teaching, and assessing: A revision of Bloom's taxonomy of educational objectives* (abridged ed.). New York: Longman.

Angelo, T. A., & Cross, K. P. (1993). *Classroom assessment techniques: A handbook for college teachers* (2nd ed.). San Francisco: Jossey-Bass.

Aronson, E., Stephan, C., Sikes, J., & Snapp, M. (1978). *The jigsaw classroom.* Beverly Hills, CA: Sage.

Bloom, B. S. (1956). *Taxonomy of educational objectives—The classification of educational goals: Handbook I—Cognitive domain.* NY: David McKay.

Bransford, J. D., Brown, A. L., & Cocking, R. R. (Eds.) (2000). *How people learn: Brain, mind, experience, and school.* Commission on Behavioral and Social Sciences and Education National Research Council. Washington, DC: National Academy.

Fantuzzo, J. W., Dimeff, L. A., & Fox, S. L. (1989). Reciprocal peer tutoring: A multimodal assessment of effectiveness with college students. *Teaching of Psychology, 16*(3), 133–135.

Fantuzzo, J. W., Riggio, R. E., Connelly, S., & Dimeff, L. A. (1989). Effects of reciprocal peer tutoring on academic achievement and psychological adjustment: A component analysis. *Journal of Educational Psychology, 81*(2), 173–177.

Fink, L. D. (2003). *Creating significant learning experiences: An integrated approach to designing college courses.* San Francisco: Jossey-Bass.

Jensen, E. (2000). *Brain-based learning* (rev. ed.). San Diego, CA: The Brain Store.

Kagan, S. (1989). *Cooperative learning resources for teachers.* San Capistrano, CA: Resources for Teachers.

Kagan, S. (2009). *Cooperative learning.* San Juan Capistrano, CA: Resources for Teachers.

King, A. (1990). Enhancing peer interaction and learning in the classroom through reciprocal questioning. *American Educational Research Journal, 27*(4), 664–687.

King, A. (1995, Winter). Guided peer questioning: A cooperative learning approach to critical thinking. *Cooperative Learning and College Teaching*, 5(2), pp. 15–19. Reprinted in J. L. Cooper, P. Robinson, & D. Ball (Eds.), *Small group instruction in higher education: Lessons from the past, visions of the future* (pp. 112–121). Stillwater, OK: New Forums.

Leamnson, R. (1999). *Thinking about teaching and learning: Developing habits of learning with first year college and university students.* Sterling, VA: Stylus.

McTighe, J. (1992). Graphic organizers: Collaborative links to better thinking. In N. Davidson & T. Worsham (Eds.), *Enhancing thinking through cooperative learning* (pp 182–197). New York: Teachers College Press.

Millis, B. J. (2009, Spring). Becoming an effective teaching using cooperative learning: A personal odyssey. *Peer Review, 11*(2), 17–21.

Millis, B. J., & Cottell, P. G. (1998). *Cooperative learning for higher education faculty.* Phoenix, AZ: American Council of Education/Oryx.

Rhem, J. (1995). Close-Up: Going deep. *The National Teaching & Learning Forum,* 5(1), 4.

Rogers, T. B., Kuiper, N. A., & Kirker, W. S. (1977). Self-reference and the encoding of personal information. *Journal of Personality and Social Psychology, 35,* 677–688.

Walvoord, B. E., & Anderson, V. J. (2010). *Effective grading: A tool for learning and assessment* (2nd ed.). San Francisco: Jossey-Bass.

Wiggins, G., & McTighe, J. (1998). *Understanding by design.* Alexandria, VA: Association for Supervision and Curriculum Development.

Zull, J. E. (2002). *The art of changing the brain: Enriching teaching by exploring the biology of learning.* Sterling, VA: Stylus.

Appendix A

GUIDING CRITICAL THINKING

Generic Questions	Specific Thinking Processes Induced
Explain why ____. (Explain how ____.)	analysis
What would happen if ____?	prediction / hypothesizing
What is the nature of ____?	analysis
What are the strengths and weaknesses of ____?	analysis / inferencing
What is the difference between ___ and ___?	comparison-contrast
Why is ___ happening?	analysis / inferencing
What is a new example of ____?	application
How could ____ be used to ____?	application
What are the implications of ____?	analysis / inferencing
What is ____ analogous to?	identification / creation of analogies and metaphors
How does ___ effect ____?	analysis of relationship (cause effect)
How does ___ tie in with what we learned before?	activation of prior knowledge
Why is ___ important?	analysis of significance
How are ____ and ____ similar?	comparison-contrast
How does ____ apply to everyday life?	application—to the real world
What is a counter-argument for ____?	rebuttal to argument

GUIDING CRITICAL THINKING (*continued*)

Generic Questions	Specific Thinking Processes Induced
What is the best ____, and why?	evaluation and provision of evidence
What is the solution to the problem of ____?	synthesis of ideas
Compare ____ and ____ with regard to.	comparison-contrast & evaluation based on criteria
What do you think causes ____? Why?	analysis of relationship (cause-effect)
Do you agree or disagree with this statement: ____?	evaluation and provision of evidence
What evidence is there to support your answer?	
What is another way to look at ____?	taking other perspectives
What does ____ mean?	comprehension
Describe ____ in your own words.	comprehension
Summarize ____ in your own words.	comprehension

King, 1995.

10

Implementing Cooperative Learning in Introductory Economics Courses

Mark H. Maier, KimMarie McGoldrick, and Scott Simkins

Despite the reported low use of cooperative learning strategies in economics relative to other disciplines, we believe that this pedagogy is particularly well-suited for economics instruction.[1] Because economics is both an empirical and a social science, common cooperative learning techniques, such as Think-Pair-Share, Send-a-Problem, Jigsaw, and Cooperative Controversy, are readily adaptable to economics content and concepts.

In addition, cooperative learning strategies can easily be used to extend a wide variety of teaching techniques that faculty members are already employing in their classrooms, including traditional lecture and discussion formats and more innovative pedagogies such as Just-in-Time Teaching, games, simulations, classroom experiments, and debates. In each case, integrating cooperative learning into existing teaching strategies provides the opportunity for enhanced student learning.

In this chapter, we emphasize cooperative learning examples for introductory economics courses because of their potential positive impact on undergraduate education. Salemi and Siegfried (1999) estimate that over 40% of all undergraduate students at 4-year colleges complete at least one economics course, most commonly at the introductory level. Further, we focus on in-class activities because these are most relevant to the largest number of introductory economics instructors. Within this framework, we provide a variety of examples to show how cooperative learning can be used to expand economists' pedagogic tool kits and enhance student learning in the economics classroom.

---

[1] Michael Watts and William E. Becker have conducted national surveys of economics instructors at 5-year intervals since 1995. In their most recent survey (Becker & Watts, 2008), the median proportion of class time dedicated to cooperative learning is reported at only 6%, far less than the frequency measured across other disciplines (Cooper & Mueck, 1990).

We begin by illustrating the use of the simplest form of cooperative learning—the Think-Pair-Share technique—and addressing the most common objections (as voiced by economists) associated with this pedagogy—loss of content coverage and the negative impact of "free riders." Next, we introduce more advanced cooperative learning structures, including (1) Send-a-Problem, (2) Jigsaw, and (3) Cooperative Controversy. Finally, we show how cooperative learning can be used in conjunction with a variety of innovative pedagogies that have already been implemented by some economics instructors. Throughout our discussion, we include brief examples to stimulate the reader to consider the wide range of potential adaptations of cooperative learning in introductory economics courses.

INTRODUCING COOPERATIVE LEARNING TO ECONOMICS INSTRUCTORS

Two common objections raised by economists regarding cooperative learning exercises include an expected loss of course content and concerns about "free riding" by students. Our experience suggests that economists' trepidation on both issues can be overcome when instructors understand the importance of building structure into cooperative learning exercises.

As others in this volume note, cooperative learning facilitates the greatest enhancements in learning—and addresses the previously noted concerns—when its structure fulfills four well-established criteria: (1) positive interdependence, (2) individual accountability, (3) equal participation, and (4) simultaneous interaction (Kagan, 2009; Millis & Cottell, 1998).

Content Coverage

Introductory economics courses at most institutions are characterized by their breadth of content and their shallowness of coverage. Although leading economic educators argue that students would be better served by courses that focus more deeply on a few core concepts (Hansen, Salemi, and Siegfried, 2002), there is little evidence that either economics textbooks or classroom instruction is moving in this direction. However, even in an environment characterized by a perceived need to cover expansive course content, cooperative learning can enhance student learning without a significant loss of content coverage.

Few learners are able to retain significant portions of a continual steam of new ideas in the absence of breaks or shifts in activity, an observation supported by considerable educational research (Nilson, 2003). Many economics instructors address this learning challenge by breaking up lectures using whole-class, teacher-directed discussion. Although this is a potential enhancement to traditional lecture methods, whole-class discussions relegate most students to a passive spectator role as a result of time constraints. In addition, whole-class discussions conducted in larger classes have been found to generate learning environments dominated by only a few students (Davis, 1993).

Cooperative learning provides an opportunity for all students to contribute ideas, critique arguments, and summarize concepts in a relatively short period, even in large auditorium-style classrooms. For example, the Think-Pair-Share technique—mentioned by virtually all the authors in this volume—can be used in the middle of a lecture to quickly involve all students in a brief problem-solving session or a discussion of a course concept. Because this technique requires equal participation by all students, it is more likely to actively engage the entire class in the learning process. The following Think-Pair-Share example illustrates both the efficiency and potential learning gains provided by this teaching pedagogy.

> After a lecture on sunk costs, the instructor raises the question: *You bought a ticket for a movie and now discover that you lost it. Should you buy a second ticket, or should you go home?* Students first consider their answer individually, and everyone votes by showing thumbs up (buy the ticket) or thumbs down (go home). After viewing the distribution of responses, students are given two minutes to pair and take turns explaining the reason for their answer to their partner. Students reconsider their answer based on this discussion, followed by a re-polling of the class. A small sample of students may be asked to share their reasoning with the class. Learning is reinforced by formally connecting their responses to the economic concept of sunk costs.

In practice, the Think-Pair-Share method is neither foolproof nor homogenous in its application. As Millis and Cottell (1998) note, instructors can enhance its effectiveness by allowing for sufficient individual think time (frequently neglected), by being intentional about how pairing occurs (so that students are required to vary the partner they work with), and by considering carefully the sharing process (rotating who initiates the sharing process and varying the sharing format so that it does not become stale).

The content of Think-Pair-Share questions can vary from Quick-Think questions—written on-the-fly in reaction to what is currently occurring in the classroom (Robinson and Cooper, chapter 7)—to more carefully scripted questions, each designed to gauge the level of student understanding. In the latter category, economists could mimic the practices of science education researchers by developing a set of multiple-choice concept test questions that address common student preconceptions or present material in new contexts, testing students for deeper understanding rather than a simple recall of the preceding lecture.[2] Overall, well-structured cooperative learning pedagogy allows instructors to provide students with a more effective learning environment without sacrificing content.

Free Riding

Economists are generally skeptical of group-based learning activities because of concerns about the free riding that occurs when students take advantage of others' contributions to the group without contributing in kind. Similarly, student resistance to cooperative learning is often based on prior experiences with peers who failed to contribute to group projects and were not held individually accountable.

Well-structured cooperative learning exercises that incorporate individual accountability and positive interdependence offer the best antidote to such negative learning experiences. For example, in Think-Pair-Share exercises student accountability is generated by randomly choosing one student from the pair to report out (pairs accountability) and by developing follow-up with individually completed writing assignments (individual accountability). Positive interdependence is integrated into the Think-Pair-Share technique through the partner-sharing process.

When we first introduce Think-Pair-Share exercises in our courses, we are careful to explain the benefits of both speaking and listening, reinforcing this process through the use of a time signal requiring the first student to offer his or her thoughts before allowing the second student to share. Over the course of a term, we find that students learn appropriate expectations for cooperative learning practices—if we initially are quite specific in our instructions and provide explicit explanations about why we use these techniques, even demonstrating with a sample group how the exercise is structured.

MORE STRUCTURED COOPERATIVE LEARNING TECHNIQUES

Although the integration of Think-Pair-Share exercises serves as a significant improvement over the passive lectures that dominate most economics classrooms, additional learning gains are likely to be achieved through the imple-

---

[2] See the Field-tested Learning Assessment Guide (FLAG) at http://www.flaguide.org/cat/contests/contests1.php for additional information about Concept Tests, including examples.

mentation of more complex structured cooperative learning exercises. In this section, we focus on three such exercises—Send-a-Problem, Jigsaw, and Cooperative Controversy—and provide examples of how they can be used effectively in introductory economics courses.

Because many students have grown accustomed to "chalk and talk" or "PowerPoint karaoke" teaching formats, they have learned to become passive learners. To successfully break students of this habit, more complex cooperative learning structures require careful preparation by the instructor, clear instructions for students, and the encouragement of positive group interactions.

In our classrooms, we assign students to base groups in which students work together for most, if not all, of the semester. Base groups provide many advantages, including introducing procedural efficiencies such as time saved in creating groups, building familiarity with group roles and tasks, and establishing group decision-making processes. Base groups also provide the opportunity to pay more careful attention to group composition, following the consensus among cooperative learning experts that three to five is an ideal group size and that heterogeneous groups are most successful.

In our experience, it is also important to place close friends in different groups. Other considerations in group formation, such as the mix of student skills, ethnicity, and personality, are best dealt with on a case-by-case basis. On occasion, it is helpful to create homogeneous groups, such as placing two very highly skilled students in the same group so that they can enhance each other's learning or pairing two women or two students from a similar minority or ethnic background so that they are not isolated (Barkley, Cross, & Major, 2005; Felder & Brent, 1996; Millis & Cottell, 1998.)

In addition, more complex cooperative learning tasks need to be appropriately structured. If, for example, the task can best be completed by one student or by breaking a project into separate tasks with no interdependence, there is little incentive for students to work cooperatively. Michaelsen, Fink, and Knight (1997) point out that, although most writing assignments are appropriately relegated to a single individual, problem-solving activities, which are common in economics, naturally lend themselves to cooperative learning exercises.

Research by mathematics educators Vidakovic (1997) and Martin (with Vidakovic, 2004) shows that groups are able to solve problems more accurately than individuals working alone. Even when one member is more skilled, the collective group is able to correct errors that remain unnoticed when the skilled problem solver works independently without explaining his or her procedure.

In economics, Maier (2003a) used tape recordings of group work to show that students assist one another in the learning process, resolving relatively minor barriers to understanding that are difficult to deal with in a full-class discussion because they are so varied and students are reluctant to articulate them. In small groups, economics students were quite good at discussing and correcting errors in vocabulary, historical events, mathematical procedures, and graphing techniques. These activities also strengthened students' problem-solving abilities.

Send-a-Problem

As a problem-solving discipline, effective economics instruction often relies on activities in which students construct and interpret diagrams or carry out mathematical computations. Research on learning (Bransford, Brown, & Cocking, 2000) suggests that this process is most effective when problems use varying contexts and when students explicitly think about their problem-solving methods.

The Send-a-Problem cooperative learning structure is especially well-suited for building these learning transfer skills. In this technique small groups solve problems in a sequential manner, passing problems from one small group to another, sometimes adding to a solution and sometimes analyzing previous groups' answers. The following three variations of the Send-a-Problem technique are particularly beneficial for introductory economics courses.

(1) Students Compare Answers or Ways of Solving a Provided Problem

In the most common Send-a-Problem application, the instructor distributes a unique problem to small groups (three to four students) to solve within a given time limit. At the end of the allotted time, members of each group place their solution to the problem in an envelope and pass the envelope to another group.

In each round, every group receives a problem its members have not yet seen; they proceed to generate a solution without looking at the previous groups' work contained in the envelope. The process repeats, typically for three or four cycles depending on the problem's complexity, generating multiple solutions in each envelope.

After passing the envelope one final time, members of each group evaluate the collection of solutions contained in the envelope they are holding. For example, students can be asked to compare and contrast the process that the students in each group used to answer the problem. Did they begin with relevant definitions? Were assumptions outlined? Was a graphical solution provided? In this final stage, students begin to think critically and metacognitively about the components and construction of a well-formulated answer, improving their preparation for similar exercises that are subsequently included on exams or other evaluative assessments.

The following example illustrates how the Send-a-Problem protocol could be used to investigate the concept of elasticity in a principles course.

> Small groups are presented with a problem in which a business or government must make a decision based on one of the following: price elasticity of demand, price elasticity of supply, cross price elasticity, or income elasticity. The problems are solved in four cycles, so that each group solves a problem involving each elasticity category. In the last (fifth) cycle, group members evaluate the answers in their envelope and the arguments made to support those decisions.

(2) Students Build on One Another's Answers to a Provided Problem

The Send-a-Problem technique can also be used as an iterative process with students initiating a solution and passing the incomplete solution to another group for a continuation of the process. For example, students can receive a problem that is already segmented into key components necessary for a well-formulated answer. In the first stage, groups work to identify and describe background information such as definitions and assumptions necessary for grounding the final solution. In the second stage, groups receive the initial groups' work evaluating background information and use it—if valid—to generate the first segment of the solution.

Ideally, problems have multiple components, so that the evaluation and solution process can be developed over several rounds. The following example illustrates how this sequential solution-building process can be used near the end of a macroeconomics principles course class.

> As a group you have 5 minutes to answer one component of the following problem. If you are the first group to work on this problem, you are required to complete the first stage of this exercise. Subsequent groups build off this answer until all components have been completed. When your answer is complete or time has been called, place your answer in the attached envelope.

Problem: The country of Econation is operating at full employment, but policy makers believe the current inflation rate of 10% is too high to be consistent with economic efficiency and long-term economic growth.

1. **First group**: Provide a graphical presentation (along with a brief explanation) of current economic conditions in Econation.

2. **Second group**: You have been charged with recommending a policy change to rectify the problem noted by policy makers. Provide a description of this change and a justification for using this as opposed to an alternative policy.

3. **Third group**: Show (and explain) this policy change using the graph completed by the first group.

As a follow-up question for groups that finish the exercise earlier than their peer groups, a "sponge" or "extension activity" is recommended for all group work (Millis & Cottell, 1998): Describe two drawbacks or problems associated with the policy change that you recommend.

(3) **Students Create Multiple Problems for Exchange and Solving**

One downside of instructor-created problems is the students' expectation that the instructor will ultimately provide the answers, reducing their motivation to engage fully in the exercise.

However, Send-a-Problem can be structured so that a student or group creates a problem to be solved by classmates. In our experience, student-created problems raise the level of classroom engagement significantly. When applied to simple concepts, this process requires students to individually create a problem that is passed to another student.

For more complex problems, small groups can create a problem for other groups to solve. In either case, providing criteria and guidance in the problem construction phase of this exercise is critical to ensure that the problem has a meaningful solution and requires the intended skill set. The following example illustrates this variation of the Send-a-Problem technique.

An individual student designates two sets of future incomes and an interest rate and sends this information to another student "accountant" to calculate present discounted value and determine which set of incomes is more valuable. The solution is passed back to the first student to check for correctness. If there is a disagreement regarding the answer, both students discuss the reasons for their decision.

Jigsaw

Jigsaws should be especially attractive to economists who are worried about free-riding behaviors because positive interdependence is built into the structure of the activity itself. The typical Jigsaw begins with individual students or groups developing expertise in one aspect of a problem. The full solution to the problem, however, can be achieved only after bringing together experts on each component of the problem—similar to the way in which a picture is revealed only when all pieces of a puzzle fit into place.

The inherently social nature of the Jigsaw may be especially important in economics because the nature of the discipline may encourage students to act more out of narrow short-term self-interest than in the interest of the group, even if such social behavior may be beneficial for everyone in the long run (Frank, Gilovich, & Regan, 1996). Jigsaw exercises can be used to help counteract these competitive tendencies because the activity simply cannot be completed by a student working alone; input from others is required to complete the activity. The following examples illustrate the importance of this interdependence in Jigsaw cooperative learning exercises.

(1) Pair Jigsaws Solving Mirror-Image Problems

Mirror-image problems are designed to enhance student understanding of economics concepts through examples that include parameters that can take opposing values. A student in each pair is given one version of a problem; the other student receives the opposite version. After solving their problems individually and developing expertise in a single version of the application, students compare answers and explain the impact of the parameter's value on the outcome of the problem.

For example, student pairs analyze the impact of increased immigrant labor by having one pair examine a scenario with an inelastic demand for labor; the other pair examines the same scenario under the condition of an elastic demand for labor. Students obtain a better understanding of the importance of elasticity of demand when one pair then compares results with the other. A similar format can be used to compare the impact of elastic versus inelastic demand (or supply) in the case of tax incidence or the minimum wage.[3]

---

[3] This example was created by Maya Federman, Department of Economics, Pitzer College. Used with permission.

(2) Three-Person Jigsaws Using Numerical Problems

Many numerical economics problems can be written as a Jigsaw in which each student does a separate calculation on one component of the entire problem. In this format, students first practice a series of calculations and then reinforce their understanding of the motivation for such calculations as they combine their solutions (demonstrating the interdependent nature of the problem) and work toward a final solution to the problem. Two examples follow:

> *Economies of scale.* To determine whether economies of scale are present, students must calculate cost values for different scales of operation. Instead of each student conducting a series of repetitive, time-consuming calculations associated with, say, three separate scales of production, students are divided into three groups and begin the exercise by focusing their efforts on calculating cost values associated with only one of the three scales of production. "Expert groups"—those students who calculated cost values for the same scale of production—first compare their answers for consistency before forming a triad with members of the other two scales of operation expert groups and comparing results. In this way, students learn to perform the necessary calculations without focusing solely on algebraic procedures, allowing them to develop greater confidence and facility in the use of economy of scale concepts.

> *Tax Simulation.* Similarly, a Jigsaw can be used to analyze results of a simple tax simulation. In this case, each student calculates the amount of a particular type of tax paid by individuals representing a single income group. Students next form groups, pooling results across income groups to compute the total tax incidence and evaluate the extent to which the total tax system is progressive or regressive.

Cooperative Controversy

As an "unsettled" science with political disputes underlying many core concepts, economics provides the opportunity for students to learn to deal with strong and internally consistent yet opposing arguments, an approach advocated by W. E. Becker (2007).

According to William Perry (1970), one of the most significant intellectual developments for college students is the shift from the need for a single correct answer to a position in which competing answers are tolerated and understood as logically consistent (Nelson, chapter 8).[4] Cooperative

---

[4] In economics, two recent examples include Borg and Borg (2001) and Knoedler and Underwood (2003).

learning structures help students with this transition by requiring students to articulate arguments about core concepts.

Cooperative Controversy (Smith, Matusovich, Meyers, and Mann, chapter 6) is a process that helps students identify and evaluate multiple perspectives on an issue. In introductory economics courses, such viewpoints arise in discussions regarding the impact of minimum wage legislation, trade restrictions, marginal tax rate increases, antitrust decisions, and macroeconomic policy decisions, among others.

By carefully choosing articles with opposing viewpoints, such as those provided in widely available "course readers" (Bonello and Lobo, 2008), and thoughtfully designing cooperative structures, instructors can generate a more thorough understanding of multiple perspectives on such issues.

The most common form of this exercise begins with students being randomly assigned to read an article covering one of the multiple perspectives. Each student is then assigned to a pair representing the same article and given the task of identifying key arguments associated with that perspective. Pairs then combine with another pair of students who were required to complete the same process for an article representing an alternative perspective.

First one side, then the other, summarizes the key arguments. As a group of four, students identify the strongest argument on each side of the debate, prepare an explanation of the criteria on which they based their decision, and report their findings to the class.

For example, students are asked to evaluate the implications for competitive markets of a proposed merger. Based on a set of readings from the business press that include market shares of the merging firms and their competitors, students use the Cooperative Controversy structure to identify arguments supporting or rejecting the merger.

Another useful variant of this technique encourages students with divergent viewpoints on economic issues to defend their positions using economic theory. For example, students position themselves along a continuum based on the strength of their agreement with a controversial topic, such as "The minimum wage should be increased to $12 per hour."

Students first pair with a student standing next to them (having a relatively similar strength of agreement) to practice their position on the issue. Then the line is split in two, and students with the strongest positions on either end match up with students in the middle (from the other half of the line).

These new pairs exchange views in a structured format, allowing for justification of existing positions. For particularly complex or emotionally laden issues, students may be asked to employ the Think-Pair-Share technique by first listening and then summarizing the other person's argument before responding with their own position.

In each of these variations, Cooperative Controversy provides a useful starting point for follow-up individual assignments in which students are asked to take a position on an issue and complete a related task.

USING COOPERATIVE LEARNING IN CONJUNCTION WITH OTHER TEACHING INNOVATIONS

Although economists use cooperative learning techniques less frequently than many other disciplines, during the past ten years economic instruction has broadened its use of other pedagogical innovations. In fact, economists are at the forefront in one pedagogical technique, classroom experiments, which has grown out of the theoretical field of experimental economics.

In this section, we consider how cooperative learning can be used to extend pedagogical innovations that are already being used by some economics faculty to improve student learning, including classroom experiments, simple games, simulations, surveys, Just-in-Time Teaching (JiTT), service-learning, and undergraduate research. Experience from other disciplines represented in this volume suggests that adding a cooperative learning component to these teaching strategies further improves student learning.

Experiments, Simple Games, and Simulations

(1) Experiments

Once a field relegated to the margins, experimental economics now influences high-level economic theory, as indicated by the awarding of the Nobel Prize in economics to Vernon Smith in 2002. Not surprisingly, the use of experiments in introductory economics classroom is supported by an extensive set of resources for economics instructors.[5]

Despite this increasing support for economics experiments as a teaching tool, the associated pedagogical research has focused on the development of experiments that address traditional economics concepts rather than on determining the best pedagogical processes for implementing economics experiments in the classroom. Durham, McKinnon, and Schulman (2007)

---

[5] See for example, Bergstrom and Miller (2000), the journal Experimental Economics, and Web resources at VECONLAB http://veconlab.econ.virginia.edu/admin.htm, EconPort http://www.econport.org/econport/request?page=web_home, and Aplia http://www.aplia.com/economics/ for a wide variety of supporting materials.

provide evidence that economic experiments increase student learning, interest in the discipline, and course enjoyment, but there is little research on the impact of experimental design or differences in student characteristics on learning.[6]

However, learning sciences research (Bransford, Brown, & Cocking, 2000) offers insights into ways that classroom experiments can be adapted to improve student learning. In particular, cooperative learning structures that incorporate more opportunities for active student reflection—on both the processes involved in the experiment and the expected outcomes—are likely to lead to deeper and more durable student learning.

Consider the double oral auction, the most commonly used economics experiment, which can be implemented using direct face-to-face interaction, classroom personal response systems (clickers), or online programs. The goal of double oral auction experiments is to illustrate the interaction of buyers and sellers in a market, the usual emergence of an equilibrium price, and the impact of various conditions (e.g., price floors or ceilings and asymmetric information) on market equilibria.

Although the results often are elegant, few experimental designs require students to interact in other than explicit and predetermined roles. In most cases, once the experiment itself concludes, so does the interaction. One way to enhance classroom experiments in economics is to consider the results of educational research on experiments in the physical sciences. This research (Crouch, Fagen, Callan, & Mazur, 2004) suggests that student learning increases when students are forced to make predictions about the experiment's outcome prior to the experiment and to reflect on how their predictions compared with actual outcomes after the experiment. Adding this component to economics classroom experiments takes little time or effort, yet it is likely to pay off in increased student learning.

For example, it is easy to add Think-Pair-Share exercises at various points during an economics experiment, initially asking students to use economic theory to predict what might happen during the experiment and later asking them to interpret experiment outcomes and to reflect on why they were generated.

When students are expected to participate in a number of related experiments (for example, the double oral auction with and without product quality differences), a version of the cooperative learning Jigsaw structure can be used, distributing different sample experiment outcomes to each student in a small group and asking them to match the outcome with the experiment.

---

[6] One notable exception regarding student characteristics is found in Emerson and Taylor (2007).

Individuals in these groups rely on work completed during each experiment (serving as their "expert group") in collaboration with others to enhance their understanding of the effect of economic conditions on experiment outcomes. The Jigsaw structure can also be used prior to the experiment as a method of generating predicted outcomes.

In most experiments, students must make strategic decisions while assuming the role of, for example, a consumer, a producer, an employer, or an employee. Here, too, student learning could be improved if the activity included the opportunity for students to discuss potential strategies prior to the experiment.

In some experiments, working in pairs enhances student learning because participants are required to explicitly identify, articulate, and choose between alternative strategies rather than simply putting one into practice. Thoughtful consideration of cooperative learning theory can enhance learning in these situations by ensuring adequate time for students to individually identify a strategy before reflecting on their partner's strategy choice.

Finally, cooperative learning exercises can be employed during the reporting out period of classroom experiments, providing an efficient process for gauging student comprehension. If the experiment is basic, simple techniques such as Think-Pair-Share may be appropriate.

However, in the case of more complicated experiments, cooperative learning groups can be used to sequentially improve on the analysis by employing the Send-a-Problem structure. Furthermore, when students have different roles in an experiment, groups can be formed to include representatives for each role, creating a Jigsaw in which subsequent analysis requires input from each perspective.

(2) Simple Games

Many economists promote "expert-like learning" in the classroom by having students link economic concepts to real-world examples. For instance, instructors may ask students to match alternative narratives describing reasons for unemployment with the concepts of frictional, seasonal, cyclical, and structural unemployment.

Such categorization techniques are a valuable precursor to more advanced critical and analytical thinking processes that characterize an "economic way of thinking." Games that employ this type of matching or categorization process can take advantage of the efficiencies of small groups while minimizing adverse outcomes (such as the free rider problem) by requiring a different student to take the lead in discussing each example. This process forces students to consider each example at greater length while also allowing each group member to participate.

Narrative cards, kept face down until used and then turned over by different students, provide an efficient process to facilitate focused attention and involve all group members. For example, in a national income and product accounting game, students turn over one card at time, each with one expenditure example, and must determine whether it is included in the accounts and, if so, under which category (Keenan & Maier, 2009). Similarly, board games, such as "Masters of the Economy" (Hansen, 2006), and other games in which decisions are made sequentially are more likely to have equal participation among group members if cards are drawn in turn.

(3) Simulations

Online and classroom-based economic simulations represent additional opportunities to incorporate cooperative learning. Cooperative learning structures can be used to develop group projects that require students to be more reflective in their decision process, explaining and defending choices in ways that ensure equal participation and accountability. For example, Simkins (1999) discusses the use in an introductory economics course of a simulated meeting of the Federal Open Market Committee (FOMC). In this simulation, students work in "expert groups" representing different regional Federal Reserve banks. Over a two week period, the student groups use current macroeconomic data to develop a monetary policy recommendation after conducting regional, national, and international economic analyses. All of the "expert groups" come together for an in-class simulated FOMC meeting where groups debate the merits of changing interest rates in the economy, based on their respective analyses. The simulation concludes with an interest rate vote and a debriefing.

Another macroeconomic simulation activity puts students in control of the federal budget process using an online budget simulator to increase or decrease values for a range of federal government spending categories while either staying within a predetermined budget or raising or lowering taxes to accommodate the spending changes. In this simulation, individuals can be required to make their own initial spending and taxation decisions, share their results with peers, and finally come to a group consensus on each decision with the results reported out to the class.

Alternatively, instructors can use computer-based simulations of the U.S. economy as the basis for a Jigsaw in which each student in a small group receives a policy change and economic impact pair that does not match. Students are challenged to determine whether the policy change leads to the listed economic impact and, if not, to determine the correct economic impact of the listed policy change.

For many simulation exercises, the reporting out process is an ideal time to inject a cooperative learning exercise. Reporting back to the larger class is an important component of any individual or group-completed exercise, but it can easily become tedious and repetitive. Although in some cases it may be sufficient for the instructor to simply offer comments on what he or she observed during group work—emphasizing concepts that all groups should know or common errors that were observed—formal cooperative learning structures offer an alternative approach for conducting the reporting out process. The following two examples, based on Millis and Cottell (1998), provide an illustration of this point.

> *Reporting Out—One Stay, the Rest Stray.* Using this structure, all but one group member rotate to another group for an explanation of that group's choices. A few rounds of rotating among the groups provides students with a sense of the wide range of potential outcomes associated with other group decisions; thus it is not necessary for every group to see every other group's work.
>
> Alternatively, one can provide students with the opportunity to practice explaining alternative choices and their associated reasoning as they reconvene in their original groups and share insights into the different choices other groups made (Millis & Cottell, 1998, p. 106).

> *Reporting Out—Poster Rotation.* This technique integrates visual components into the reporting out process. Groups display results on posters that are viewed in rotation by groups moving around the room from one poster to another. View-ing groups may be asked to either reflect on the presented outcomes—by answer-ing questions linked to the content of each poster—or to provide comments to other groups through the use of a comment section on the poster. Combining this with the One Stay, the Rest Stray technique allows students to practice explaining their visually represented answers (Millis and Cottell, 1998, pp. 108–109).

Surveys

Like classroom experiments, anonymous surveys are often used to gather information regarding student behaviors. Using their peers as survey sub-jects, students collect and analyze data related to variables such as willingness to purchase an item or provide labor services, along with demographic information such as levels of family income, gender, ethnicity, and age. Positive interdependence is inherent in the survey methodology because subsequent analysis depends on data contributions from all group members.

In addition, cooperative learning techniques can be used to assign roles to conduct the analysis and facilitate reporting out, reinforcing individual accountability and reducing the likelihood of free riders. Consider the two following examples of classroom surveys that can be used to reinforce basic microeconomic concepts.[7]

> *Labor Supply Curve.* Simulating the decision to work, group members generate and collect data associated with a survey on willingness to provide their labor at different wage rates. Applications that are contextually linked to students' environment, such as those associated with on-campus jobs, including tutoring or library book reshelving, provide realistic data. Aggregating the number of hours that students are willing to work over the range of wage rates generates a labor supply curve.

> *Price Elasticity of Demand.* The Jigsaw can also be used to collect data through the interview process. Requiring students in one group to interview students in a second group concerning the quantity of a good they would purchase at differing prices provides individual demand data.
>
> Using the Three Stay, One Stray method (Millis & Cottell, 1998) and moving between groups, a representative from each group can conduct interviews of members of another group about quantity of an item demanded at two different prices. Returning to their original group, students have multiple observations from which to construct the "market" demand curve and to generate estimates of the price elasticity of demand.

Just-in-Time Teaching

Just-in-Time Teaching (JiTT), originally developed by Novak, Gavrin, Christian, and Patterson (1999) for physics education, is a technique that allows both students and instructors to gauge understanding in a timely manner, prior to moving on to new material. To begin, students complete carefully constructed exercises focusing on material to be covered in the next class by a preassigned deadline a few hours prior to that class.

Students typically submit their answers digitally using course management systems such as Blackboard or Moodle. Once the answers have

---

[7] For additional examples, see Maier (2003b).

been submitted, instructors review students' JiTT responses and use them to organize and modify the upcoming classroom session in the hours leading up to the class—hence the "just-in-time" label. Selected student responses are projected in class (with identifying names removed) at the start of class and are used to develop in-class cooperative learning exercises.[8]

Adapting JiTT for use in economics, Simkins and Maier (2004) find that students come to class better prepared and gain more from each class session as a result of completing JiTT exercises, leading to better performance on exams. In addition, students receive immediate feedback on their understanding of concepts covered in the JiTT exercises, providing a "teachable moment" that is absent with traditional homework assignments or quizzes, which provide feedback only after a (sometimes considerable) lag.

At the same time, instructors also receive valuable feedback that allows them to alter their instructional plans and thus make in-class teaching and learning more effective. Because JiTT exercises are completed between classes, instructors can uncover students' misunderstandings of economic concepts prior to class and design classroom activities to overcome these misunderstandings while the concepts are still fresh in students' minds.

JiTT exercises can be combined with cooperative learning in several ways using excerpts from students' submissions as the basis for in-class exercises. Consider the following JiTT question:

> Describe the role of the price of a good in moving a competitive market to equilibrium if there is currently a shortage in this market. To fully answer this question, consider the following two questions: (1) What will happen to the price of the good in this case? Why? (2) How does the change in the price of a good provide an incentive for demanders and suppliers to change their behavior in this situation, thus bringing the market to equilibrium? Explain.

The following (unedited) responses were selected for presentation in class because they represented clusters of common student errors found in the JiTT submissions.

> Response 1: Whenever a good is sold at a low price, the demand for that good is higher than the supply; there will be a shortage in the market. The price of the

---

[8] For more information about the use of JiTT pedagogy, see Simkins and Maier (2010).

good will decrease because of the shortage in the market. This is because the quantity demanded decreases; therefore the price of the good would decrease.

Response 2: The shortage of a good, if viewed on a supply and demand model, would cause the supply curve to shift to the left.

Response 3: The price of the good is now higher because there is not enough of the good supplied to keep the price where it was before the shortage. Because the price has changed, less of the good will be bought by demanders. Suppliers of the good will try to put more of the good into the market, and some suppliers who can supply this good may enter the market and increase the supply of the good. The end result should be for the supply curve to shift back to the right and the market to be back at equilibrium.

In this case, cooperative learning groups could determine whether any of the responses accurately describe the process of moving to equilibrium in competitive markets and, if not, describe what is incorrect about the reasoning included in the response. A Send-a-Problem approach could be used to generate multiple groups' feedback on each of the individual responses, or Round-Robin (Barkley, Cross, & Major, 2005) and Think-Pair-Share exercises could be used to generate a list of suggested modifications to the responses that could be reported out to the class.

If a JiTT exercise generates several points of view, the submissions can be used as the basis of a Jigsaw in which "expert" groups each evaluate submissions associated with one viewpoint. Then, small groups comprising one representative from each expert group meet to compare answers. This technique forms the basis for the following example.

> In preparation for a class covering tax incidence, the JiTT exercise asks students to prepare an argument in favor of raising or lowering one U.S. tax. In the following class session, students leave their base group and join an expert group for one tax type. The expert groups analyze all student submissions relevant to that tax, looking at arguments in favor of raising the tax and those in favor of lowering the tax. After mastering their understanding of the associated arguments, students rejoin their base groups to report on their expert group discussion and determine which taxes the base group agrees should be increased or decreased.

Service-Learning

Service-learning is a method of experiential learning that links the classroom with the local community. It requires students to spend time in volunteer service and relate their experiences to the educational theories that they learn in the classroom. As McGoldrick and Ziegert (2002) show, the use of service-learning is particularly applicable to economics instruction.

Demonstration of learning associated with such experiences relies heavily on a student's ability to integrate his or her experiences with course material through structured reflection. The Think-Pair-Share technique is especially useful in facilitating this process because it requires students to demonstrate learning to their partners by describing applications of economic theory to their own practical experiences. This type of learning is further enhanced when the student takes the role of reflective listener, ultimately challenging the descriptions of learning provided by his or her partner.

Undergraduate Research

Think-Pair-Share exercises can also be applied to more traditional course work such as the development of research projects. Students participating in undergraduate research experiences, for example, can be motivated to refine the focus of their thesis and the extent to which evidence supports their conclusions through a series of Think-Pair-Share exercises.

One of the most difficult steps in developing a viable research project is the construction of an effective research question. The Think-Pair-Share technique enhances this component of the project because it requires each student to justify his or her question to a partner and evaluate the justification of the partner's research question. The following example illustrates how this process can be used to encourage student engagement in the research question development stage.

> Students prepare for this in-class exercise by reviewing the characteristics of an effective economic research question (Greenlaw, 2006): problem-oriented, analytical rather than descriptive, interesting and significant, amenable to economic analysis, and feasible, given time and resources.
>
> In addition, students are required to submit a "class ticket" to enter the classroom and participate in the exercise. The "ticket" is a document containing three potential research questions and their associated justifications based on each characteristic of an effective research question. In class, students pair, and the first student, choosing his or her best question, presents a justification. The task of the reflective student is to offer suggestions for modifications to the original question that bring it more in line with the provided justification (such as narrowing the focus to enhance the feasibility of the question) or provide insight for stronger justifications (such as an alternative context that might appeal to other interest groups).

This technique can be repeated two or three times, rotating student pairs, providing additional insights that are used when students revise their questions and justifications, turning in both the original and revised versions in the subsequent class period.

SUMMARY

The chapters in this volume clearly illustrate that the benefits of cooperative learning extend across disciplines, course levels, institutions, instructors, and students. As noted in the introduction to this chapter, we believe that cooperative learning strategies for classroom use are particularly well-suited for introductory economics courses, both because of the nature of the discipline—which emphasizes a wide variety of empirical, theoretical, graphical, and analytical reasoning skills—and because of the flexibility of the pedagogy, which allows it to be adopted with traditional lecture methods, as well as adapted for use with more innovative teaching strategies.

In each of these cases, cooperative learning offers structures that encourage students to verbalize or write about their learning process. This deliberate focus on students' metacognition is strongly supported by learning theory.

Perhaps most important, well-designed cooperative learning activities have the potential to address directly the issues of free riding and course coverage that economics instructors often are concerned about. The examples in this chapter illustrate how student learning can be enhanced using cooperative learning. These cooperative activities can easily be integrated into traditional introductory economics classroom settings with little sacrifice of time or content.

These examples are intended to provide a "quick start" for economics instructors who may now be convinced to begin adding cooperative learning activities in their courses. The wide range of cooperative learning strategies documented here means they can be adopted incrementally, beginning with the Think-Pair-Share technique. When instructors feel ready, they can introduce more complex structures with teams of students by using approaches such as Send-a-Problem, Jigsaw, and Cooperative Controversy.

We hope that this chapter offers a framework for instructors wishing to expand their use of small group work, including those wishing to adapt specific cooperative learning structures for use with other active-student learning techniques that they may already use.

References

Barkley, E. F., Cross, K. P., & Major, C. H. (2005). *Collaborative learning techniques: A handbook for college faculty*. San Francisco: Jossey-Bass.

Becker, W. E. (2007). Quit lying and address the controversies: There are no dogmata, laws, rules or standards in the science of economics. *American Economist, 51*(1), 3–14.

Becker, W. E., & Watts, M. (2008). A little more than chalk and talk: Results from a third national survey of teaching methods in undergraduate economics courses. *Journal of Economic Education, 39*(3), 273–286.

Bergstrom, T. C., & Miller, J. H. (2000). *Experiments with economic principles: Microeconomics*. Boston: McGraw-Hill.

Bonello, F. J., & Lobo, I. (2008). *Taking sides. Clashing views on economic issues.* Dubuque, IA: McGraw-Hill/Contemporary Learning Series.

Borg, J. R., & Borg, M. O. (2001). Teaching critical thinking in interdisciplinary economics courses. *College Teaching, 49*, 20–25.

Bransford, J., Brown, A. L., & Cocking, R. R. (2000). *How people learn: Brain, mind, experience, and school.* Washington, DC: National Academy.

Cooper, J. L., & Mueck, R. (1990). Student involvement in learning: Cooperative learning and college instruction. *The Journal on Excellence in College Teaching, 1*(1), 68–76.

Crouch, C. H., Fagen, A. P., Callan, J. P., & Mazur, E. (2004). Classroom demonstrations: Learning tools or entertainment? *American Journal of Physics, 72*, 835–838.

Davis, B. G. (1993). *Tools for teaching*. San Francisco: Jossey-Bass.

Durham, Y., McKinnon, T., & Schulman, C. (2007). Classroom experiments: Not just fun and games. *Economic Inquiry, 45*(1), 162–178.

Emerson, T. L. N., & Taylor, B. A. (2007). Interactions between personality type and the experimental methods. *Journal of Economic Education, 38*(1), 18–35.

Felder, R. M., & Brent, R. (1996). Navigating the bumpy road to student-centered instruction. Retrieved February 3, 2010, from http://www4.ncsu.edu/unity/lockers/users/f/felder/public/Papers/Resist.html.

Frank, R. H., Gilovich, T. D., & Regan, D. T. (1996). Do economists make bad citizens? *Journal of Economic Perspectives, 10*(1), 187–192.

Greenlaw, S. A. (2006). *Doing economics: A guide to understanding and carrying out economic research*. Boston: Houghton Mifflin.

Hansen, M. E. (2006). Masters of the economy. Retrieved March 9, 2010, http://academic2.american.edu/~mhansen/MastersGame.

Hansen, W. L., Salemi, M. K., & Siegfried, J. J. (2002). Use it or lose it: Teaching literacy in the economics principles course. *American Economic Review, 92*, 463–472.

Kagan, S. (2009). *Cooperative learning*. San Juan Capistrano, CA: Resources for Teachers.

Keenan, D., & Maier, M. (2009). *Economics live! Learning economics the collaborative way*. New York: McGraw-Hill.

Knoedler, J. T., & Underwood, D. A. (2003). Teaching the principles of economics: A proposal for a multi-paradigmatic approach. *Journal of Economic Issues, 37*, 697–726.

Maier, M. (2003a). You can learn a lot by listening. *National Teaching and Learning Forum, 12*(2), 10–11.

Maier, M. (2003b). Surveys and cooperative learning: Using student experiences as the basis for small-group work. In J. L. Cooper, P. Robinson & D. Ball (Eds.), *Small group instruction in higher education: Lessons from the past, visions of the future* (pp. 311–320). Stillwater, OK: New Forums.

McGoldrick, K., & Ziegert, A. L. (2002). *Putting the invisible hand to work: Concepts and models for service learning in economics.* Ann Arbor: University of Michigan Press.

Michaelsen, L. K., Fink, L. D., & Knight, A. (1997). Designing effective group activities: Lessons for classroom teaching and faculty development. In D. DeZure (Ed.), *To improve the academy: Resources for faculty, instructional and organizational development* (pp. 373–398). Stillwater, OK: New Forums.

Millis, B. J., & Cottell, P. G. (1998). *Cooperative learning for higher education faculty.* Phoenix, AZ.: American Council of Education/Oryx.

Nilson, L. B. (2003). *Teaching at its best: A research-based resource for college instructors* (2nd ed.). Boston, MA: Anker.

Novak, G., Gavrin, A., Christian, W., & Patterson, E. (1999). *Just-in-time teaching: Blending active learning with web technology.* Upper Saddle River, NJ: Prentice Hall.

Perry, W. G., Jr. (1970). *Forms of intellectual and ethical development in the college years: A scheme.* NY: Holt, Rinehart and Winston.

Salemi, M. K., & Siegfried, J. J. (1999). The state of economic education. *American Economic Review, 89*(2), 355–361.

Simkins, S. P. (1999). Promoting active student learning using the world wide web in economics courses. *Journal of Economic Education, 30*(3), 278–291.

Simkins, S. P., & Maier, M. (2004). Using just-in-time teaching techniques in the principles of economics course. *Social Science Computer Review, 22*(4), 444–456.

Simkins, S. P., & Maier, M. (2010). *Just-in-time teaching: Across the disciplines, across the academy.* New pedagogies and practices for teaching in higher education series. Sterling, VA: Stylus.

Vidakovic, D. (1997). Learning the concept of inverse functions in a group versus individual environment. In E. Dubinsky, D. M. Mathews, & B. E. Reynolds (Eds.), *Readings in cooperative learning for undergraduate mathematics* (pp. 173–195). Washington, DC: Math Association of America.

Vidakovic, D., & Martin, W. O. (2004). Small-group searches for mathematical proofs and individual reconstructions of mathematical concepts. *The Journal of Mathematical Behavior, 23*(4), 465–492.

11

Cooperative Learning in Geological Sciences

Edward Nuhfer

Unique aspects of the geological sciences affect cooperative learning, the focus of this chapter. Geology curricula provide boundless opportunities for group approaches to learning. In fact, small group learning may be the only effective way to learn some of the content of this science.

To learn in-depth conceptual designs of cooperative learning exercises from specialists, the reader should obtain the work of Johnson, Johnson, and Smith (2006); Millis and Cottell (1998); or Cooper, Robinson, and Ball (2003) and do a thorough cover-to-cover read before picking any exercise crafted by another party. Rather than duplicate any of these resources, this chapter seeks to show the benefits of using cooperative learning in geoscience courses as part of lesson design, course design, and extending personal teaching philosophies.

SCIENTIFIC METHOD OF MULTIPLE WORKING HYPOTHESES (HISTORICAL METHOD OF SCIENCE)

Geology contributed a cornerstone to science in the scientific method of multiple working hypotheses (Chamberlin, 1897)—a method that the late Stephen Jay Gould often emphasized as the method of historical sciences. This historical method tests scientific hypotheses that are either impossible or inappropriate to test through controlled experiments.

Textbooks that state that science only tests hypotheses through controlled experiments contribute to the science illiteracy that science professors try to eradicate. If science produced only knowledge that was confirmable by controlled experiments, we would know nothing about evolution, the history of life on Earth, past extinction events, paleoclimates, plate tectonics, age of the Earth, or any other aspect of deep time. Most environmental science and field biology would not exist.

The historical method uses the growing body of knowledge that comes mainly from field investigations to deduce which of several competing hypotheses best explains observed phenomena. The body of knowledge grows slowly through the efforts of hundreds, perhaps thousands, of generally forgotten workers who produced a map here, a paper there, and an occasional summary document. Eventually, sufficient cumulative knowledge allows scientists to discard hypotheses that prove untenable, leaving standing the hypothesis that best explains phenomena.

The historical method of science excels in detecting natural changes and reconstructing in detail when and how changes occurred. Employing the historical method requires use of evidence, the scientific framework of reasoning, and evaluative decisions. Employing the method on actual problems provides a special experience in the kind of practice that moves students toward higher-level thinking. Developing skill in using available evidence to decide which among several competing hypotheses best explains phenomena offers a learning challenge that is ideally met through peer discussions and structured cooperative learning.

This method is also pertinent to this book because deducing whether students learn better in a cooperative environment than through a standard lecture format offers competing hypotheses. The problem is analogous to deducing which depositional environments produce particular sedimentary rocks. Likewise, deducing whether students' pertinent knowledge and skills changed during a college course is similar to deducing whether climate changes have occurred during the past ten thousand years.

Researchers (Bloom, 1984; Hake, 1998; Springer, Stanne, & Donovan, 1999) examined large numbers of students who were exposed to many teachers and both pedagogies to deduce whether one had a closer association with successful learning. All concluded that cooperative interactions more effectively supported learning success than did standard lectures.

Becker (2004) criticized these and similar studies, both for their design and for the numerical methods employed to analyze and present data. He suggested that cooperative interaction might not generally be more effective in support of learning success than standard lecturing. Becker's criticisms, even if legitimate, constitute neither a test of a competing hypothesis nor an explanation of the evidence available.

A strong competing hypothesis would explain how alternate research design or different numerical analyses in the studies criticized could likely produce opposite conclusions. It would also explain how researchers with long experience, operating independently, and using large data sets could all deduce a similar positive association between interactive engagements and successful learning.

Neuroscience (summarized in practical terms as it applies to college teaching by Leamnson, 1999) offers pertinent evidence. Learning occurs by the formation and stabilization of synaptic connections. A pedagogy that increases such connections by enlisting many areas of the brain should surpass a pedagogy that enlists fewer. Interactive engagement enlists all of the brain involved during attending lecture, plus additional parts of the brain involved in speaking, arguing, and listening to different viewpoints.

Thus, a positive association between interactive engagement and learning success does seem expected from the consideration of learning as the development of synaptic networks. A competing hypothesis must either gain comparable support from neuroscience research or refute the biological explanation for the basis of learning.

When phenomena that we seek to understand are amenable to study by a controlled experiment, the method of replicable experiments is the correct choice. The problem with using controlled experiments to explain some real-world phenomenon is that after one does any controlled experiment, the inevitable collateral hypothesis arises: that the conclusions made based on the results of the controlled experiment can be safely extrapolated to explain the complex real world.

The historical method employing field data taken from the real world offers the only appropriate way to test such collateral hypotheses. Geology is replete with examples in which field data that contradicted explanations and predictions generated from well-designed, controlled experiments eventually led to understanding. Someone who understands the function of the scientific method of multiple working hypotheses realizes why knowledge accumulated from disparate studies done in actual classroom conditions, although imperfect, is essential. It is equivalent to the field data of geology.

From data collected under classroom conditions, one dominant hypothesis emerges: classes that employ interactive methods are generally more effective at producing learning than classes that employ conventional lecture. It seems to have better evidence and supporting explanations than its converse hypothesis. For this reason, I employ interactive engagements and cooperative methods in my classes.

GEOLOGY, GEOLOGISTS, AND COOPERATION

Geology is a science of (1) materials—mostly rocks, minerals, water, and air; (2) energy-driven processes such as landslides, weathering, erosion, and volcanoes, through which materials are formed, altered, and moved; and (3) changes through time. This last concept, which is the hallmark of geology, involves conceptual thinking about ages, order of events, patterns, frequencies, rates, magnitudes, and duration of events.

Geology tends to attract people who love the outdoors, remote areas, and lots of space from crowds. Geologists constitute a strange hybridization of rugged individual and scientific geek. They are unusually independent thinkers and rarely joiners. Their professional fragmentation reflects this: geological societies are scattered according to specialty interests, some of which duplicate one another across two or more geological societies.

If geologists ever envied the benefits afforded by a centralized organization that chemists enjoy in the American Chemical Society (Shadle, chapter 3), they never envied it enough to create such an organization. It's so unclear where geology ends and related disciplines begin that "geoscience" now replaces "geology" in some circles in order to be more inclusive. After 1995, *The Journal of Geological Education* became *The Journal of Geoscience Education.*

In spite of the independent nature of geologists, geology usually ends up being the most cooperative of all the natural sciences on a campus. Geology departments have traditions of intense interaction beyond classrooms between student majors and professors. Most have active geology student clubs, and undergraduates routinely participate in geology professors' research. These tendencies were common decades before higher education embraced "undergraduate research."

The tradition of cooperation springs from geology's origin as a field science. This science was a hazardous profession before the era of two-way radios, global positioning satellite (GPS) units, helicopters, detailed maps, aerial photos, and antibiotics. Rather than having a map to follow, early geologists were usually the mapmakers.

Early mapping equipment required a minimum of two people to operate. For safety and labor, fieldwork required teams of people. Creating new field knowledge thus was a cooperative learning experience, and classroom lectures alone could not provide the skills required for such work.

Although academic geologists practiced cooperative learning, they weren't necessarily doing it reflectively or investigating its value. Academic geologists' sophisticated thinking about cooperative learning started about 1991, when the Johnson brothers and Karl Smith produced their first edition of *Active Learning: Cooperation in the College Classroom.* This book spoke easily to geologists and challenged professors to see potential uses of cooperation that they had not previously considered. That book quickly became cited in posters and theme sessions sponsored by the rapidly growing education division at the annual meetings of the Geological Society of America.

Despite increased penetration of active learning methods into geosciences, Macdonald, Manduca, Mogk, and Tewksbury (2005) showed that lecture with discussion remains the prevalent teaching method used in geology. Courses that are dominantly cooperative, although growing, are rare. I suggest three reasons for this:

1. Since 1991, teaching loads, research demands, and service loads increased in most schools (Gappa, Austin, & Trice, 2007; Milem, Berger, & Dey, 2000). Because preparing a lecture requires less time and less creativity than designing a cooperative learning experience, increased loads drive professors toward lecturing.

2. Student ratings—now the most important factor in retention and reward for teaching—rely on established rating forms that arose from research on lecture-based classes. These forms tend to perpetuate teacher-centered lecture modalities through items such as "The teacher was well prepared for each day's lecture" or "The presentation of the material is well organized" (Feldman 2007). By preferentially rewarding teacher-centered instruction, schools unintentionally discourage learner-centered pedagogies.

3. Students who expect to have a lecture-based experience often react so negatively when their experience in class conflicts with their preconceptions about learning that professors become intimidated and return to lecturing (Rhem, 2006; Thorn, 2003).

Nevertheless, most instructors who discovered the benefits that cooperative methods produce in learning content and developing professional skills (Smith, Matusovich, Meyers, and Mann, chapter 6) introduced some cooperative learning into their geology classes.

Professors eventually learned to reduce student resistance to these unfamiliar methods by introducing cooperative learning in the syllabus and employing cooperative methods on the first day of class. A short note in the syllabus provides the needed advance notice: "The course will use many learning approaches. We'll use visual aids, cooperative work, writing, and short projects done in class with fellow students."

The instructor who intends to teach by using interactive engagements should emphasize the "cooperative work" phrase in the syllabus and then employ an interactive learning exercise on the opening day of class. One such exercise, "The Unique Earth," follows.

Example 1. The Unique Earth—Opening Day of Class in Introductory Courses

Introductory courses overwhelmingly serve non-geology majors. Even though students' prior exposure to the subject varies greatly, according to the status and quality of each state's K–12 earth science program, most students have conceptual ideas about the physical world that arise from commonsense explanations that don't accurately represent reality (Kalman, 2008; Wolpert, 1992).

Preconceptions about science also come with preconceptions about learning it. Students' ideas about good learning experiences don't generally reflect what research reveals as good practices (Feldman, 1989).

Many science instructors wonder: "How do I connect initially with students who know nothing about my subject?" It's helpful to be aware of the power of affect (Nuhfer, 2008a) and to realize that feelings of desire to learn must precede all decisions to learn. Fear or anxiety (Panitz, chapter 4) reduce the desire to learn.

Like Nelson (chapter 8), I've found the work of Perry (1999) to be very helpful in selecting pedagogy, especially when one becomes aware of the affective levels (Krathwohl, Bloom, & Masia, 1964) that accompany the Perry stages (Nuhfer, 2008b). Most students in introductory courses operate at Perry stages 2 and 3. These are the stages when students become suspicious of authority and seek to differentiate themselves from it. They are willing to learn, but they prefer the company of students of about the same or similar stage.

Many learn more easily from one another than from a professor. We can take advantage of this quality and design classes with cooperative activities that maximize students' learning from one another. A good rule to success with introductory-level courses is to connect first with students' affect through a cooperative exercise.

In an introductory geoscience course, it is a safe bet that young adults relish the beauty of their home planet. This affinity offers an opportunity to promote their learning through their caring. "Brainstorming Poster" conveys on the first day: (1) "This is going to be a topic we do care about," and (2) "We will learn together."

The instructor enters the room early and places large poster-sized Post-it® sticky notes on wall areas around the room—about one poster per six or eight students, with one colored marker at each poster. A single question begins the *Unique Earth* exercise: "How is Earth unique and unlike any other place we know about in the universe?" The instructor can use a few prompts to convey how other places in the universe are different, such as projecting images of other planets, the solar system, and Earth seen from space.

One prompt might be: "You left home this morning in a coat or jacket. What was the temperature? What range of temperatures can you live in without that coat? What is the range of temperatures on this planet? Consider the wider universe. What are the ranges of temperatures there? Now, we are going to brainstorm answers to our original question about how Earth is unique and unlike any other place we know."

Next, the instructor gives some quick directions such as, "Get up from your desks and gather in groups of six or eight around each poster. Introduce yourselves to one another, and pick a person with good handwriting as a recorder. In the next ten minutes, your group is to record as many unique aspects of Earth as you can think of. Remember, you have one entry already—Earth's temperature range is unique. If it were outside this range, we almost certainly would not be here today talking geology. What other unique attributes of Earth can you think of?"

A nice PowerPoint slide of our beautiful blue planet seen from satellite orbit remains on the screen as a prompt.

Soon, the room buzzes with ideas, as the instructor moves among groups, listening and giving a prompt here and there. Common things start to appear on the posters: temperature, water, life, an atmosphere, gravity, oxygen, ozone, people, oceans, magnetic field, continents, pollution, seasons, a moon, the sun.

At the end of about ten minutes, students return to their chairs, and the instructor starts with a bit of reflection: "Let's see a show of hands: How many of you obtained a new insight from your group—one you probably would not have thought of if you had to make this list on your own?" Nearly all hands go up. At this point, the instructor can talk a minute—maybe two at most—about how the power of group discussion helps us learn quickly what would take us much longer to achieve alone.

The instructor next chooses a topic from one poster, then another. At each point, the instructor considers aloud: "I wonder . . . what if this one attribute were different? We have a unique atmosphere; why this atmosphere? What does gravity have to do with this; what does our planet's size have to do with this? What if our planet's size (mass) was only half its present size? How might this change our odds of being here today?"

Another poster may list "seasons," "day and night," and "magnetic field." The instructor can posit: "What if all else was the same, and our planet didn't spin at a rate of once in 24 hours? Suppose it spun at a rate of once every hour or once every year? Would we still be here?" Another question might be "What might be different for us, if Earth didn't have a magnetic field?"

The point of Brainstorming Poster is to have students join the instructor in a spirit of mutual discovery, rather than as individual students answering an instructor's question. The group begins to reflect together on the question "What if that one characteristic were different?"

In a short time, students realize that their group-based discussions led them to identify conditions that defy insurmountable odds in coming together in one place. The planet has to be just the right size, just the right distance from just the right kind of star, and spinning at just the right speed and at an inclination. The temperature range must allow water to cycle in its three states.

A long and unique history was necessary to make the planet habitable for human beings. Students begin to realize that the odds of moving to another planet, should we degrade this one, are impossibly small—there likely isn't another planet like our own. Understanding the Earth in ways that encourage us to value it and care for it is a serious matter of survival for modern humanity. This is more than just an esoteric learning exercise.

Appreciation occurs when students reflect upon the result of pooling their existing knowledge with that of others. A capstone exercise occurs when each individual creates and submits his or her own list of ten ways in which the Earth is unique.

Brainstorming Poster portrays cooperative learning as a valid way to learn and gain understanding. Students are eager to follow an unconventional pedagogy when they understand its relevance and its value.

REFLECTIONS ON COOPERATIVE LEARNING RELATED TO FIRST-DAY-OF-CLASS COOPERATIVE EXERCISES

Like students, instructors, too, need to reflect on our teaching practices. Why do we choose to teach as we do? Mastering several congruent pedagogies—ones that research show to be promising—offers choices. Cooperative learning is a well-researched approach to learning; simple cooperative exercises in science classes increase learning in science courses by about one-half standard deviation (Springer, Stanne, & Donovan, 1999) beyond the usual lecture and discussion methods.

Instructors need a very good plan for first day of class because the tenor we set there will be what students expect to continue all term. Students may not know how to work well together, initially, to do a learning exercise that we design. We have to enlist their interest and guide them through unfamiliar learning exercises.

This means we need to start their "learning how to learn" in the same way that we start their learning a new discipline: start small, start simple, and strive to leave no person behind. This focus must continue throughout the term, as we introduce additional cooperative learning exercises such as the examples that follow.

Example 2. Opportunistic Cooperative Learning: Geological Materials

To find opportunities to match content learning with a cooperative learning strategy, instructors must look at content learning that actually requires students to take an action and do something. Identifying rocks and minerals with skill is an act that requires an evaluative decision. Students must overcome their conditioned propensity to memorize what specimen samples look like because that tactic limits their development of required skills. Instead, students need to reflect on *why* they assign a particular name to a material; they must know the basis for their judgment that leads to their decision.

Assigning names involves a complex process of systematically looking for a few diagnostic properties and using these to assign a correct name based upon systematic frameworks of classification. Many properties needed to assign a name are subtle. Gaining the ability to see these subtle properties is a learning experience that is tailor-made for students teaching other students. When one student in a group fails to see the property, another usually sees it and shares his or her insights with the rest of the group.

In freshman laboratories, the initial sites for students' introduction to materials identification, the lab kits consist of boxes with about twenty different specimens. Because only one lab kit is often available for every two to four students, it isn't surprising that this scarcity prompted some of the early reported uses of structured cooperative learning in geology (Constantopoulos, 1994).

Indeed, sharing kits and working together result in a better learning arrangement than if each student had his or her own laboratory kit. Students in groups can help one another find the subtle properties. When students see, for example, the nature of the cleavage, fabric, or the grain size, they can teach those properties to other students.

Further, the students can monitor one another by asking individuals to explain why they assigned a particular name to a specimen. In informal cooperative learning, short games provide valuable, motivating practice—learning experiences that can place the knowledge required for specimen identification into long-term memory.

Example 3. Rock and Mineral Bingo

At the start, the instructor guides students to identify one specimen at a time from their kits, using cues such as "Now, pick up the pyrite specimen from your kits," with the stipulation that anyone from the group must be able to explain to class members why the group assigned that identification name.

The instructor allows time for peer coaching and physical testing of diagnostic properties such as luster, hardness, and streak (color of the powdered mineral shown by scratching the mineral across an unglazed porcelain plate called a "streak plate" by geologists), until every group member is ideally prepared to respond.

The instructor then calls on random members from each group to explain the "why" for each specimen. Once all specimens are out of the box, the instructor has the group mix the specimens around on the table and then initiates a type of Bingo game. The instructor calls out a name such as "orthoclase" or "arkose." The student team must respond by correctly identifying the specimen, agreeing why they picked up that particular specimen, and return it to the box. This proceeds at a guided slow pace until all specimens are back in the box in their proper places and peer coaching has occurred.

Next, the game becomes more challenging. Groups exchange rock and mineral boxes and immediately pour the specimens onto the table and mix them. Each group now has a different set, and individuals cannot rely on remembering what single specimens look like. The pace picks up as the instructor calls out the name of a substance but waits only so long as he or she sees the first student group agree on the properties through which they selected that specimen and return that specimen to the box.

The instructor immediately calls out the name of another specimen, and so on. The first group to return its correctly identified specimens to the box wins. If this approach sounds a bit harsh for groups that come in last, the activity conveys a message about the level of proficiency that one must obtain to acquire permanent learning in the field of geology. Students come to realize not only that they must gain the ability to identify material, but also that they must be able to make the identification quickly and confidently.

Following this relatively low-stakes competition, a more complex drill can ensue. Two groups of students pour the contents of their two boxes together on a table and mix up the specimens. Now teams of four to eight compete to identify the specimens correctly, as fast as the instructor calls them out, and return them to their correct places in each box. To promote learning, the students are still required to call out each name and to explain why they assigned it to a substance.

Instead of boxes, instructors can have large sheets of paper arranged in squares like Bingo cards with names and properties of the specimens from the box written randomly on each paper, so that, like Bingo cards, no two papers are alike. A variant is using Bingo cards created in patterns that mimic the classification scheme for the rock.

For example (Figure 11.1), igneous rock names are assigned based upon texture and a color index; a name such as "basalt" is assigned because it is dark—nearly black—and fine-grained. "Granite" is the most common igneous rock, with a light color and coarse-grained texture. Having students place specimens correctly in a two-dimensional matrix that captures the basic logic of the igneous rock classification scheme teaches them the framework of reasoning for classifying the specimens.

Students must place their specimens correctly on the square with the matching label as the instructor randomly chooses materials from an identical set of specimens and calls out the name of the material or the diagnostic properties of a particular material. The students must find the correct material from the specimens scattered on the desktop and play it onto their Bingo card until one team wins by filling its card.

Well-designed courses may cover minerals in the first two weeks, then igneous rocks, sedimentary rocks, and, in the next week, the metamorphic rocks. However, the learning shouldn't stay compartmentalized. Using Bingo, last week's specimens get dumped in with the current week's; the pile of unknowns gets larger, and the critical properties to identification get more diverse.

As this occurs, a student who masters the "why" of identification has no problem. With this kind of practice over several weeks, students have placed their knowledge of "why I assigned this name" into long-term memory.

	Texture	
COLOR	**Coarse-Grained**	**Fine-Grained**
Light	*granite*	*rhyolite*
Intermediate	*diorite*	*andesite*
Dark	*gabbro*	*basalt*
	Pyroclastic	**Glassy**
Any	*tuff*	*scoria/obsidian*

Figure 11.1 Color shades and textures are the basis for assigning most igneous rock names. This rudimentary igneous rock classification chart, when enlarged, allows placement of specimens on it in Bingo drill games to enhance specimen identification skills.

Proficiency in materials identification is basic to geology. In practice, geologists cannot carry reference books into the field or use expensive instrumentation to do a task that is easily accomplished in seconds by a well-trained brain. Courses that try to cram identification into one lab produce a rather meaningless exposure to "covering the material," without any useful design for deep learning. They also offer a sad disservice to most students who really do want to know how to identify the rocks and minerals they find; this is their only opportunity to learn these skills. Students who do not become geology majors nevertheless see and collect rocks and want to respond to questions that their children may later ask.

It may seem that the acquisition of such basics involves only memorization and operations at the lower levels of Bloom's (1956) cognitive domain. However, understanding the process through which one assigns a correct name is really an evaluative exercise—one that requires a decision that is based on the use of evidence through a framework of reasoning. To understand this process is to understand the basis for scientific interpretations.

Learning through speaking, listening, writing, and arguing with others activates more synaptic connections than occurs when studying alone in silence. A student learning alone has less emotional support and less inspiration to stay on task. Further, studying alone without the benefit of peer regulation incurs a higher risk of acquiring erroneous systems for identification. These erroneous identifications build counterproductive neural networks that the user needs to later replace, requiring still more labor.

The best situations provide time for students to return to the laboratories when classes are not in session so that they can study the specimens with needed individual quiet reflection. Cooperative exercises done in class do not negate the need to study and again engage with the content outside of class. Specimen sets placed on reserve in the library are another way to allow individual study.

REFLECTIONS ON COOPERATIVE LEARNING RELATED TO SEIZING OPPORTUNITY

Learning material well and lecturing about it year after year leads to boredom. Being fully alive in our work means taking risks, being opportunistic, and looking perpetually for creative ways to teach topics. Cooperative learning structures, such as Turn to Your Neighbor, Teach Your Neighbor, Think-Pair-Share, or Write-Pair-Share, take any question we might ask and turn it into an interactive exercise for our whole class instead of just an interaction between us and one or two students. Cooperative techniques offer countless opportunities to convert something we teach routinely into a better learning experience.

When we find ourselves telling students, "Study the sedimentary rock sets. You'll have a quiz next week," we need to stop and ask ourselves: "Is there anything fun or motivating about this, and is this the best I can do to bring about that desired learning?" Realize: We have a right to enjoy this business of "professoring"!

Example 4. Optimal Designs: Students' Deep Learning and Continued Course Improvement

Next, we look at designs that integrate cooperative methods with other tools and methods. Optimal designs produce deep learning, but they are not trivial to design and polish. A realistic goal is to produce only one such new experience each time we teach a course. Once developed, these superior opportunities exist for students for as long as the topic remains relevant. After several years, instructors can teach courses dominated by sophisticated learning-centered engagements.

Cooperative methods prove to be most useful when they are incorporated with varied engagements inside and outside of class (Table 11.1). Optimal learning exercises address big-picture concepts. Most require enactment over several class periods.

A tool, discussed in the following, that facilitates design for extreme learning experiences is a good Knowledge Survey (Nuhfer & Knipp, 2003). The instructor constructs the course plan in the detail required before enacting the course. To appreciate the advantages this provides, see Figure 11.2, which is a segment of an evolved knowledge survey created by a professor with over two decades of teaching experience. It is not merely a list of topics. It discloses to students a plan within which an instructor can design learning experiences and choose effective pedagogy to address specific items.

Examining a few items that address the topic of deep time and change through time (Figure 11.2) helps us see how the detailed organization allows a focus on pedagogy.

Item 39 is a rote memorization challenge. The instructor devised a visual mnemonic that conveys this learning in under ten minutes of class time.

Items 42 and 49 are also factual items that conventional lecture can convey reasonably well. It makes little sense to use cooperative learning for such learning challenges. Once students know item 49, pairs of students engage item 50, and groups of four engage item 51.

Table 11.1 Checklist for design of optimal learning exercises.

Design considerations	Pedagogical Design Elements	Function in building and stabilizing synaptic connections
1. Appropriate to our students' abilities and needs?	Meets a planned outcome disclosed in class organization. Is appropriate to levels of thinking and present knowledge of students in class	Connects with existing knowledge and perceptions to enable building rather than resulting in confusion
2. Carries an affective "hook?"	Conveys relevance, worth, links to individuals' personal interests and/or experience	Enlists neurons associated with feeling a desire to learn
3. Requires individual reflection out of class?	Structured reading and double-entry journals, solving a "puzzle" or confronting "why" or "how" a discovery or insight occurred and what method of thinking or reasoning framework was involved	Enlists neurons active during reflection; helps brain to develop and establish synaptic connections on problem during sleep overnight
4. Makes use of interactive engagement in class?	Problem begun by individuals is completed through cooperative in-class group or pair work and whole-class summarization. Can include role-play, interviews, and structured debate	Enlists neurons used in listening, speaking, responding, arguing. Develops confidence and sense of being supported in learning
5. Encourages visualization?	"Explain by diagram," map concepts, construct flow chart	Builds and stabilizes by engaging psychomotor domain in drawing plus synaptic connections to build a mental picture from information
6. Requires writing and encourages revision?	Assigned writing of abstracts, stories, summaries along with peer editing & review	Engages psychomotor domain through writing. Stabilizes synapses by repeated editing, reorganizing, and polishing
7. Requires metacognitive reflection?	What learning resulted; what seemed difficult, what seemed easy and why?	Stabilizes synapses through repetition and self-organization by review of content, process and current self assessment
8. Possesses an effective assessment and rubric?	Rubric conveys to students the specific meaning of high quality achievement.	Embed assessments to promote learning. Be sure that the product or performance required relates clearly to the outcome intended.

Understanding Change through Time
32. **GCI 36.** Which of the following statements do you think best describes the relationship between people and dinosaurs? **(A)** People and dinosaurs co-existed for about five thousand years. **(B)** People and dinosaurs co-existed for about five hundred thousand years. **(C)** Dinosaurs died out about five thousand years before people appeared on Earth. **(D)** Dinosaurs died out about five hundred thousand years before people appeared on Earth. **(E)** Dinosaurs died out about 50 million years before people appeared on Earth.
37. Besides age, other qualities of change through time need consideration. Pick a single geologic process and explain its qualities of age, pattern, rates, order, frequency, magnitude, and duration.
39. Name in order from oldest to youngest the established time periods and eras of the geologic time scale.
42. What was the first absolute date published for age of Earth, who published it, what was the age, and on what was it based?
43. The following contributed to our concept of deep time: Nicolaus Steno (Neils Stensen) (1669), William Smith (1769–1839), Baron Georges Cuvier (1769–1832), James Hutton (work of 1795), Charles Lyell (1797–1875), Charles Darwin (work of 1859), William Thomson (Lord Kelvin - work in 1897), John Joly (work of 1908), Thomas Chamberlin (work of 1899–1909), Madame Curie (1867–1934), Bertram B. Boltwood (work 1905–1909), Stephen Jay Gould (work 1972–2000). In a 500-word essay that includes all of the names, summarize why their contributions were essential for allowing the discovery of deep time and understanding change through deep time.
44. If we placed all of Earth's history on a 24-hour scale and held a party beginning at midnight, what time would humans arrive at the party?
49. The population of the world doubles about every **A.** 3800 years. **B.** 380 years. **C.** 38 years. **D** 3.8 years. **E** 38 months.
50. If Earth's population (currently at about 6 billion) is at about 50% of the planet's capacity to maintain it, barring any change in the current growth/death trend, how long should we have before our population exceeds the planet's capacity to support us?
51. Explain why the situation existing at a 50% carrying capacity would convey no sense of a problem or urgency to "common sense" observation.
263. In general, rock is worn away on Earth's surface at the rate of (A) about 1mm/yr. (B) about 1mm/decade. (C) about 1mm/century. (D) about 1mm/1000 yrs. (E) About 1mm/10,000 yrs.

Figure 11.2 Ten of many knowledge survey items for an introductory geology course that pertain to learning the concept of change through deep time in an introductory geology course. The designation "GCI 36" on item 32 indicates that the item came from the Geoscience Concept Inventory (Libarkin and Anderson, 2005). Readers can download such knowledge surveys through the case studies at <http://elixr.merlot.org/>.

For item 44, the instructor uses storytelling and a spreadsheet to convert 4.6 billion years of Earth history into a 24-hour scale. If an instructor in a higher-level course wanted students to learn to construct their own spreadsheet model, assigning the task as homework to pairs presents a better learning plan than an assignment to individuals. Pairs guided via good assignment instructions support one another and check one another's assumptions.

Item 37 invites an exercise for groups of four or five. The learning structure assigns roles to group members to deduce the rate, age, etc., as a division of labor. The resulting discussion helps clarify the terms that students often confuse.

Item 263 involves a field trip to a graveyard where individuals make measurements on actual dated headstones and return to the following class to reach consensus within groups of about four. The groups compare these against published rates that they find on the Web and choose a "best" rate.

Next, individuals use these "best" rates in homework to estimate durability of varied phenomena that they encounter every day. Note that this item is a direct application of the method of multiple working hypotheses, and students can learn the method through direction to reflect on the process of choosing a rate.

Item 43, on deep time, uses an exercise and a game. Teaching item 43 employs all checklist points of Figure 11.2. The exercise takes several periods, and high-quality final products require an average of two revisions. It involves individual work, group work, limited role-play, the interactive lecture described by Robinson and Cooper (chapter 7), writing, reflection, and concept mapping.

Nuhfer and Mosbrucker (2007) detailed the exercises in items 43 and 263 and performed assessments to show that the interactive exercise produced high learning gains. All exercises in that 2007 article, along with materials needed to enact the lessons, are available in a single large zip folder at http://profcamp.tripod.com/NuhferTimefiles.zip.

Item 43 reveals that the geoscience community developed major concepts by grappling with problems afforded by growing knowledge. It took time before scientists realized unifying connectedness and expressed these realizations as concepts. Students must engage in similar grappling over extended time before they master conceptual thinking.

Item 32, designed to test for conceptual awareness, comes from the Geoscience Concept Inventory (GCI; Libarkin & Anderson, 2005—available from http://gci.lite.msu.edu/). The authors used item analysis and a national sampling of students to standardize this inventory. This item, and other items that challenge conceptual awareness, offer ideal challenges for students to master through structured small group discussions after they complete optimal learning exercises that employ the criteria outlined in Figure 11.2.

Instructors commonly come to class overprepared to deliver content knowledge and underprepared to engage students' learning through creative exercises. Busy professors tend to prepare for classes the night before and, as a result, lecture on everything. The Knowledge Survey changes that situation (Nuhfer & Fleisher, 2008).

Constructing a knowledge survey helps us produce more interactive, engaged classes. The content we want to teach now is available in writing and in detail. Having the plan detailed as previously described makes the enactment of interactive lessons more attractive. It also makes clear how much planning is necessary for effective teaching. We can know a few weeks ahead when we must teach an item such as 43 or 263 and begin to prepare. Preparation of a good exercise for these may require several days of work.

Knowledge Surveys make it easy to look at each item and see opportunities by asking: "What is a really effective way to teach that content?" For items such as 50 and 51, we can change in minutes something that we might have taught by lecture into paired or group exercises simply by adding one or two PowerPoint® slides into our lecture presentation to guide students through the group activities.

The ultimate learning experiences that result from such gradual improvement over the long term are perhaps studio courses (Perkins, 2005). To learn more about studio courses, see the website at http://serc.carleton.edu/introgeo/studio/index.html.

Additional Resources

The Web offers an increasing wealth of demonstrations and exercises that we can use on specialty topics such as those hosted at the Incorporated Research Institutions for Seismology "IRIS" site http://web.ics.purdue.edu/~braile/indexlinks/educ.htm for earthquakes.

Compilations of cooperative learning exercises in geoscience exist via the links of Science Education Resource Center (SERC) http://serc.carleton.edu/introgeo/index.html and On the Cutting Edge http://serc.carleton.cdu/NAGT-Workshops/index.html. Since its inception, the latter site has collected classroom resources and disseminated them on the Web as a searchable collection. Both sites feature submissions from geoscience professors who use cooperative learning.

California State University's new ELIXR MERLOT site http://elixr.merlot.org/ increasingly provides examples of classroom instruction innovations as short Web movies. The ELIXR/MERLOT project offers faculty development lessons—with demonstrations of actual class enactments on video, coupled with links to very in-depth resources. Most of us enact cooperative learning more easily by seeing it done than by reading about it.

REFLECTIONS ON PLANNING IN DETAIL AS KEY TO CREATING AN INTERACTIVE CLASS

Many authors in this volume emphasize the need for structure and organization. Knowledge Surveys offer the transparency needed to allow us to create organized, content-rich, interactive courses. Good planning involves knowing both what we should teach and how we should teach it. Original deep-learning experiences take time to construct, but their use in subsequent years reduces preparation time. As we gradually add engaging strategies, each subsequent course becomes stronger. Eventually, using this iterative process leads to using deep-learning exercises to address all major learning outcomes.

References

Becker, W. E. (2004). Quantitative research on teaching methods in tertiary education. In W. E. Becker and M. L. Andrews (Eds.), *The scholarship of teaching and learning in higher education: Contributions of research universities* (pp. 265–309). Bloomington: Indiana University Press.

Bloom, B. S. (1956). *Taxonomy of educational objectives—The classification of educational goals: Handbook I.—Cognitive domain.* New York: David McKay.

Bloom, B. S. (1984). The 2 sigma problem: The search for methods of group instruction as effective as one-to-one tutoring. *Educational Researcher, 4*(6), 4–16.

Chamberlin, T. C. (1897). The method of multiple working hypotheses. *Journal of Geology, 5,* 837–848. (An 1890 version of this paper). Retrieved February 3, 2010, from http://www.accessexcellence.org/RC/AB/BC/chamberlin.html.

Constantopoulos, T. L. (1994). A cooperative approach to teaching mineral identification. *Journal of Geological Education, 42,* 261–63. Retrieved February 3, 2010, from http://nagt.org/files/nagt/jge/abstracts/constantopoulos.pdf.

Cooper, J. L., Robinson, P., & Ball, D., (Eds.) (2003). *Small group instruction in higher education: Lessons from the past, visions of the future.* Stillwater, OK: New Forums.

Feldman, K. A. (1989). The association between student ratings of specific instructional dimensions and student achievement: Refining and extending the synthesis of data from multisection validity studies. *Research in Higher Education, 30,* 583–645.

Feldman, K. A. (2007). Identifying exemplary teachers and teaching: Evidence from student ratings. In R. Perry & J. Smart (Eds.), *The scholarship of teaching and learning in higher education: An evidence-based approach* (pp. 93–129). New York: Springer.

Gappa, J. M., Austin, A. E., & Trice, A. G. (2007). *Rethinking faculty work: Higher education's strategic imperative.* San Francisco: Jossey-Bass.

Hake, R. R. (1998). Interactive-engagement versus traditional methods: A six-thousand-student survey of mechanics test data for introductory physics courses. *American Journal of Physics, 66*(1), 64–74. Retrieved February 3, 2010, from http://tinyurl.com/3xuyqe.

Johnson, D. W., Johnson, R. T., & Smith, K. A. (2006). *Active learning: Cooperation in the college classroom* (3rd ed.). Edina, MN: Interaction Books.

Kalman, C. S. (2008). *Successful science and engineering teaching: Theoretical and learning perspectives.* New York: Springer.

Krathwohl, D. R., Bloom, B. S., & Masia, B. B. (1964). *Taxonomy of educational objectives: The affective domain.* New York: McKay.

Leamnson, R. (1999). *Thinking about teaching and learning: Developing habits of learning with first-year college and university students.* Sterling, VA: Stylus.

Libarkin, J. C., & Anderson, S. W. (2005). Assessment of learning in entry-level geoscience courses: Results from the geoscience concept inventory. *Journal of Geoscience Education, 53,* 394–401.

Macdonald, R. H., Manduca, C. A., Mogk, D. W., & Tewksbury, B. J. (2005). Teaching methods in undergraduate geoscience courses: Results of the 2004 On the Cutting Edge Survey of U.S. Faculty. *Journal of Geoscience Education, 53,* 237–252.

Milem, J., Berger, J., & Dey, E. (2000). Faculty time allocation: A study of change over twenty years. *The Journal of Higher Education, 71,* 454–475.

Millis, B. J., & Cottell, P. G. (1998). *Cooperative learning for higher education faculty.* Phoenix, AZ: American Council on Education/Oryx.

Nuhfer, E. B. (2008a). The affective domain and the formation of the generator: Educating in fractal patterns XXIII, part 1: *National Teaching and Learning Forum, 18*(2), 8–11, and part 2, *National Teaching and Learning Forum, 18*(3), 9–11.

Nuhfer, E. B. (2008b). The feeling of learning: Intellectual development and the affective domain: Educating in fractal patterns XXVI. *National Teaching and Learning Forum, 18*(1), 7–11.

Nuhfer, E. B., & Fleisher, S. (2008). The utility of knowledge surveys in a culture of over work: Design of introductory courses that meet institutional educational and assessment requirements. Geological Society of America Abstracts with Programs. Boulder, CO. Retrieved February 3, 2010, from http://a-c-s.confex.com/crops/2008am/webprogram/Paper49187.html.

Nuhfer, E. B., & Knipp, D. (2003). The knowledge survey: A tool for all reasons. In C. M. Wehlburg & S. Chadwick-Blossey (Eds.), *To Improve the academy: Resources for faculty, instructional, and organizational development, 21,* 59–78. San Francisco: Jossey-Bass. Retrieved February 3, 2010, with addenda, from http://www.isu.edu/ctl/facultydev/KnowS_files/KnowS.htm.

Nuhfer, E., & Mosbrucker, P. (2007). Developing science literacy using interactive engagements for conceptual understanding of change through time. *Journal of Geoscience Education. 55*(5), 36–50. Retrieved February 3, 2010, from http://www.nagt.org/files/nagt/jge/abstracts/nuhfer-v55p36.pdf.

Perkins, D. (2005). The case for a cooperative studio classroom: Teaching petrology in a different way. *Journal of Geoscience Education, 53*(1), 101–109.

Perry, W. G., Jr. (1999). *Forms of intellectual and ethical development in the college years: A scheme* (Reprint of the 1st ed., published in 1968 and 1970 by Holt Rinehart and Winston, with 1999 introduction by L. Knefelkamp). San Francisco: Jossey-Bass.

Rhem, J. (2006). The high risks of improving teaching. *National Teaching and Learning Forum, 15*(6), 1–2.

Springer, L., Stanne, M. E., & Donovan, S. S. (1999). Effects of small-group learning on undergraduates in science, mathematics, engineering, and technology: A meta-analysis. *Review of Educational Research, 69,* 21–51.

Thorn, P. M. (2003). Bridging the gap between what is praised and what is practiced: Supporting the work of change as anatomy and physiology instructors introduce active learning into their undergraduate classroom. Unpublished doctoral dissertation, The University of Texas at Austin. Retrieved February 3, 2010, from http://www.lib.utexas.edu/etd/d/2003/thornpm032/thornpm032.pdf#page=3.

Wolpert, L. (1992). *The unnatural nature of science.* Cambridge, MA: Harvard University Press.

12

Concluding Thoughts on This Volume

Barbara J. Millis

I am struck by the level of sophistication that these seasoned teachers and authors bring to the challenge of describing their cooperative learning efforts. Their essays go far beyond paeans to structured group work and speak also of good teaching practices in general. These authors, for example, are not "lecture-bashing": they recognize that the lecture has a long and venerable tradition and that experts such as Stephen Brookfield can write candidly of its virtues.

But they are also aware of compelling research that suggests that a rigid adherence to unrelieved "teacher talk" alone does not strengthen the student synapses essential for learning. A straight lecture approach can also have a negative impact on a host of other important effects, such as feelings of efficacy, connection, and persistence.

Virtually all of the authors place cooperative learning within a far broader context of teaching and learning. Many authors—Cohen, Nuhfer, and Panitz, for example—focus on the importance of establishing positive cooperative norms during the first class meeting. Often, this can be accomplished through an interactive review of a learning-centered syllabus, another common feature of several of the chapters.

The syllabus is often the first place where faculty can introduce students to the value of cooperative group work, but the student "buy-in" needs to be continually reinforced as faculty members share with students why they are selecting particular teaching and learning approaches. Cohen, in particular, emphases this need for transparency. These approaches seem to emphasize the need for the teacher to emerge from behind the instructor dominated "Oz Screen" by letting students in on the so-called research secrets of human learning, which they may have previously regarded as "smoke and mirrors."

I am struck, too, by the depth of reflection that informed all of these essays. The authors were not mindlessly trying the latest "fad of the semester." They have carefully thought-out teaching and learning philosophies and have used research to inform their practice. They are continuously refining their approaches. Their classes are "works in progress," but the progress is evidence-based.

They also show tremendous respect for their students and for their "calling." These are caring people: they care about their students, their students' learning, and their own contributions to their profession and to society as a whole.

It is an affirmation of college teaching that so many people in so many disciplines can care so deeply about what matters in college. They care not only about the deep learning that cooperative approaches can engender, but also about the affective parts of teaching that less dedicated faculty—often overwhelmed by large class sizes, heavy work demands, and other stresses— tend to ignore.

Students who persist and succeed need to feel connected to teachers and to other students; they need peer support as they struggle with difficult topics; they need to feel respected and valued as human beings. All of these affective factors are critically important, and these authors recognized long ago that cooperative learning approaches have both cognitive and affective impacts on learning.

Bibliography

Allen, D. E., Dutch, B. E., & Groh, S. E. (1996). The power of problem-based learning in teaching introductory science courses. New Directions for Teaching and Learning. In L. Wilkerson, LuAnn & W. H. Gijselaera, (Eds.) *Bringing problem-based learning to higher education: Theory and practice.* (pp. 43–52). San Francisco: Jossey-Bass.

Ames, C., & Ames, R. (1981). Competitive versus individualistic goal structures: The salience of past performance information for causal attributions and affect. *Journal of Educational Psychology, 73,* 411–418.

Anderson, D. L., Fisher, K. M., & Norman, G. J. (2002). Development and evaluation of the conceptual inventory of natural selection. *Journal of Research in Science Teaching, 39,* 952–978.

Anderson, L. W., Krathwohl, D. R., Airasian, P. W., Cruikshank, K. A., Mayer, R. E., Pintrich, P. R., Raths, J., & Wittrock, M. C. (Eds.) (2001). *A taxonomy for learning, teaching, and assessing: A revision of Bloom's taxonomy of educational objectives* (abridged ed.). New York: Longman.

Anderson, W. T. (1990). *Reality isn't what it used to be: Theatrical politics, ready-to-wear religion, global myths, primitive chic, and other wonders of the postmodern world.* San Francisco: Harper and Row.

Angelo, T. A., & Cross, K. P. (1993). *Classroom assessment techniques* (2nd ed.). San Francisco: Jossey-Bass.

Arons, A. B. (1976). Cultivating the capacity for formal operations: Objectives and procedures in an introductory physical science course. *American Journal of Physics, 44,* 834–838.

Arons, A. B. (1997). *Teaching introductory physics.* New York: Wiley.

Aronson, E., Stephan, C., Sikes, J., & Snapp, M. (1978). *The jigsaw classroom.* Beverly Hills, CA: Sage.

Association of American Colleges and Universities (2002). *Greater expectations: A new vision for learning as a nation goes to college.* Washington, DC: Author. Retrieved February 3, 2010, from http://www.greaterexpectations.org/.

Association of American Colleges and Universities. (2007). *College learning for the new global century: A report from the National Leadership Council for Liberal Education & America's Promise.* Washington, DC: Association of American Colleges and Universities.

Astin, A. (1993). *What matters in college? Four critical years revisited.* San Francisco: Jossey-Bass.

Barkley, E. F., Cross, K. P., & Major, C. H. (2005). *Collaborative learning techniques: A handbook for college faculty.* San Francisco: Jossey-Bass.

Barr, R. B., & Tagg, J. (1995, November/December). From teaching to learning: A new paradigm for undergraduate education. *Change: The Magazine of Higher Learning, 27*(6), 13–25.

Becker, W. E. (2004). Quantitative research on teaching methods in tertiary education. In W. E. Becker & M. L. Andrews (Eds.), *The scholarship of teaching and learning in higher education: Contributions of research universities* (pp. 265–309). Bloomington: Indiana University Press.

Becker, W. E. (2007). Quit lying and address the controversies: There are no dogmata, laws, rules or standards in the science of economics. *American Economist, 51*(1), 3–14.

Becker, W. E., & Watts, M. (2008). A little more than chalk and talk: Results from a third national survey of teaching methods in undergraduate economics courses. *Journal of Economic Education, 39*(3), 273–286.

Belenky, M., Clinchy B., Goldberger N., & Tarule, J. (1986). *Women's ways of knowing: The development of self, voice, and mind.* New York: Basic Books.

Bellas, C. J., Marshall, J., Reed, M. M., Venable, J. M., & Whelan-Berry, K. S. (2000, October). *PBL in business—Understanding Problem-Based Learning and trying PBL in your business discipline: An interactive approach.* Paper presented at PBL 2000, Birmingham, AL.

Bergstrom, T. C., & Miller, J. H. (2000). *Experiments with economic principles: Microeconomics.* Boston: McGraw-Hill.

Bligh, D. A. (1972). *What's the use of lectures?* London: Penguin.

Bligh, D. A. (2000). *What's the use of lectures?* New York: Wiley.

Bloom, A. (1987). *The closing of the American mind.* New York: Simon and Schuster.

Bloom, B. S. (1956). *Taxonomy of educational objectives—The classification of educational goals: Handbook I.—Cognitive domain.* New York: David McKay.

Bloom, B. S. (1984). The 2 sigma problem: The search for methods of group instruction as effective as one-to-one tutoring. *Educational Researcher, 4*(6), 4–16.

Bonello, F. J., & Lobo, I. (2008). *Taking sides. Clashing views on economic issues.* Dubuque, IA: McGraw-Hill/Contemporary Learning Series.

Bonwell, C. C., & Eison, J. A. (1991). *Active learning: Creating excitement in the classroom.* Washington, DC: ERIC Clearinghouse on Higher Education, George Washington University.

Borg, J. R., & Borg, M. O. (2001). Teaching critical thinking in interdisciplinary economics courses. *College Teaching, 49*, 20–25.

Bransford, J. D., Brown, A. L., & Cocking, R. R. (Eds.) (2000). *How people learn: Brain, mind, experience, and school.* Commission on Behavioral and Social Sciences and Education National Research Council. Washington, DC: National Academy Press.

Braxton, J. M., Jones, W. A., Hirschy, A. S., & Hartley, H. V., III. (2008). The role of active learning in college persistence. In J. M. Braxton (Ed.), *The role of the classroom in college student persistence: New directions for teaching and learning, no. 115* (pp. 71–83). San Francisco: Jossey-Bass.

Brookfield, S. D. (1987). *Developing critical thinkers: Challenging adults to explore alternative ways of thinking and acting.* San Francisco: Jossey-Bass.

Brown, A. L., Campion, J., & Day, J. (1981). Learning to learn: On training students to learn from texts. *Educational Researcher, 10*(2), 14–21.

Burchfield, C. M., & Sappinton, J. (2000). Compliance with required reading assignments. *Teaching of Psychology, 27*(1), 58–60.

Chamberlin, T. C. (1897). The method of multiple working hypotheses. *Journal of Geology, 5,* 837–848. (An 1890 version of this paper). Retrieved February 3, 2010, from http://www.accessexcellence.org/RC/AB/BC/chamberlin.html.

Constantopoulos, T. L. (1994). A cooperative approach to teaching mineral identification. *Journal of Geological Education, 42,* 261–63. Retrieved February 3, 2010, from http://nagt.org/files/nagt/jge/abstracts/constantopoulos.pdf.

Cooper, J. (1990, May). Cooperative learning and college teaching: Tips from the trenches. *The Teaching Professor, 4*(5), 1–2.

Cooper, J. L., & Mueck, R. (1989). Cooperative/collaborative learning: Research and practice (primarily) at the collegiate level. *The Journal of Staff, Program, and Organization Development, 7*(3), 149–151.

Cooper, J. L., & Mueck, R. (1990). Student involvement in learning: Cooperative learning and college instruction. *The Journal on Excellence in College Teaching, 1*(1), 68–76.

Cooper, J. L., Robinson, P., & Ball, D. (Eds.) (2003). *Small group instruction in higher education: Lessons from the past, visions of the future.* Stillwater, OK: New Forums.

Cooper, M. M. (1995). Cooperative learning: An approach for large enrollment courses. *Journal of Chemical Education, 72,* 162–164.

Cooper, M. M. (2005). An introduction to small-group learning. In N. J. Pienta, M. M. Cooper, & T. J. Greenbowe (Eds.), *Chemists' guide to effective teaching* (pp. 117–128). Upper Saddle River, NJ: Pearson.

Cottell, P. G., & Millis, B. J. (1993, Spring). Cooperative learning structures in the instruction of accounting. *Issues in Accounting Education, 8*(1), 40–59.

Crouch, C. H., Fagen, A. P., Callan, J. P., & Mazur, E. (2004). Classroom demonstrations: Learning tools or entertainment? *American Journal of Physics, 72,* 835–838.

Crouch, C. H., & Mazur, E. (2001). Peer instruction: Ten years of experience and results. *American Journal of Physics, 69,* 970–977.

Cusco, J. (1992, Winter). Collaborative and cooperative learning in higher education: A proposed taxonomy. *Cooperative Learning and College Teaching, 2*(2), 2–4. Reprinted in J. L. Cooper, P. Robinson, & D. Ball (Eds.), *Small group instruction in higher education: Lessons from the past, visions of the future* (pp. 18–26). Stillwater, OK: New Forums.

Davidson, J. E., & Sternberg, R. (2003). *The psychology of problem solving.* Cambridge, UK: Cambridge University Press.

Davis, B. G. (1993). *Tools for teaching*. San Francisco: Jossey-Bass.

Dembo, M. H. (2004). *Motivation and learning strategies for college success: A self-management approach*. Mahwah, NJ: Lawrence Erlbaum.

Duch, B. J. (2001). Writing problems for deeper understanding. In B. J. Duch, S. E. Groh, & D. E. Allen (Eds.), *The power of problem-based learning: A practical "how to" for reaching undergraduate courses in any discipline* (pp. 47–53). Sterling, VA: Stylus.

Duch, B. J., Groh, S. E., & Allen, D. E. (Eds.) (2001). *The power of problem-based learning: A practical "how to" for reaching undergraduate courses in any discipline*. Sterling, VA: Stylus.

Duit, R. (2009). Bibliography—STCSE: Students' and teachers' conceptions and science education. Retrieved February 3, 2010, from www.ipn.uni-kiel.de/aktuell/stcse/bibint.html.

Durham, Y., McKinnon, T., & Schulman, C. (2007). Classroom experiments: Not just fun and games. *Economic Inquiry, 45*(1), 162–178.

Dweck, C. S. (1986). Motivational processes affecting learning. *American Psychologist, 41*, 1040–1048.

Ebert-May, D., & Hodder, J. (Eds.) (2008). *Pathways to scientific teaching*. Sunderland, MA: Sinauer.

Emerson, T. L. N., & Taylor, B. A. (2007). Interactions between personality type and the experimental methods. *Journal of Economic Education, 38*(1), 18–35.

Fantuzzo, J. W., Dimeff, L. A., & Fox, S. L. (1989). Reciprocal peer tutoring: A multimodal assessment of effectiveness with college students. *Teaching of Psychology, 16*(3), 133–135.

Fantuzzo, J. W., Riggio, R. E., Connelly, S., & Dimeff, L. A. (1989). Effects of reciprocal peer tutoring on academic achievement and psychological adjustment: A component analysis. *Journal of Educational Psychology, 81*(2), 173–177.

Farrell, J. J., Moog, R. S., & Spencer, J. N. (1999). A guided inquiry general chemistry course. *Journal of Chemical Education, 76*, 570–574.

Felder, R. M., & Brent, R. (1994). *Cooperative learning in technical courses: Procedures, pitfalls, and payoffs*. Eric Document Reproduction Service Report ED 377038. Retrieved February 3, 2010, from http://www4.ncsu.edu/unity/lockers/users/f/felder/public/Papers/Coopreport.html.

Felder, R. M., & Brent, R. (1996). Navigating the bumpy road to student-centered instruction. Retrieved February 3, 2010 from http://www4.ncsu.edu/unity/lockers/users/f/felder/public/Papers/Resist.html.

Feldman, K. A. (1989). The association between student ratings of specific instructional dimensions and student achievement: Refining and extending the synthesis of data from multisection validity studies. *Research in Higher Education, 30*, 583–645.

Feldman, K. A. (2007). Identifying exemplary teachers and teaching: Evidence from student ratings. In R. Perry & J. Smart (Eds.), *The scholarship of teaching and learning in higher education: An evidence-based approach* (pp. 93–129). New York: Springer.

Fink, L. D. (2003). *Creating significant learning experiences: An integrated approach to designing college courses*. San Francisco: Jossey-Bass.

Finkel, D. (2000). *Teaching with your mouth shut.* Portsmouth, NH: Heinemann.

Frank, R. H., Gilovich, T. D., & Regan, D. T. (1996). Do economists make bad citizens? *Journal of Economic Perspectives, 10*(1), 187–192.

Fullilove, R. E., & Treisman, P. U. (1990). Mathematics achievement among African American undergraduates at the University of California, Berkeley: An evaluation of the Mathematics Workshop Program. *Journal of Negro Education, 59*(3), 463–478.

Gappa, J. M., Austin, A. E., & Trice, A. G. (2007). *Rethinking faculty work: Higher education's strategic imperative.* San Francisco: Jossey-Bass.

Gardner, H. (1993). *Multiple intelligences: The theory in practice.* New York: Basic Books.

Gibbs, G., & Jenkins, A. (1992). *Teaching large classes in higher education: Maintaining quality with reduced resources.* London: Kogan Page.

Greenlaw, S. A. (2006). *Doing economics: A guide to understanding and carrying out economic research.* Boston: Houghton Mifflin.

Grossman, R. W. (2005). Discovering hidden transformations: Making science and other courses more learnable. *College Teaching, 53*(1), 33–40.

Hake, R. R. (1998a). Interactive-engagement versus traditional methods: A six-thousand student survey of mechanics test data for introductory physics courses. *American Journal of Physics, 66*(1), 64–74.

Hake, R. R. (1998b). Interactive-engagement methods in introductory mechanics courses. Retrieved March 9, 2010, from http://www.physics.indiana.edu/~sdi/IEM -2b.pdf.

Hake, R. R. (2002). Lessons from the physics education reform effort. Conservation Ecology, 5(2): 28. Retrieved March 9, 2010, from http://www.consecol.org/vol5/iss2/ art28/.

Halloun, I., & Hestenes, D. (1985a.) The initial knowledge state of college physics. *American Journal of Physics, 53*, 1043–1055.

Halloun, I., & Hestenes, D. (1985b.) Common sense concepts about motion *American Journal of Physics, 53*, 1056 1065.

Handelsman, J., Ebert-May D., Beichner, R., Bruns, P., Chang, A., & DeHaan, R. (2004). Scientific Teaching. *Science, 304*, 521–522.

Hansen, M. E. (2006). Masters of the Economy. Retrieved March 9, 2010, from http:// academic2.american.edu/~mhansen/MastersGame.

Hansen, W. L., Salemi, M. K., & Siegfried, J. J. (2002). Use it or lose it: Teaching literacy in the economics principles course. *American Economic Review, 92*, 463–472.

Hanson, D. M. (2006). *Instructor's guide to process-oriented guided-inquiry learning.* Lisle, IL: Pacific Crest.

Hanson, D. M., & Wolfskill, T. (2000). Process workshops—A new model for instruction. *Journal of Chemical Education, 77*, 120–130.

Herreid, C. F. (2004). Using case studies in science—And still "covering the content." In L. K. Michaelsen, A. Bauman Knight, & L. D. Fink (Eds.), *Team-based learning: A transformative use of small groups in college teaching* (pp. 105–114). Sterling, VA: Stylus.

Hilton, J. M., Kopera-Frye, K., & Millis, B. (2007). Techniques for student engagement and classroom management in large (and small) classes. *Journal of Teaching in Marriage and Family, 6,* 490–505.

Hobson, E. H. (2003, November). Encouraging students to read required course material. Workshop presented at the 28th Annual Conference of the Professional and Organizational Development (POD) Network in Higher Education, Denver, CO.

Hobson, E. H. (2004, July). *Getting students to read: Fourteen tips.* IDEA Paper #40. Kansas State: IDEA Paper Series. Retrieved February 3, 2010, from http://www.theideacenter.org/IDEAPaper40.

Hofer, B. K., & Pintrich, P. R. (1997). The development of epistemological theories: Beliefs about knowledge and knowing and their relation to learning. *Review of Educational Research, 67,* 88–140.

Jacobs, D. C. (2000). *An alternative approach to general chemistry: Addressing the needs of at-risk students with cooperative learning strategies.* Retrieved March 9, 2010, from http://cms.carnegiefoundation.org/collections/castl_he/djacobs/index.html.

Jensen, E. (2000). *Brain-based learning* (rev. ed.). San Diego, CA: The Brain Store.

Johnson, D. W., & Johnson, R. T. (1975). *Learning together and alone: Cooperation, competition, and individualization.* Englewood Cliffs, NJ: Prentice-Hall.

Johnson, D. W., Johnson, R. T., & Smith, K. A. (1991). *Active learning: Cooperation in the college classroom.* Edina, MN: Interaction Book.

Johnson, D. W., Johnson, R. T., &. Smith, K. A. (1991). *Cooperative learning: Increasing college faculty instructional productivity.* ASHE-ERIC Higher Education Report No. 4. Washington, DC: The George Washington University School of Education and Human Development.

Johnson, R. T., Johnson, D. W., & Holubec, E. J. (Eds.) (1987). *Structuring cooperative learning: Lesson plans for teachers.* Edina, MN: Interaction Book.

Johnson, R. T., Johnson, D. W., & Smith, K. A. (n.d.) *Cooperative learning.* Minneapolis: Cooperative Learning Center. Retrieved February 13, 2010, from http://www.ce.umn.edu/~smith/docs/CL%20College-604.doc.

Johnston, S., & Cooper, J. (1997). Quick-thinks: Active thinking in lecture classes and televised instruction. *Cooperative Learning and College Teaching, 8*(1), 2–6.

Johnston, S., & Cooper, J. (1999). Supporting student success through scaffolding. *Cooperative Learning and College Teaching, 9*(3), 3–6.

Johnston, S., & Cooper, J. (2007). Quick-thinks: The interactive lecture. *Tomorrow's Professor, Msg. #818.* Retrieved March 9, 2010, from http://cgi.stanford.edu/~dept-ctl/cgi-bin/tomprof/posting.php.

Johnston, S., & Cooper, J. (2008). Supporting student success through scaffolding. *Tomorrow's Professor, Msg. #849.* Retrieved March 9, 2010, from http://cgi.stanford.edu/~dept-ctl/cgi-bin/tomprof/posting.php.

Johnstone, K. M., & Biggs, S. F. (1998). Problem-based learning: Introduction, analysis, and accounting curricula implications. *Journal of Accounting Education, 16*(3/4), 407–427.

Kagan, S. (1989). *Cooperative learning resources for teachers.* San Capistrano, CA: Resources for Teachers.

Kagan, S. (2009). *Cooperative learning.* San Juan Capistrano, CA: Resources for Teachers.

Kalman, C. S. (2008). *Successful science and engineering teaching: Theoretical and learning perspectives.* New York: Springer.

Keenan, D., & Maier, M. (2009). *Economics live! Learning economics the collaborative way.* New York: McGraw-Hill.

King, A. (1990). Enhancing peer interaction and learning in the classroom through reciprocal questioning. *American Educational Research Journal, 27*(4), 664–687.

King, A. (1995, Winter). Guided peer questioning: A cooperative learning approach to critical thinking. *Cooperative Learning and College Teaching, 5*(2), pp. 15–19. Reprinted in J. L. Cooper, P. Robinson, & D. Ball (Eds.), *Small group instruction in higher education: Lessons from the past, visions of the future* (pp. 112–121). Stillwater, OK: New Forums.

Knoedler, J. T., & Underwood, D. A. (2003). Teaching the principles of economics: A proposal for a multi-paradigmatic approach. *Journal of Economic Issues, 37,* 697–726.

Kolb, D. A. (1984). *Experiential learning: Experience as the source of learning and development.* Upper Saddle River, NJ: Prentice Hall.

Krathwohl, D. R., Bloom, B. S., & Masia, B. B. (1964). *Taxonomy of educational objectives: The affective domain.* New York: McKay.

Kuh, G. D. (2003). What we're learning about engagement from NSSE: Bookmarks for effective educational practices. *Change, 35*(2), 24–32.

Kuh, G. D., Kinzie, J., Schuh, J. H., Whitt, E. J., & associates (2005). *Student success in college: Creating conditions that matter.* San Francisco: Jossey-Bass.

Lasry, N. (2008, April). Clickers or flashcards: Is there really a difference? *Physics Teacher, 46,* 242–244.

Lawson, A. E., Abraham, M. R., & Renner, J. W. (1989), *A theory of instruction: Using the learning cycle to teach science concepts and thinking skills [Monograph Number One].* Kansas State University, Manhattan, KS: National Association for Research in Science Teaching.

Leamnson, R. (1999). *Thinking about teaching and learning: Developing habits of learning with first year college and university students.* Sterling, VA: Stylus.

Levine, A., & Cureton, J. S. (1998). Collegiate life: An obituary. *Change, 30*(3), 14.

Lewis, S. E., & Lewis, J. E. (2005). Departing from lectures: An evaluation of a peer-led guided inquiry alternative. *Journal of Chemical Education, 82,* 135–139.

Libarkin, J. C., & Anderson, S. W. (2005). Assessment of learning in entry-level geoscience courses: Results from the geoscience concept inventory. *Journal of Geoscience Education, 53,* 394–401.

Maier, M. (2003a). You can learn a lot by listening. *National Teaching and Learning Forum, 12*(2), 10–11.

Maier, M. (2003b). Surveys and cooperative learning: Using student experiences as the basis for small-group work. In J. L. Cooper, P. Robinson, & D. Ball (Eds.), *Small group instruction in higher education: Lessons from the past, visions of the future* (pp. 311–320). Stillwater, OK: New Forums.

Marshall, P. (1974). How much, how often? *College and Research Libraries, 35*(6), 453–456.

Marzano, R., Pickering, D., Norford, J., & Paynter, D. (2001). *Handbook for classroom instruction that works.* Alexandria, VA: Association for Supervision and Curriculum Development.

Macdonald, R. H., Manduca, C. A., Mogk, D. W., & Tewksbury, B. J. (2005). Teaching methods in undergraduate geoscience courses: Results of the 2004 On the Cutting Edge Survey of U.S. Faculty. *Journal of Geoscience Education, 53,* 237–252.

McCombs, B. L., & Whisler, J. S. (1997). *The learner-centered classroom and school: Strategies for increasing student motivation and achievement.* San Francisco: Jossey-Bass.

McGoldrick, K., & Ziegert, A. L. (2002). *Putting the invisible hand to work: Concepts and models for service learning in economics.* Ann Arbor: University of Michigan Press.

Michaelsen, L. K., Fink, L. D., & Knight, A. (1997). Designing effective group activities: Lessons for classroom teaching and faculty development. In D. DeZure (Ed.), *To improve the academy: Resources for faculty, instructional, and organizational development* (pp. 373–398). Stillwater, OK: New Forums.

Milem, J., Berger, J., & Dey, E. (2000). Faculty time allocation: A study of change over twenty years. *The Journal of Higher Education, 71,* 454–475.

Millis, B. J. (2002, October) Enhancing learning—and more!—through cooperative learning. IDEA Paper #38. Kansas State University: IDEA Center. Retrieved February 13, 2010, from http://www.theideacenter.org/sites/default/files/IDEA_Paper_38.pdf.

Millis, B. J. (2005). Helping faculty learn to teach better and "smarter" through sequenced activities. In S. Chadwick-Blossy & D. R. Robertson (Eds.), *To improve the academy: Resources for faculty, instructional, and organizational development, 24* (pp. 216–230). Bolton, MA: POD Network and Anker.

Millis, B. J. (2006). Structuring complex cooperative learning activities in 50-minute classes. In S. Chadwick-Blossy & D. R. Robertson (Eds.), *To improve the academy: Resources for faculty, instructional, and organization development* (pp. 153–171). Bolton, MA: POD Network and Anker.

Millis, B. J. (2009, Spring). Becoming an effective teaching using cooperative learning: A personal odyssey. *Peer Review, 11*(2), 17–21.

Millis, B. J., & Cottell, P. G. (1998). *Cooperative learning for higher education faculty.* Phoenix, AZ: American Council on Education/Oryx.

Moog, R. S., & Farrell, J. J. (2008). *Chemistry: A guided inquiry* (4th ed.). Hoboken, NJ: Wiley.

Moog, R. S., & Spencer, J. N. (Eds.) (2008). *Process-Oriented Guided Inquiry Learning,* ACS Symposium Series, No. 994. New York: Oxford University Press.

Nelson, C. E. (1994). Critical thinking and collaborative learning. In K. Bosworth & S. Hamilton (Eds.), *Collaborative learning and college teaching* (pp. 45–58). San Francisco: Jossey-Bass.

Nelson, C. E. (1996). Student diversity requires different approaches to college teaching, even in math and science. *American Behavioral Scientist, 40,* 165–175.

Nelson, C. E. (1999). On the persistence of unicorns: The trade-off between content and critical thinking revisited. In B. A. Pescosolido & R. Aminzade (Eds.), *The social worlds of higher education: Handbook for teaching in a new century* (pp. 168–184). Thousand Oaks, CA: Pine Forge.

Nelson, C. E. (2000). Effective strategies for teaching evolution and other controversial subjects. In W. James, J. W. Skehan, & C. E. Nelson (Eds.), *The creation controversy and the science classroom* (pp. 19–50). Arlington, VA: National Science Teachers Association.

Nelson, C. E. (2001). What is the most difficult step we must take to become great teachers? *National Teaching and Learning Forum, 10*(4), 10–11.

Nelson, C. E. (2007). Teaching evolution effectively: A central dilemma and alternative strategies. *McGill Journal of Education, 42*(2), 265–283.

Nelson, C. E. (2008a). Teaching evolution (and all of biology) more effectively: Strategies for engagement, critical reasoning, and confronting misconceptions. *Integrative and Comparative Biology, 48*, 213–225.

Nelson, C. E. (2008b). The right start: Reflections on a departmentally based graduate course on teaching. *Essays on Teaching Excellence, 11*(7), 1–4.

Nilson, L. B. (2003). *Teaching at its best: A research-based resource for college instructors* (2nd ed.). Bolton, MA: Anker.

Novak, G., Gavrin, A., Christian, W., & Patterson, E. (1999). *Just-in-time teaching: Blending active learning with web technology.* Upper Saddle River, NJ: Prentice Hall.

Nuhfer, E. B. (2008a). The affective domain and the formation of the generator: Educating in fractal patterns XXIII, part 1: *National Teaching and Learning Forum, 18*(2), 8–11, and part 2, *National Teaching and Learning Forum, 18*(3), 9–11.

Nuhfer, E. B. (2008b). The feeling of learning: Intellectual development and the affective domain: Educating in fractal patterns XXVI. *National Teaching and Learning Forum, 18*(1), 7–11.

Nuhfer, E. B., & Fleisher, E. (2008). The utility of knowledge surveys in a culture of overwork: Design of introductory courses that meet institutional educational and assessment requirements. Geological Society of America Abstracts with Programs. Boulder, CO. Retrieved February 3, 2010, from http://a-c-s.confex.com/crops/2008am/webprogram/Paper49187.html.

Nuhfer, E. B., & Knipp, D. (2003). The knowledge survey: a tool for all reasons. In C. M. Wehlburg & S. Chadwick-Blossey (Eds.), *To improve the academy: Resources for faculty, instructional, and organizational development, 21*, 59–78. San Francisco: Jossey-Bass. Retrieved February 3, 2010, with addenda, from http://www.isu.edu/ctl/facultydev/KnowS_files/KnowS.htm.

Nuhfer, E., & Mosbrucker, P. (2007). Developing science literacy using interactive engagements for conceptual understanding of change through time. *Journal of Geoscience Education. 55*(5), 36–50. Retrieved February 3, 2010, from http://www.nagt.org/files/nagt/jge/abstracts/nuhfer-v55p36.pdf.

Oblinger, D. G., & Oblinger, J. L. (Eds.) (2005). *Educating the net generation.* Boulder, CO: Educause.

Osterman, D. N. (1985). *The feedback lecture.* (Idea Paper No. 13). Manhattan, KS: Center for Faculty Development and Evaluation, Kansas State University.

Pascarella, E., & Terenzini, P. (2005) *How college affects students: A third decade of research* (vol. 2). San Francisco: Jossey-Bass.

Perkins, D. (2005). The case for a cooperative studio classroom: Teaching petrology in a different way. *Journal of Geoscience Education, 53*(1), 101–109.

Perry, W. G., Jr. (1968). *Forms of intellectual and ethical development in the college years: A scheme.* Cambridge, MA: Bureau of Study Counsel, Harvard University.

Perry, W. G., Jr. (1970). *Forms of intellectual and ethical development in the college years: A scheme.* New York: Holt.

Perry, W. G., Jr. (1999). *Forms of intellectual and ethical development in the college years: A scheme.* (Reprint of the 1970 edition with a new introduction by L. Knefelkamp). San Francisco: Jossey-Bass.

Pink, D. H. (2005). *A whole new mind.* Riverhead, NY: Riverhead Books.

Rhem, J. (1995). Close-up: Going deep. *The National Teaching and Learning Forum, 5*(1), 4.

Rhem, J. (2006). The high risks of improving teaching. *National Teaching and Learning Forum, 15*(6), 1–2.

Rogers, T. B., Kuiper, N. A., & Kirker, W. S. (1977). Self-reference and the encoding of personal information. *Journal of Personality and Social Psychology, 35,* 677–688.

Rosenshine, B., & Meister, C. (1995). Scaffolds for teaching higher-order cognitive strategies. In A. C. Ornstein (Ed.), *Teaching: Theory into practice* (pp. 134–153). Boston: Allyn & Bacon.

Ruder, S. M., & Hunnicutt, S. S. (2008). POGIL in chemistry courses at a large urban university: A case study. In R. S. Moog, & J. N. Spencer (Eds.), *Process-Oriented Guided Inquiry Learning.* ACS Symposium Series 994 (pp. 131–145). New York: Oxford University Press.

Russell, D. (2008). Math anxiety. About.com: Mathematics. Retrieved February 3, 2010, from http://math.about.com/od/reference/a/anxiety.htm.

Russell, J., Hendricson, W. D., & Herbert, R. J. (1984). Effects of lecture information density on medical student achievement. *Journal of Medical Education, 59,* 881–889.

Salemi, M. K., & Siegfried, J. J. (1999). The state of economic education. *American Economic Review, 89*(2), 355–361.

Self, J. (1987). Reserve readings and student grades: Analysis of a case study. *Library and Information Science Research, 9*(1), 29–40.

Simkins, S. P. (1999). Promoting active student learning using the world wide web in economics courses. *Journal of Economic Education, 30*(3), 278–291.

Simkins, S. P., & Maier, M. (2004). Using Just-in-Time Teaching techniques in the principles of economics course. *Social Science Computer Review, 22*(4), 444–456.

Simkins, S. P., & Maier, M. (2010). *Just-in-Time Teaching: Across the disciplines, across the academy.* New pedagogies and practices for teaching in higher education series. Sterling, VA: Stylus.

Slavin, R. E. (1995). Cooperative learning and intergroup relations. In J. A. Banks & M. Banks (Eds.), *Handbook of research on multicultural education* (pp. 628–634). New York: Macmillan.

Smith, K. A., Sheppard, S. D., Johnson, D. W., & Johnson, R. T. (2005). Pedagogies of engagement: Classroom-based practices. *Journal of Engineering Education: Special Issue on the State of the Art and Practice of Engineering Education Research, 94*(1), 87–102.

Spikell, M. (1993). *Teaching mathematics with manipulatives: A resource of activities for the K–12 teacher.* New York: Allyn and Bacon.

Springer, L., Stanne, M. E., & Donovan, S. S. (1997). *Effects of small-group learning on undergraduates in science, mathematics, engineering and technology: A meta-analysis.* Madison: National Institute for Science Education, University of Wisconsin.

Springer, L., Stanne, M. E., & Donovan, S. S. (1999, Spring). Effects of small-group learning on undergraduates in science, mathematics, engineering, and technology: A meta-analysis. *Review of Educational Research, 69*(1), 21–51.

Staley, C. C. (2003). *Fifty ways to leave your lectern.* Belmont, CA: Wadsworth/Thompson.

Straumanis, A., & Simons, E. A. (2008). A multi-institutional assessment of the use of POGIL in organic chemistry. In R. S. Moog & J. N. Spencer (Eds.), *Process-Oriented Guided Inquiry Learning*, ACS Symposium Series 994 (pp. 224–237). New York: Oxford University Press.

Sundberg, M. D. (2003, Mar–Apr). Strategies to help students change naive alternative conceptions about evolution and natural selection. *Reports of the National Center for Science Education, 23,* 23–26.

Sundberg, M. D., & Dini, M. L. (1993). Science majors vs. nonmajors: Is there a difference? *Journal of College Science Teaching, 23,* 299–304.

Sundberg, M. D., Dini, M. L., & Li, E. (1994). Improving student comprehension and attitudes in first-year biology by decreasing course content. *Journal of Research in Science Teaching, 31,* 679–693.

Sugar, S. (n.d.). *Quizo Game System.* Retrieved February 2, 2010, from www.thegamegroup.com

Svinicki, M. D. (2004). *Learning and motivation in the postsecondary classroom.* Bolton, MA: Anker.

Svinicki, M.D., & Dixon, N. M. (1987). The Kolb Model modified for classroom activities. *College Teaching, 35,* 141–146.

Thorn, P. M. (2003). Bridging the gap between what is praised and what is practiced: Supporting the work of change as anatomy and physiology instructors introduce active learning into their undergraduate classroom. Unpublished doctoral dissertation, University of Texas at Austin. Retrieved February 3, 2010, from http://www.lib.utexas.edu/etd/d/2003/thornpm032/thornpm032.pdf#page=3.

Tobias, S. (1993). *Overcoming math anxiety.* New York: Norton.

Treisman, U. (1992). Studying students studying calculus: A look at the lives of minority mathematics students in college. *College Mathematics Journal, 23,* 362–372.

Vidakovic, D. (1997). Learning the concept of inverse functions in a group versus individual environment. In E. Dubinsky, D. M. Mathews, & B. E. Reynolds (Eds.), *Readings in cooperative learning for undergraduate mathematics* (pp. 173–195). Washington, DC: Math Association of America.

Vidakovic, D., & Martin, W. O. (2004). Small-group searches for mathematical proofs and individual reconstructions of mathematical concepts. *The Journal of Mathematical Behavior, 23*(4), 465–492.

Vygotsky, L. (1978). *Mind in society: The development of higher psychological processes.* Cambridge, MA: Harvard University Press.

Wasley, P. (2006, November 17). Underprepared students benefit most from "engagement." *Chronicle of Higher Education* (pp. A39–A40).

Walvoord, B. E., & Anderson, V. J. (2010). *Effective grading: A tool for learning and assessment* (2nd ed.). San Francisco: Jossey-Bass.

Webb, N. M. (1989). Peer interaction and learning in small groups. *International Journal of Educational Research, 13,* 21–39.

Weimer, M. (2002). *Learner-centered teaching: Five key changes to practice.* San Francisco: Jossey-Bass.

Wiggins, G., & McTighe, J. (1998). *Understanding by design.* Alexandria, VA: Association for Supervision and Curriculum Development.

Wolpert, L. (1992). *The unnatural nature of science.* Cambridge, MA: Harvard University Press.

Yezierski, E. J., Bauer, C. F., Hunnicutt, S. S., Hanson, D. M., Amaral, K. E., & Schneider, J. P. (2008). POGIL implementation in large classes: Strategies for planning, teaching, and management. In R. S. Moog & J. N. Spencer (Eds.), *Process-Oriented Guided Inquiry Learning,* ACS Symposium Series 994 (pp. 60–71). New York: Oxford University Press.

Zull, J. E. (2002). *The art of changing the brain: Enriching teaching by exploring the biology of learning.* Sterling, VA: Stylus.

Contributors

Margaret W. Cohen is the Associate Provost for Professional Development and founding Director of the Center for Teaching and Learning at the University of Missouri-St. Louis (UMSL). She joined the UMSL faculty in 1980 and chaired the Division of Educational Psychology, Research and Evaluation in the College of Education before adding her current responsibilities in the Office of Academic Affairs in 2000. She designs campus programs for faculty, teaching assistants, academic leaders, and peer tutors; she also supports new initiatives for faculty and chairs at the four campuses in the University of Missouri System. She is the co-author, with Barbara Millis, of the revision of Judith Grunert's *The Course Syllabus: A Learning-Centered Approach* (2008). Cohen serves on the Core Committee of the Professional and Organizational Development Network. Her recent honors include an UMSL Trailblazer Award and the Yellow Rose Award from Zonta International. She earned her PhD in educational psychology from Washington University in St. Louis.

James L. Cooper is the author of over seventy chapters, technical monographs and articles dealing with teaching and learning in higher education. From 1990-1999 he served as editor of *Cooperative Learning and College Teaching*, an international newsletter that he founded with an FIPSE grant that he administered from 1990 to 1993. He has published three books on small group instruction, most recently *Small Group Instruction in Higher Education: Lessons from the Past, Visions of the Future* (2003): second edition published in 2009. In 2005 he was named the Outstanding Professor at CSU, Dominguez Hills, where he serves as Professor of Graduate Education and Coordinator of the Curriculum and Instruction M.A. Program. His newest book on college teaching will be published in 2010 by New Forums Press. It will deal with active and small group learning and will be co-edited with Pamela Robinson.

Philip G. Cottell, Jr., Professor of Accountancy at Miami University, received his DBA in Accounting from the University of Kentucky. He has served as the facilitator for several diverse faculty learning communities at Miami University, including the Senior Faculty Community for Teaching Excellence, the Community Using Cooperative Learning to Enhance Teaching, the Community Using Problem-Based Learning to Enhance Teaching, and the Community Using Small Groups to Enhance Teaching. He has had numerous articles published on cooperative learning, as well as on classroom assessment techniques. He also conducts workshops on these topics. He and Barbara Millis are the co-authors of *Cooperative Learning for Higher Education Faculty* (ACE/Oryx Press). Phil has worked with several large public accounting firms to develop realistic problem-based learning scenarios for use in accounting classrooms. He and his wife, Lin Cottell, have two children and four grandchildren. He enjoys gardening and dog training.

Mark Maier is a Professor of Economics at Glendale Community College (California). He is co-principal investigator (with Scott Simkins, KimMarie McGoldrick, and Cathy Manduca) for a National Science Foundation (NSF) project called "Starting Point: Teaching and Learning Economics" (DUE 0817382). Previously, he was co-principal investigator with Scott Simkins on NSF projects adapting successful pedagogies from the natural sciences to economic education (DUE 0088303) and developing Just-In-Time Teaching methods in economics (DUE 0411037). Between 2001 and 2004, Maier was a Scholar and Lead Scholar in the CASTL program at the Carnegie Foundation for the Advancement of Teaching. Most recently, he served as a staff member in the Teaching Innovations Program (TIP), co-sponsored by the American Economic Association's Committee on Economic Education. He has published several articles on cooperative learning and is the co-editor (with Scott Simkins) of the book, *Just-in-Time Teaching: Across the Disciplines, Across the Academy.* In addition, Mark is the author of *Introducing Economics: A Critical Guide for Teaching* (with Julie Nelson), *The Data Game: Controversies in Social Science Statistics,* and *City Unions: Managing Discontent in New York City.*

Llewellyn Mann is a lecturer and the Associate Program Director, Foundation Studies at CQ University in Queensland, Australia. After completing a dual degree in Mechanical and Space Engineering and Physics at the University of Queensland, he went on to earn a PhD in engineering education, focusing on sustainable design. He then completed a year's postdoctoral research at Purdue University in the School of Engineering Education, researching cross-disciplinary practice. His research interests include understanding how students develop their engineering identity, next-generation learning spaces, and sustainable design. He has extensive experience in developing and teaching engineering courses using project-based learning, particularly in engineering design.

Holly Matusovich is an Assistant Professor in the Department of Engineering Education at Virginia Polytechnic Institute and State University. Holly received her PhD in Engineering Education from Purdue University. She also has a BS in Chemical Engineering and an MS in Materials Science. Holly has more than ten years of industrial experience, working first as an engineering consultant and then in a variety of technical and quality systems roles at an aerospace supplier. Holly participated in cooperative learning activities as a student of Karl Smith's at Purdue. She is now very passionate about incorporating cooperative learning into her own classroom.

KimMarie McGoldrick is a Professor of Economics at the University of Richmond. She currently serves on the American Economic Association's Committee on Economic Education and on the Board of Editors of the *Journal of Economic Education*. Her research spans a wide range of education topics, including service-learning, undergraduate research, cooperative learning, and liberal education skills as applied in economics. Her research regularly appears in leading education journals, including the *Journal of Economic Education*. In 2008, she received the *State Council of Higher Education of Virginia Outstanding Faculty Award* and in 2009 was awarded the *Kenneth G. Elzinga Distinguished Teaching Award* from the Southern Economic Association. McGoldrick is co-principal investigator (with Scott Simkins, Mark Maier, and Cathy Manduca) on a National Science Foundation project (DUE 0817382), "Starting Point: Teaching and Learning Economics," creating a web-based "pedagogic portal" that will make it easier for economists to integrate and assess pedagogical innovations in their classrooms. McGoldrick has co-organized 11 economics education workshops since 1996. Her most recent efforts contribute to the Teaching Innovations Program (TIP), an NSF-funded project designed to improve undergraduate education in economics by offering instructors an opportunity to expand their teaching skills and participate in the scholarship of teaching and learning. McGoldrick has served on the American Economic Association's Committee on the Status of Women in the Economics Profession and was a co-principal investigator for the project "CeMENT: Workshops for Female Untenured Faculty in Economics" (HRD ADVANCE 0317755), which aims to reduce professional barriers for female economics professors by assisting in the development of cross-institutional mentoring relationships.

Kerry Meyers is an Associate Professional Faculty member in the College of Engineering at the University of Notre Dame. She completed her PhD in Engineering Education at Purdue University in December 2009. She also has a B.S. and M.S. in Mechanical Engineering. Kerry has over 7 years of industrial experience (automotive industry), but has since shifted her focus to engineering education with the first-year engineering program at the University of Notre Dame.

Barbara J. Millis, Director of the Teaching and Learning Center (TLC) at the University of Texas at San Antonio, received her PhD in English literature from Florida State University. She frequently offers workshops at professional conferences (Teaching Professor Conference, Lilly Teaching Conferences, Association of American Colleges and Universities, Council of Independent Colleges, etc.) and for over three hundred colleges and universities. She publishes articles on a variety of faculty development topics, such as cooperative learning, peer classroom observations, the teaching portfolio, microteaching, syllabus construction, classroom assessment and research, critical thinking, focus groups, academic games, and course redesign. She is the co-author of three books: *Cooperative Learning for Higher Education Faculty* (with Philip Cottell, 1998), *Using Simulations to Enhance Learning in Higher Education* (2002, co-authored with John Hertel), and a revision of Judith Grunert's *The Course Syllabus: A Learning-Centered Approach* (2008, co-authored with Margaret Cohen). While at the U.S. Air Force Academy, Barbara won both a teaching award and a research award. Barbara loved being a Visiting Scholar at Victoria University, Wellington, New Zealand, in 2002.

Craig E. Nelson is a Professor Emeritus of Biology at Indiana University where he has been on the faculty since 1966 (retiring from teaching in 2004). He received his PhD in Zoology from the University of Texas. His biological research has been on evolution and ecology. He has taught biology, intensive freshman seminars, honors courses, several collaboratively taught interdisciplinary courses, and a graduate biology course on alternative approaches to teaching college biology. His teaching papers address critical thinking and mature valuing, diversity, active learning, teaching evolution, and the scholarship of teaching and learning (see http://mypage.iu.edu/~nelson1/ for titles). He has been invited to present workshops at many national meetings and at hundreds of individual institutions in 37 states and 8 countries. He has served on the editorial boards of several journals on pedagogy and the scholarship of teaching and learning, and on teaching grant review panels for the National Science Foundation and other federal programs. He has won several awards for distinguished teaching, and is a winner of the Indiana University President's Medal for Excellence. He was named the Outstanding Research and Doctoral University Professor of the Year by the Carnegie Foundation in 2000.

Edward Nuhfer is California State University at Channel Islands' Director of Faculty Development. He is a geologist by training (PhD from the University of New Mexico) and is the author of many geological publications, including *The Citizens' Guide to Geologic Hazards* (1993, 2005), which received a *Choice* award as Outstanding Academic Book in 1995 by the Association of College and Research Libraries. He holds several national awards in both geology and in faculty development. Ed founded and manages the Boot Camp for Profs® faculty development program and is a regular columnist for *National Teaching and Learning Forum*. His research interests involve fractal characteristics of teaching and learning, assessment, and curriculum design. His teaching interests are promoting science literacy and practical applications of geology to everyday life for laypersons.

Theodore Panitz, Chair of the Department of Mathematics at Cape Cod Community College and former Coordinator for the Developmental Mathematics Program at the college, has been active in regional and national mathematics associations, including the American Mathematical Association of Two-Year Colleges (AMATYC) and the New England Mathematical Association of Two-Year Colleges (NEMATYC), where he has made numerous presentations focused upon adopting cooperative learning methods in developmental mathematics courses. He has published many articles on cooperative learning, both in journals and as book chapters. New Forums Press published his book *Learning Together: Keeping Teachers and Students Actively Involved in Learning by Writing Across the Curriculum*. He also consults with colleges and universities on the subjects of cooperative learning and writing in mathematics. He holds an EdD from Boston University in the area of Adult Education. A more detailed résumé may be accessed at http://tpanitz.jimdo.com/about-ted/.

Pamela Robinson, Assistant Chair of the Department of Liberal Studies and Coordinator of the Integrated Option at California State University, Dominguez Hills, received her EdD from the University of Southern California. She has written and co-written a number of articles and book chapters on research-based active learning strategies, including cooperative learning and college instruction. She presents workshops and conference presentations on effective teaching and has co-edited several book chapters. Her latest book, co-edited with Jim Cooper, is focused on college teaching and will be published by New Forums Press in 2010.

Susan Shadle is the Director of the Center for Teaching and Learning and is a Professor of Chemistry and Biochemistry at Boise State University. She received her PhD in inorganic chemistry from Stanford University and spent a decade on the faculty at Boise State before moving into her current position. She has received a number of teaching accolades, including the Boise State College of Arts and Science Award for Distinguished Teaching (2000), the Boise State University Foundation Scholar Award for Teaching (2004), and the Boise State University Honors College Professor of the Year (2005). In her current role, she works with faculty across the campus to support teaching effectiveness and facilitate engagement in student learning. In addition, she is involved in the national POGIL project, a project involved in disseminating the Process-Oriented Guided Inquiry Learning pedagogy. She facilitates workshops designed to introduce POGIL to faculty in a variety of disciplines, and provides leadership for the POGIL project on the Scholarship of Teaching and Learning.

Scott Simkins is the Director of the Academy for Teaching and Learning and is an Associate Professor of Economics at North Carolina A&T State University in Greensboro, North Carolina. Over the past decade, he and Mark Maier have led multiple National Science Foundation (NSF)-funded projects exploring the adaptability of teaching innovations originally developed in the natural and physical sciences, for use in economics (DUE 0088303 and DUE 0411037). Simkins is currently co-principal investigator (with KimMarie McGoldrick, Mark Maier, and Cathy Manduca) on an NSF project (DUE 0817382), "Starting Point: Teaching and Learning Economics," creating a "pedagogic portal" that will make it easier for economists to use and assess a variety of innovative pedagogical practices in their classroom teaching. Scott is a frequent presenter on Scholarship of Teaching and Learning (SoTL) topics at workshops and conferences regionally, nationally, and internationally, focusing on cross-disciplinary sharing of educational research and pedagogical practices. He has published a number of articles and book chapters on pedagogical innovation and is co-editor (with Mark Maier) of the book, *Just-in-Time Teaching: Across the Disciplines, Across the Academy.*

Karl A. Smith is the Cooperative Learning Professor of Engineering Education in the School of Engineering Education at Purdue University West Lafayette. He has been at the University of Minnesota since 1972 and is in phased retirement as Morse-Alumni Distinguished Professor of Civil Engineering. Karl has worked with thousands of faculty all over the world on pedagogies of engagement, especially cooperative learning, problem-based learning, and constructive controversy. Please refer to his website for details— http://www.ce.umn.edu/~smith/ He has co-authored eight books, including *How to Model It: Problem Solving for the Computer Age; Active Learning: Cooperation in the College Classroom* (3rd ed.); *Cooperative Learning: Increasing College Faculty Instructional Productivity; Strategies for Energizing Large Classes: From Small Groups to Learning Communities;* and *Teamwork and Project Management* (3rd ed.).

Index